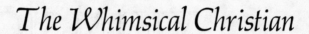

The Whimsical Christian

The WHIMSICAL

18 ESSAYS BY

CHRISTIAN

Dorothy L. Sayers

MACMILLAN PUBLISHING CO., INC.

NEW YORK

Permission to reprint selections from the works of Dorothy L. Sayers has been granted by the Dorothy L. Sayers estate as follows: from *The Mind of the Maker*, Copyright, 1941, by Dorothy L. Sayers: "The Image of God," "Problem Picture"; from *Unpopular Opinions*, Copyright, 1947, by Dorothy L. Sayers: "What Do We Believe?", "A Vote of Thanks to Cyrus," "The Dates in *The Red-Headed League*," "Towards a Christian Aesthetic," "Creative Mind," "Christian Morality"; from *Creed or Chaos*, Copyright, 1949, by Dorothy L. Sayers: "The Greatest Drama Ever Staged," "Strong Meat," "The Dogma is the Drama," "Creed or Chaos?", "The Other Six Deadly Sins"; from *The Poetry of Search and the Poetry of Statement*, © Anthony Fleming 1963: "Charles Williams: Poet's Critic," "The Writing and Reading of Allegory," "Oedipus Simplex: Freedom and Fate in Folk-Lore and Fiction," "The Faust Legend and the Idea of the Devil"; from *Punch* magazine: "Calendar of Unholy & Dead-Letter Days" and "The Cosmic Synthesis" (Nov. 2, 1953), Copyright, 1953, by Dorothy L. Sayers, "Creed of Euthanasia" (Jan. 13, 1954), Copyright, 1954, by Dorothy L. Sayers, "The Polar Synthesis" (Jan. 20, 1954), Copyright, 1954, by Dorothy L. Sayers.

Excerpts from T. S. Eliot's *The Family Reunion* and *Murder in the Cathedral* used by permission of Harcourt Brace Jovanovich, Inc.

Excerpts from Stephen Spender's *The Making of a Poem* used by permission of the author, with agreement of the reprint publisher, Greenwood Press, Inc.

(Previously published under the title *Christian Letters to a Post-Christian World*)

Macmillan Publishing Co., Inc.
866 Third Avenue, New York, N.Y. 10022
Collier Macmillan Canada, Ltd.

Library of Congress Cataloging in Publication Data

Sayers, Dorothy Leigh, 1893–1957.
    The whimsical Christian.

    Previous ed. published under title: Christian letters
to a post-Christian world.
    1. Theology, Doctrinal—Addresses, essays, lectures.
BT15.S27 1978   201.1   78-5613
ISBN 0-02-606930-X

FIRST MACMILLAN EDITION 1978

Printed in the United States of America

Contents

v

Foreword

Dorothy L. Sayers (1893–1957) is known to most as a mystery writer, to many as a translator, to some as a playwright, to few as an apologist for Christianity, and to almost none as an advertising copywriter.

From 1921 to 1929 she worked at Benson's, a London advertising agency. She had come from Oxford where she received a Master of Arts from the university and worked as an editor at Blackwell's. She brought with her from the academic world three qualities prized by the world of commerce: She could think logically in metaphysics and therefore would deal efficiently with margarine. She knew how to handle words, whether it was a sonnet she was to compose or a slogan. And she had no reticence about sharing her knowledge, which would mean only good vibrations with the rest of the office staff.

Sayers was hired at Benson's as "an idea man and copy-writer," and she contributed enormously to the success of a now-famous campaign for Colman's mustard. A declining ad budget and the essential dullness of mustard were the problems to be solved. A club was invented, characters concocted, situations devised, and soon members of the Mustard Club and the message of mustard for the masses were appearing on posters and billboards, in newspapers and magazines, all over England.

It was during her years at Benson's that she began to write mystery stories. She read everything she could find of the theory and practice of the genre, and not long after there sprang from her brow, bemused and bemonocled, Lord Peter Wimsey. *Whose Body?* was published in 1923, and the ultra-suave Lord Peter appeared in ten more novels and twenty-one stories. Though she stopped writing Wimseys in 1937, the second son of the Duke of Denver has lived on in the United Kingdom and the United States, not only in book form, but also in versions dramatized for television.

Sayers' last Wimsey novel began as a play. *Busman's Holiday* was produced in Birmingham in 1936 and later published in London. She was encouraged by this to write more plays. Two of them were presented at the Canterbury Festival: *The Zeal of Thy House* in 1937, a pageant not unlike Eliot's *Murder in the Cathedral;* and *The Devil to Pay* in 1939, a version of the Faust legend. Two more plays were commissioned and broadcast by the B.B.C.: *He That Should Come* in 1938, a nativity play; and *The Man Born to Be King* in 1941, a series of plays on the life of Christ. There are two more plays in her canon: *The Just Vengeance,* written to celebrate Lichfield Cathedral's 750th anniversary in 1946; and *The Emperor Constantine,* written for the Festival of Britain at Colchester in 1951.

Although Sayers' plays are mostly religious in nature, her novels are largely secular. Wimsey does say some place that he was "brought up religious." At least he seems to have read the Book, and in several translations; he and

Bunter parse the same passage in the Vulgate, Revised, and King James versions until they find a missing clue. And Chief Detective Inspector Parker, when not tracking down criminals at large, is sleuthing through New Testament hermeneutics. But Lord Peter was not a convinced Christian and could never become one, or so his creator said—something about his inability to deduce the existence of a soul.

The man Sayers married in 1926 was Oswold Atherton Fleming, and if he was not her intellectual equal during their twenty-four-year marriage, at least he was not an obstacle. It was he who, with the assistance of V1 rockets sailing over London, brought Dorothy and Dante together. When the air-raid sirens wailed, he grabbed her, she grabbed a book, and they both ran for the cellar. When the all-clear sounded, she had read enough of the *Divina Commedia* in medieval Italian to convince her to translate the work into modern English. *Hell* was published in 1949 and *Purgatory* in 1955. *Paradise* was completed after her death by Barbara Reynolds; it was published in 1962.

If there were one word to describe Sayers' view of Christianity, it would be *whimsy*. Like C. S. Lewis, she saw that the world was divided, not into many Christian communities, each professing more or less the same thing, but into two camps, the believers and the non-believers. The intellectuals like herself who believed in the Incarnation were considered whimsical, frivolous, capricious. But to Sayers the fact that "God . . . was made in the year when Caesar Augustus was taking a census in connection with a scheme of taxation" was the divinest whimsy, and the point on which she turned all of her apologetical thinking.

Sayers could give as good as she got, as the essays in *The Mind of the Maker* (1941), *Unpopular Opinions* (1946), and this book clearly show. The secularists she dresses in sacred clothes and mercilessly mocks in the selections from "The Pantheon Papers." The churchmen who found dogma dull as mustard she excoriates in "The Dogma Is the Drama."

The biblical exegetes who would destroy the integrity of the
Bible she destroys in "The Dates in *The Red-Headed
League*," an essay in which she treats whimsically—that is
to say, solemnly and thus hilariously—Sherlock Holmes as a
real person and the novel itself as a historical document.
The other essays in *The Whimsical Christian* deal in one way
or another with the creative mind as an image of God the
Creator.

In addition to the whimsicality surrounding Sayers' literary and apologetical efforts, there was a touch of whimsy
about the way she looked and the way she sounded. She
was slender as a young girl, stout as an adult, and tall
enough to fill G. K. Chesterton's robes as president of the
Detection Club—and he was six feet from crown to ground
and four feet around the middle. She could sing, and her
voice in conversation could be like a high wind, according
to C. S. Lewis; no small wind himself, he ascribed the tone
to her keen mind and extraordinary zest. She liked parties,
and when the women withdrew from the room to discuss
their ailments, she continued to converse with the men on
the great theological and philosophical issues. She smoked
and drank in the manner of the best-known Christian apologists of the century.

The heraldry developed for Lord Peter by C. W. Scott-
Giles might well be applied, with miniscule changes, to
Sayers herself.

Crest: a huge tabby cat crouched, ready to prey.

Arms: three mice, cringing secularists no doubt, about to
pray.

Motto: "As my whimsical Lord takes me."

WILLIAM GRIFFIN
Macmillan Publishing Co., Inc.
April 1, 1978

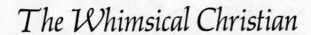

The Whimsical Christian

Selections from "The Pantheon Papers"

THE COSMIC SYNTHESIS

To DIDYMUS PANTHEON, Esq., M.A., Ph.D., etc. Professor of
   Comparative Irreligion in Mansoul University, Cos-
   mopolis.

   Dear Professor Pantheon:

   In an incomplete copy of that very scarce publication,
Blimey's *Monumental Monstrosities of the Age of Unreason*,
I have come across the enclosed color plate. The reference is lacking; but it appears to represent a stained-glass
window, of debase neo-Gothic type, dedicated to some
kind of devotional cult. A few of the personages depicted
seem vaguely familiar, but others are quite unknown to
me. Can you help?

Yours very truly,

DOROTHY L. SAYERS

To Miss Dorothy L. Sayers, M.A., D. Litt.,
  c/o Mr. Punch, 10 Bouverie Street, E.C. 4
    Dear Dr. Sayers:

I am deeply indebted to you for the rare "extra" plate to Blimey, which I had not seen before; it is not included in either the B.M. or the Bodleian copy. I do not know for what building the window was designed, but I think I may say without undue hesitation that it is in some way connected with that widely distributed though elusive community (so to call it, though it specifically repudiates communion) whose adherents are variously known as Stylites, Polarites, Animamundanes, Egregians, Cacophonophilists (or Discordants), Umbragians, Nolimetangerines, etc. It is claimed that its following embraces almost the whole population of the Western world (with the exception of a few strict Jews and fanatical Christian sects), and this makes it the more remarkable that the secret of its organization and cult should be so well kept. It is perhaps a *secret de Polichinelle* so obvious as to escape observation.

So far as I can ascertain, this community resembles the early Gnostic churches in that it consists of an Outer Diffusion of Simple Followers, or "Nebulous," and an Inner Concentration of Initiates, or "Sufficients." The former practice the rites associated with the innumerable cult-divinities, and subscribe to the ethical code and esoteric doctrine provided for them, but have no access to the Mysteries. The latter are jealous guardians of the *arcana*, and alone know the true name of the esoteric Deity who is worshipped under so many protean disguises.

There is also said to be a dissident body calling themselves Galactics, who affirm that the general following has become corrupt and are concerned to recover and restore the sincere Milk of the Way.

I have been for some time engaged in research on this subject, and in return for your most valuable window (which illumines a number of problems) I have pleasure in sending you a few items that have come into my hands. The sketch represents a fragment of an oak screen (discovered in a tithe barn in Norfolk), which is of much greater antiquity than the window, and shows that the cult goes back to at least the fifteenth century. The notes on the saints depicted are culled from the *Legenda Plumbea* of Jacques de Voracity (? Veracity)—a curious book, of which no two copies are alike. I have also added a so-called Polar Hymn from a MS in a private collection and (though this very tentatively) my own conjectural reconstruction of part of the Polar Calendar, showing the succession of the Seasons, with Movable Feasts and a few of the Unholy and Dead-Letter Days. This last item has been put together from isolated hints and indications, and it must be regarded as *entirely* provisional and subject to modification in the light of future research.

Yours gratefully and sincerely,
DIDYMUS PANTHEON

I confess myself puzzled by the frequent allusions to "poles" and "polarity." Dr. Grubbenbücher believes them to have an electrical signification, but I am inclined to associate them with some kind of totem cult.

The Calendar

The Polar Year is divided into eight Seasons. ADVERTISE-MENT, a season of solemn preparation leading up to the *Birth of Science* (Winter Solstice), is followed by CACO-PHONY, which extends from *Circumlocution* to *Derogation Day;* after which Trash Wednesday brings us to the pestilential season of UMBRAGE. Then comes the great equinoctial Feast of the ENLIGHTENMENT, whose season ends on *Civilization Sunday.* The season of COMPRESSION (devoted to the celebration of the Masses in Urbanity) begins with *Ignition Sunday* and ends in *Explosion.* Immediately after comes the *Theophany of the Spirit of Progress* (commonly called *Petrol Sunday*), which marks the Summer Solstice. After the brisk series of Sundays in PETROL (briefly interrupted by the Feast of the *Unholy Name*), we break out into EXPANSION, which lasts from *Bank Holiday* (first Monday in August) to *Exhaust Sunday* and *All Hollows*, celebrated at the Autumn Equinox. The Sunday following, *Pole Star Sunday*, devoted to the cult of Isolation, ushers in the season of POLARITY, a period of peculiar and awful sanctity, in which the cycle of the year completes its revolution.

Hagiological Notes

ST. LUKEWARM OF LAODICEA, MARTYR

St. Lukewarm was a magistrate in the city of Laodicea under Claudius (Emp. A.D. 41–54). He was so broadminded as to offer asylum and patronage to every kind of religious cult, however unorthodox or repulsive, saying in answer to all remonstrances: "There is always some truth in everything." This liberality earned for him the surname of "The Tolerator." At length he fell into the hands of a sect of Anthropophagi (for whom he had erected a sacred kitchen and cooking stove at the public expense), and was duly set on to stew with appropriate ceremonies. By miraculous intervention, however, the water continually went off the boil; and when he was finally served up, his flesh was found to be so tough and tasteless that the Chief Anthropophagus spat out the unpalatable morsel, exclaiming: *"Tolerator non tolerandus!"* (A garbled Christian version of this legend is preserved in Revelations 3:16.)

St. Lukewarm is the patron saint of railway caterers and is usually depicted holding a cooking pot.

SS. URSA AND URSULINA
(*Popularly called SS. Ursa Major and Minor*)

These two sisters are sometimes said to have belonged to the famous medieval family of the Orsini, and sometimes to a patrician *gens* of ancient Rome, but their legend clearly goes back to a much more remote antiquity. Though as beautiful and accomplished as they were nobly born, they nevertheless dedicated themselves from early maidenhood to a life of Arctic severity, practicing the Polar virtues of frigidity and superiority to a truly heroic degree. Rejecting all suitors and resolutely detaching themselves from the society of their kindred and inferiors, they immured themselves in a tower of blue looking glass, and for the last forty years of their lives spoke only to each other. Lest death should reduce them to the level of common humanity, the Spirit of Proper Pride miraculously turned them into White Bears and translated them to the North Pole, whence they perpetually contemplate their own reflections in the starry heavens. They are usually represented in the bodies of their transformation.

ST. SIMIAN STYLITES

This fifth-century saint is reputed to have spent his entire life on a pedestal. When told that this behavior might cause him to be confused with a certain superstitious Christian who was similarly engaged, he made the crushing rejoinder: *"Istud corpus exaltatum mentem humilem habet; ego autem omnino superior."* He added that the attitudes, not the platitudes, of the virtuous were to be imitated.

St. Simian is one of the most important saints in the calendar, his feast being celebrated on the day following All Hollows. Roughly carved effigies belonging to his cult are found in every nursery, where, under the familiar name of "monkey-on-a-stick," they are the objects of much infant devotion.

ST. SUPERCILIA

St. Supercilia, born in Paris about the year 1400, was a maiden of remarkable erudition, who steadfastly refused to marry anyone who could not defeat her in open disputation. When the best scholars of all the universities in Europe had tried and failed, her unworthy father brutally commanded her to accept the hand of a man who, though virtuous, sensible, and of a good estate, knew only six languages and was weak in mathematics. At this, the outraged saint raised her eyebrows so high that they lifted her right off her feet and out through a top-story window, whence she was last seen floating away in a northerly direction.

St. Supercilia is the patron of pedants. Her feast, Eyebrow Sunday, falls in Cacophony, between Lowbrow Sunday and Derogation Day.

For an Evening Service

*This hymn is suitable for
the Vigil of the Enlightenment*

The day that Nature gave is ending,
　　The hand of Man turns on the light;
We praise thee, Progress, for defending
　　Our nerves against the dreadful night.

As o'er each continent and island
　　The switches spread synthetic day,
The noise of mirth is never silent,
　　Nor dies the strain of toil away.

We thank thee that thy speed incessant
　　Provides upon this whirling ball
No time to brood on things unpleasant—
　　No time, in fact, to think at all.

Secure amid the soothing riot
　　Of crank and sound track, plane and car,
We shall not be condemned to quiet,
　　Nor left alone with what we are.

By lavish and progressive measures
　　Our neighbor's wants are all relieved;

We are not called to share his pleasures,
    And in his grief we are not grieved.

Thy winged wheels o'erspan the oceans,
    Machining out the Standard Man.
Our food, our learning, our emotions
    Are processed for us in the can.

All bars of color, caste and nation
    Must yield to movies and the mike;
We need not seek communication,
    For thou dost make us all alike.

So be it! let not sleep nor slackness
    Impede thy Progress, Light sublime;
Nor ever let us glimpse the blackness
    That yawns behind the gates of Time.
                    (Tune: *St. Clement*)

A SERMON FOR CACOPHONYTIDE

(Reprinted from the Schisminster Perish Magazine)

My Little Perishers:

Cacophony is the seedtime of the Polar Year. Not, of course, the dilatory seedtime of conquered and discredited Nature! But as from the refrigerator we cull fresh peas in December and ice cream in July, so we may plant the seeds of enmity all the year round, but especially in the Cacophonytide. Scarcely is Wishmas[1] over, with all its factitious heartiness and family friction, before bills and income-tax demands come in. Tempers are frayed, the weather is uniformly detestable; spiritually and physically, the mud is ready—that rich unwholesome mud in which the Polar seeds can germinate. Plant those seeds now. Do not be discouraged if your opportunities appear limited. The smallest

[1] *Wishmas.* This festival, which has almost everywhere superseded the superstitious commemoration of Christmas, is celebrated by domestic agglomerations and by the exchange of cards, bearing wishes for the recipients' material prosperity, and frequently adorned with ice, snow, holly, and other Polar symbols.

dispute, the most trifling misconception may, if sown with envy, watered with complaints, sprayed with clouds of verbiage, and artificially heated with unrighteous indignation, grow into a lofty and isolated Pole, up which you may climb to look down upon your neighbors.

Last week Stepfather Munchgrief gave you valuable guidance on the propagation of domestic strife; today I will say a few words on the subject of Polar apologetics.

Remember, when cultivating your coldbed of Polemic, never define, never expound, never discuss; only assert and assume. Where there is dogma, there is always a possible basis for agreement; where there is explanation, there is always the peril of mutual understanding; where there is argument, there may be victory and the dreadful prospect of peace. Again, it is often unwise, and always unnecessary, to invite examination into the merits of your case; far better to rely on a devout invocation of the sacred authorities. "Science tells us—"; "Progress demands—"; "Modern thought goes to show—." Phrases such as these, uttered with a condescending smile, are far less answerable and provoke infinitely greater irritation.

Be especially careful, when baiting Neo-Scholastics and other superstitious theologians, never to have studied their doctrines—it will only cramp your style and offer them a handle for controversy. You need only pick up at thirdhand enough of their technical jargon to use it inaccurately and so make rational debate impossible. Follow the example of the Blessed St. Hydra, and when your adversary has hewn away (as he thinks) one misconception, let two sprout in its place; that will tire out his patience. Strive earnestly to confuse every issue; there are no injuries so estranging as those that are dealt in the dark by men who do not know what the quarrel is about.

One final warning: do not fall into the error of intellectual intolerance. Reserve your resentment for people, not for ideas. Polarity thrives upon the diffusion of irresponsible opinions, which—if allowed to flourish unchecked—may easily grow into ideological tyrannies and nourish feuds of global dimensions. Any effort to oppose a new idea on the specious pretext that it is nasty, false, dangerous, or wrong should be promptly stigmatized as heresy-hunting, medieval obscurantism, or suburban prejudice. If the idea is, in fact, silly or untrue, all the better; you will then be able to sneer impartially at both those who hold and those who condemn it, and thus to enhance that sense of your own superiority that is the sole aim and reward of all Polar activity.

Let us continue, then, on the up and up—from rod to perch, from perch to pole—till at last, by modern scientific use of our own bootstraps, we shall rise to our supreme height of lordly stature, no longer dependent on any man, or even on the gods of our own invention, but every one of us in his or her own exclusive right exalted over every other.

COLLECT FOR THE THIRD SUNDAY IN CACOPHONY

O Misconstruction, that art the author of hate and lover of friction, in juggling with whom standeth our perpetual strife, and whose service is stark unreason; assist us, thy aggressive shock troops, in all our assaults upon accuracy, that we, being practiced in giving offense, may not fear the power of any argument; through the sleight of thy misleading words. *Amen.*

Preached on the Feast of the Decollation of St. Hydra by the Irrev. Garble Skimmer at the Perish Center of St. Cloud the Obscure, Schisminster.

To Professor Pantheon
Sir:

You may be interested to see the enclosed, which is the form of cultural symbol most commonly used in Segregations of the Polar Nebulus.

Yours, etc.
(Irrev.) Prometheus Upworthy
Perpetual Obscurate of
St. Scientia-in-Excelsis
Great North Road

CREED OF ST. EUTHANASIA
(Commonly called the Atheneum Creed)

I believe in man, maker of himself and inventor of all
science. And in myself, his manifestation, and captain
of my psyche; and that I should not suffer anything
painful or unpleasant.

And in a vague, evolving deity, the future-begotten child of
man; conceived by the spirit of progress, born of
emergent variants; who shall kick down the ladder by
which he rose and tell history to go to hell.

Who shall some day take off from earth and be jet-propelled
into the heavens; and sit exalted above all worlds, man
the master almighty.

And I believe in the spirit of progress, who spake by Shaw
and the Fabians; and in a modern, administrative, ethical, and social organization; in the isolation of saints,
the treatment of complexes, joy through health, and destruction of the body by cremation (with music while it
burns), and then I've had it.

The Greatest Drama Ever Staged

IS THE OFFICIAL CREED OF CHRISTENDOM

OFFICIAL CHRISTIANITY, of late years, has been having what is known as a bad press. We are constantly assured that the churches are empty because preachers insist too much upon doctrine—dull dogma as people call it. The fact is the precise opposite. It is the neglect of dogma that makes for dullness. The Christian faith is the most exciting drama that ever staggered the imagination of man—and the dogma is the drama.

That drama is summarized quite clearly in the creeds of the Church, and if we think it dull it is because we either have never really read those amazing documents or have recited them so often and so mechanically as to have lost all sense of their meaning. The plot pivots upon a single character, and the whole action is the answer to a single central problem: *What think ye of Christ?* Before we adopt any of the unofficial solutions (some of which are indeed excessively dull)—before we dismiss Christ as a myth, an idealist, a demagogue, a liar, or a lunatic—it will do no harm to find out what the creeds really say about him. What does the Church think of Christ?

The Church's answer is categorical and uncompromising, and it is this: That Jesus Bar-Joseph, the carpenter of Nazareth, was in fact and in truth, and in the most exact and literal sense of the words, the God "by whom all things were made." His body and brain were those of a common man; his personality was the personality of God, so far as that personality could be expressed in human terms. He was not a kind of demon pretending to be human; he was in every respect a genuine living man. He was not merely a man so good as to be "like God"—he was God.

Now, this is not just a pious commonplace; it is not a commonplace at all. For what it means is this, among other things: that for whatever reason God chose to make man as he is—limited and suffering and subject to sorrows and death—he [God] had the honesty and the courage to take his own medicine. Whatever game he is playing with his creation, he has kept his own rules and played fair. He can exact nothing from man that he has not exacted from himself. He has himself gone through the whole of human experience, from the trivial irritations of family life and the cramping restrictions of hard work and lack of money to the worst horrors of pain and humiliation, defeat, despair, and death. When he was a man, he played the man. He was born in poverty and died in disgrace and thought it well worthwhile.

Christianity is, of course, not the only religion that has found the best explanation of human life in the idea of an incarnate and suffering god. The Egyptian Osiris died and rose again; Aeschylus in his play, *The Eumenides,* reconciled man to God by the theory of a suffering Zeus. But in most theologies, the god is supposed to have suffered and died in some remote and mythical period of prehistory. The

Christian story, on the other hand, starts off briskly in St. Matthew's account with a place and a date: "When Jesus was born in Bethlehem of Judea in the days of Herod the King." St. Luke, still more practically and prosaically, pins the thing down by a reference to a piece of government finance. God, he says, was made man in the year when Caesar Augustus was taking a census in connection with a scheme of taxation. Similarly, we might date an event by saying that it took place in the year that Great Britain went off the gold standard. About thirty-three years later (we are informed), God was executed, for being a political nuisance, "under Pontius Pilate"—much as we might say, "when Mr. Johnson-Hicks was Home Secretary." It is as definite and concrete as all that.

Possibly we might prefer not to take this tale too seriously—there are disquieting points about it. Here we had a man of divine character walking and talking among us—and what did we find to do with him? The common people, indeed, "heard him gladly"; but our leading authorities in Church and State considered that he talked too much and uttered too many disconcerting truths. So we bribed one of his friends to hand him over quietly to the police, and we tried him on a rather vague charge of creating a disturbance, and had him publicly flogged and hanged on the common gallows, "thanking God we were rid of a knave." All this was not very creditable to us, even if he was (as many people thought and think) only a harmless, crazy preacher. But if the Church is right about him, it was more discreditable still, for the man we hanged was God Almighty.

So that is the outline of the official story—the tale of the time when God was the underdog and got beaten, when he submitted to the conditions he had laid down and became a man like the men he had made, and the men he had made broke him and killed him. This is the dogma we find so dull—this terrifying drama of which God is the victim and hero.

If this is dull, then what, in Heaven's name, is worthy to be called exciting? The people who hanged Christ never, to do them justice, accused him of being a bore—on the contrary, they thought him too dynamic to be safe. It has been left for later generations to muffle up that shattering personality and surround him with an atmosphere of tedium. We have very efficiently pared the claws of the Lion of Judah, certified him "meek and mild," and recommended him as a fitting household pet for pale curates' and pious old ladies. To those who knew him, however he in no way suggests a milk-and-water person; they objected to him as a dangerous firebrand. True, he was tender to the unfortunate, patient with honest inquirers, and humble before heaven; but he insulted respectable clergymen by calling them hypocrites. He referred to King Herod as "that fox"; he went to parties in disreputable company and was looked upon as a "gluttonous man and a winebibber, a friend of publicans and sinners"; he assaulted indignant tradesmen and threw them and their belongings out of the temple; he drove a coach-and-horses through a number of sacrosanct and hoary regulations; he cured diseases by any means that came handy, with a shocking casualness in the matter of other people's pigs and property; he showed no proper deference for wealth or social position; when confronted with neat dialectical traps, he displayed a paradoxical humor that affronted serious-minded people, and he retorted by asking disagreeably searching questions that could not be answered by rule of thumb. He was emphatically not a dull man in his human lifetime, and if he was God, there can be nothing dull about God either. But he had "a daily beauty in his life that made us ugly," and officialdom felt that the established order of things would be more secure without him. So they did away with God in the name of peace and quietness.

"And the third day he rose again." What are we to make of this? One thing is certain: if he were God and nothing else, his immortality means nothing to us; if he was man and no more, his death is no more important than yours or mine.

But if he really was both God and man, then when the man Jesus died, God died too; and when the God Jesus rose from the dead, man rose too, because they were one and the same person. The Church binds us to no theory about the exact composition of Christ's Resurrection Body. A body of some kind there had to be since man cannot perceive the Infinite otherwise than in terms of space and time. It may have been made from the same elements as the body that disappeared so strangely from the guarded tomb, but it was not that old, limited mortal body, though it was recognizably like it. In any case, those who saw the risen Christ remained persuaded that life was worth living and death a triviality—an attitude curiously unlike that of the modern defeatist, who is firmly persuaded that life is a disaster and death (rather inconsistently) a major catastrophe.

Now, nobody is compelled to believe a single word of this remarkable story. God (says the Church) has created us perfectly free to disbelieve in him as much as we choose. If we do disbelieve, then he and we must take the consequences in a world ruled by cause and effect. The Church says further, that man did, in fact, disbelieve, and that God did, in fact, take the consequences. All the same, if we are going to disbelieve a thing, it seems on the whole to be desirable that we should first find out what, exactly, we are disbelieving. Very well, then: "The right Faith is, that we believe that Jesus Christ is God and man, Perfect God and perfect man, of a reasonable soul and human flesh subsisting. Who although he be God and man yet is he not two, but one Christ." There is the essential doctrine, of which the whole elaborate structure of Christian faith and morals is only the logical consequence.

Now, we may call that doctrine exhilarating, or we may call it devastating; we may call it revelation, or we may call it rubbish; but if we call it dull, then words have no meaning at all. That God should play the tyrant over man is a dismal story of unrelieved oppression; that man should play the tyrant over man is the usual dreary record of human futility; but that man should play the tyrant over God and find him a better man than himself is an astonishing drama indeed. Any journalist, hearing of it for the first time, would recognize it as news; those who did hear it for the first time actually called it news, and good news at that; though we are likely to forget that the word *Gospel* ever meant anything so sensational.

Perhaps the drama is played out now, and Jesus is safely dead and buried. Perhaps. It is ironical and entertaining to consider that at least once in the world's history those words might have been spoken with complete conviction, and that was upon the eve of the Resurrection.

Strong Meat

> For every one that useth milk is unskilful in the word of right-
> eousness; for he is a babe.
> But strong meat belongeth to them that are of full age, even
> those who by reason of use have their senses exercised to discern
> both good and evil.
> —The Epistle of Paul the Apostle to the Hebrews 5:13–14

HERE IS A ROBUST ASSERTION of the claim of Christianity to
be a religion for adult minds. I am glad to think, now, that
it impressed me so forcibly then, when I was still comparatively young. To protest, when one has left one's youth behind, against the prevalent assumption that there is no salvation for the middle-aged is all very well; but it is likely to
provoke a mocking reference to the fox who lost his tail.
One is in a stronger position if one can show that one had
already registered the protest before circumstances rendered
it expedient.

17

There is a popular school of thought (or, more strictly, of feeling) that violently resents the operation of time upon the human spirit. It looks upon age as something between a crime and an insult. Its prophets have banished from their savage vocabulary all such words as *adult, mature, experienced, venerable;* they know only snarling and sneering epithets such as *middle-aged, elderly, stuffy, senile,* and *decrepit.* With these they flagellate that which they themselves are, or must shortly become, as though abuse were an incantation to exorcise the inexorable. Theirs is neither the thoughtless courage that "makes mouths at the invisible event," nor the reasoned courage that foresees the event and endures it; still less is it the ecstatic courage that embraces and subdues the event. It is the vicious and desperate fury of a trapped beast, and it is not a pretty sight.

Such men, finding no value for the world as it is, proclaim very loudly their faith in the future, "which is in the hands of the young." With this flattery they bind their own burden on the shoulders of the next generation. For their own failures, time alone is to blame—not sin, which is expiable, but time, which is irreparable. From the relentless reality of age, they seek escape into a fantasy of youth—their own or other people's. First love, childhood ideals, childish dreams, the song at the mother's breast, the blind security of the womb—from these they construct a monstrous fabric of pretense, to be their hiding-place from the tempest. Their faith is not really in the future, but in the past. Paradoxical as it may seem, to believe in youth is to look backward; to look forward, we must believe in age.

"Except," said Christ, "ye become as little children"—and the words are sometimes quoted to justify the flight into infantilism. Now, children differ in many ways, but they have one thing in common. Peter Pan—if indeed he exists otherwise than in the nostalgic imagination of an adult—is a case for the pathologist. All normal children (however much we discourage them) look forward to growing up. "Except ye become as little children," except you can wake on your fiftieth birthday with the same forward-looking excitement and interest in life that you enjoyed when you were five, "ye cannot see the Kingdom of God." One must not only die daily, but every day one must be born again.

"How can a man be born when he is old?" asked Nicodemus. His question has been ridiculed; but it is very reasonable and even profound. "Can he enter a second time into his mother's womb and be born?" Can he escape from time, creep back into the comfortable prenatal darkness, renounce the values of experience? The answer makes short work of all such fantasies. "That which is born of the flesh is flesh, and that which is born of the spirit is spirit." The spirit alone is eternal youth; the mind and the body must learn to make terms with time.

Time is a difficult subject for thought because in a sense we know too much about it. It is perhaps the only phenomenon of which we have direct apprehension; if all our senses were destroyed, we should still remain aware of duration. Moreover, all conscious thought is a process in time; so that to think consciously about time is like trying to use a ruler to measure its own length. The awareness of timelessness, which some people have, does not belong to the order of conscious thought and cannot be directly expressed in the language of conscious thought, which is temporal. For every conscious human purpose (including thought), we are compelled to reckon (in every sense of the word) with time.

Now, the Christian Church has always taken a thoroughly realistic view of time, and has been very particular to distinguish between time and eternity. In her view of the matter, time is not an aspect or a fragment of eternity, nor is eternity an endless extension of time; the two concepts belong to different categories. Both have a divine reality: God is the Ancient of Days and also the I AM; the Everlasting, and also the Eternal Present; the Logos and also the Father. The Creeds, with their usual practicality, issue a sharp warning that we shall get into a nasty mess if we confuse the two or deny the reality of either. Moreover, the mystics—those rare spirits who are simultaneously aware of time and eternity—support the doctrine by their knowledge and example. They are never vague, wooly-minded people to whom time means nothing; on the contrary, they insist more than anybody upon the validity of time and the actuality of human experience.

The reality of time is not affected by considering it as a dimension in a space-time continuum or as a solid having dimensions of its own. "There's a great devil in the universe," says Kay in *Time and the Conways*, "and we call it Time. . . . If things were merely mixed—good and bad—that would be all right, but they get worse. . . . Time's beating us." Her brother replies that time is "only a kind of dream," and that the "happy young Conways of the past" are still real and existing. "We're seeing another bit of the view—a bad bit if you like—but the whole landscape's still there. . . . At this moment, or any moment, we're only a cross section of our real selves. What we *really* are is the whole stretch of ourselves, all our time; and when we come to the end of this life, all our time will be *us*—the real you, the real me."

Granted all this—that the happy Conways still coexist, now, with the unhappy, middle-aged Conways; granted also the converse—that the unhappy, middle-aged Conways already coexisted, then, with the happy, young Conways. What of it? All we have done is to substitute a spatial image for a temporal one. Instead of a progress from good to evil, we have a prospect (or "landscape") of mixed good and evil, which, viewed in its entirety ("when we come to the end of this life") must necessarily contain more evil than good, since things "get worse and worse." Kay may find this "all right"; the fact remains that there is here no conquest over time, but an unconditional surrender.

That surrender is made in the moment when we assume that time is evil in itself and brings nothing but deterioration. It is a pity that the Conway family contained no saint, no artist, no one who had achieved any measure of triumphant fulfilment. His opinion would have been of great interest since he might have spoken with authority of the soul's development in time, of the dark night of the soul that precedes crucifixion and issues in resurrection.

In contending with the problem of evil, it is useless to try to escape either from the bad past or into the good past. The only way to deal with the past is to accept the whole past, and by accepting it, to change its meaning. The hero of T. S. Eliot's *The Family Reunion*, haunted by the guilt of a hereditary evil, seeks at first "to creep back through the little door" into the shelter of the unaltered past, and finds no refuge there from the pursuing hounds of heaven. "Now I know / That the last apparent refuge, the safe shelter, / That is where one meets them. / That is the way of specters . . ." So long as he flees from time and evil he is thrall to them, not till he welcomes them does he find strength to transmute them. "And now I know / That my business is not to run away, but to pursue, / Not to avoid being found, but to seek. . . . / It is at once the hardest thing, and the only thing possible. / Now they will lead me; I shall be safe with them: / I am not safe here. . . . I must follow the bright angels." Then, and only then, is he enabled to apprehend the good in the evil and to see the terrible hunters of the soul in their true angelic shape. "I feel quite happy, as if happiness / Did not consist in getting what one wanted / Or in getting rid of what can't be gotten rid of / But in a different vision." It is the release, not from, but into, reality.

This is the great way of Christian acceptance—a very different thing from so-called Christian resignation, which merely submits without ecstasy. "Repentance," says a Christian writer,* "is no more than a passionate intention to know all things after the mode of heaven, and it is impossible to know evil as good if you insist on knowing it as evil." For man's evil knowledge, "there could be but one

---

* Charles Williams: *He Came Down from Heaven.*

perfect remedy—to know the evil of the past itself as good, and to be free from the necessity of evil in the future—to find right knowledge and perfect freedom together; to know all things as occasions of love."

The story of Passiontide and Easter is the story of the winning of that freedom and of that victory over the evils of time. The burden of the guilt is accepted ("He was made Sin"), the last agony of alienation from God is passed through (*Eloi, lama sabachthani*); the temporal body is broken and remade; and time and eternity are reconciled in a single person. There is no retreat here to the paradise of primal ignorance; the new kingdom of God is built upon the foundations of spiritual experience. Time is not denied; it is fulfilled. "I am the food of the full-grown."

The Dogma Is the Drama

"ANY STIGMA," said a witty tongue, "will do to beat a dogma"; and the flails of ridicule have been brandished with such energy of late on the threshing floor of controversy that the true seed of the Word has become well-nigh lost amid the whirling of chaff. Christ, in His divine innocence, said to the woman of Samaria, "Ye worship ye know not what"—being apparently under the impression that it might be desirable, on the whole, to know what one was worshipping. He thus showed himself sadly out of touch with the twentieth-century mind, for the cry today is: "Away with the tedious complexities of dogma—let us have the simple spirit of worship; just worship, no matter of what!" The only drawback to this demand for a generalized and undirected worship is the practical difficulty of arousing any sort of enthusiasm for the worship of nothing in particular.

23

It would not perhaps be altogether surprising if, in this nominally Christian country, where the Creeds are daily recited, there were a number of people who knew all about Christian doctrine and disliked it. It is more startling to discover how may people there are who heartily dislike and despise Christiantiy without having the faintest notion what it is. If you tell them, they cannot believe you. I do not mean that they cannot believe the doctrine; that would be understandable enough since it takes some believing. I mean that they simply cannot believe that anything so interesting, so exciting, and so dramatic can be the orthodox creed of the Church.

That this is really the case was made plain to me by the questions asked me, mostly by young men, about my Canterbury play, *The Zeal of Thy House.* The action of the play involves a dramatic presentation of a few fundamental Christian dogmas—in particular, the application to human affairs of the doctrine of the Incarnation. That the Church believed Christ to be in any real sense God, or that the eternal word was supposed to be associated in any way with the word of creation; that Christ was held to be at the same time man in any real sense of the word; that the doctrine of the Trinity could be considered to have any relation to fact or any bearing on psychological truth; that the Church considered pride to be sinful, or indeed took notice of any sin beyond the more disreputable sins of the flesh:—all these things were looked upon as astonishing and revolutionary novelties, imported into the faith by the feverish imagination of a playwright. I protested in vain against this flattering tribute to my powers of invention, referring my inquirers to the creeds, to the gospels, and to the offices of the Church; I insisted that if my play were dramatic it was so, not in spite of the dogma, but because of it—that, in short, the dogma was the drama. The explanation was, however, not well received; it was felt that if there were anything attractive in Christian philosophy I must have put it there myself.

Judging by what my young friends tell me, and also by what is said on the subject in anti-Christian literature written by people who ought to have taken a little trouble to find out what they are attacking before attacking it, I have come to the conclusion that a short examination paper on the Christian religion might be very generally answered as follows:

Q.: What does the Church think of God the Father?

A.: He is omnipotent and holy. He created the world and imposed on man conditions impossible of fulfilment; he is very angry if these are not carried out. He sometimes interferes by means of arbitrary judgments and miracles, distributed with a good deal of favoritism. He likes to be truckled to and is always ready to pounce on anybody who trips up over a difficulty in the law or is having a bit of fun. He is rather like a dictator, only larger and more arbitrary.

Q.: What does the Church think of God the Son?

A.: He is in some way to be identified with Jesus of Nazareth. It was not his fault that the world was made like this, and, unlike God the Father, he is friendly to man and did his best to reconcile man to God (see *atonement*). He has a good deal of influence with God, and if you want anything done, it is best to apply to him.

Q.: What does the Church think of God the Holy Ghost?

A.: I don't know exactly. He was never seen or heard of till Whitsunday. There is a sin against him that damns you for ever, but nobody knows what it is.

Q.: What is the doctrine of the trinity?

A.: "The Father incomprehensible, the Son incomprehensible, and the whole thing incomprehensible." Something put in by theologians to make it more difficult—nothing to do with daily life or ethics.

Q.: What was Jesus Christ like in real life?

A.: He was a good man—so good as to be called the Son of God. He is to be identified in some way with God the Son (*q.v.*). He was meek and mild and preached a simple religion of love and pacifism. He had no sense of humor. Anything in the Bible that suggests another side to his character must be an interpolation, or a paradox invented by G. K. Chesterton. If we try to live like him, God the Father will let us off being damned hereafter and only have us tortured in this life instead.

Q.: What is meant by the atonement?

A.: God wanted to damn everybody, but his vindictive sadism was sated by the crucifixion of his own Son, who was quite innocent, and therefore, a particularly attractive victim. He now only damns people who don't follow Christ or who never heard of him.

Q.: What does the Church think of sex?

A.: God made it necessary to the machinery of the world, and tolerates it, provided the parties (a) are married, and (b) get no pleasure out of it.

Q.: What does the Church call sin?

A.: Sex (otherwise than as excepted above); getting drunk; saying "damn"; murder; and cruelty to dumb animals; not going to church; most kinds of amusement. "Original sin" means that anything we enjoy doing is wrong.

Q.: What is faith?

A.: Resolutely shutting your eyes to scientific fact.

Q.: What is the human intellect?

A.: A barrier to faith.

Q.: What are the seven Christian virtues?

A.: Respectability; childishness; mental timidity; dullness; sentimentality; censoriousness; and depression of spirits.

Q.: Wilt thou be baptized in this faith?

A.: No fear!

I cannot help feeling that as a statement of Christian orthodoxy, these replies are inadequate, if not misleading. But I also cannot help feeling that they do fairly accurately represent what many people take Christian orthodoxy to be.

Whenever an average Christian is represented in a novel or a play, he is pretty sure to be shown practicing one or all of the Seven Deadly Virtues just enumerated, and I am afraid that this is the impression made by the average Christian upon the world at large.

Perhaps we are not following Christ all the way or in quite the right spirit. We are likely, for example, to be a little sparing of the palms and the hosannas. We are chary of wielding the scourge of small cords, lest we should offend somebody or interfere with trade. We do not furnish up our wits to disentangle knotty questions about Sunday observance and tribute money, nor hasten to sit at the feet of the doctors, both hearing them and asking them questions. We pass hastily over disquieting jests about making friends with the mammon of unrighteousness and alarming observations about bringing not peace but a sword; nor do we distinguish ourselves by the graciousness with which we sit at meat with publicans and sinners. Somehow or other, and with the best intentions, we have shown the world the typical Christian in the likeness of a crashing and rather ill-natured bore—and this in the name of one who assuredly never bored a soul in those thirty-three years during which he passed through the world like a flame.

Let us, in heaven's name, drag out the divine drama from under the dreadful accumulation of slipshod thinking and trashy sentiment heaped upon it, and set it on an open stage to startle the world into some sort of vigorous reaction. If the pious are the first to be shocked, so much worse for the pious—others will pass into the kingdom of heaven before them. If all men are offended because of Christ, let them be offended; but where is the sense of their being offended at something that is not Christ and is nothing like him? We do him singularly little honor by watering down his personality till it could not offend a fly. Surely it is not the business of the Church to adapt Christ to men, but to adapt men to Christ.

It is the dogma that is the drama—not beautiful phrases,

nor comforting sentiments, nor vague aspirations to loving-kindness and uplift, nor the promise of something nice after death—but the terrifying assertion that the same God who made the world, lived in the world and passed through the grave and gate of death. Show that to the heathen, and they may not believe it; but at least they may realize that here is something that a man might be glad to believe.

What Do We Believe?

IN ORDINARY TIMES we get along surprisingly well, on the whole, without ever discovering what our faith really is. If, now and again, this remote and academic problem is so unmannerly as to thrust its way into our minds, there are plenty of things we can do to drive the intruder away. We can get the car out or go to a party or to the cinema or read a detective story or have a row with a district council or write a letter to the papers about the habits of the nightjar or Shakespeare's use of nautical metaphor. Thus we build up a defense mechanism against self-questioning because, to tell the truth, we are very much afraid of ourselves.

"When a strong man armed keepeth his palace, his goods are in peace. But when a stronger than he shall come upon him . . . he taketh from him all his armor wherein he trusted. . . ." So to us in wartime, cut off from mental distractions by restrictions and blackouts, and cowering in a

29

cellar with a gas mask under threat of imminent death, comes in the stronger fear and sits down beside us.

"What," he demands, rather disagreeably, "do you make of all this? Is there indeed anything you value more than life, or are you making a virtue of necessity? What do you believe? Is your faith a comfort to you under the present circumstances?"

At this point, before he has time to sidetrack the argument and entangle us in irrelevancies, we shall do well to reply boldly that a faith is not primarily a comfort, but a truth about ourselves. What we in fact believe is not necessarily the theory we most desire or admire. It is the thing that, consciously or unconsciously, we take for granted and act on. Thus, it is useless to say that we believe in the friendly treatment of minorities if, in practice, we habitually bully the office clerk; our actions clearly show that we believe in nothing of the sort. Only when we know what we truly believe can we decide whether it is comforting. If we are comforted by something we do not really believe, then we had better think again.

Now, there does exist an official statement of Christian belief, and if we examine it with a genuine determination to discover what the words mean, we shall find it is a very strange one. And whether, as Christians declare, man was made in the image of God or, as the cynic said, man has made God in the image of man, the conclusion is the same—namely, that this strange creed purports to tell us the essential facts, not only about God, but also about the true nature of man. And the first important thing it proclaims about that nature is one that we may not always admit in words, though I think we do act upon it more often than we suppose.

I believe in God the Father Almighty, Maker of all things. That is the thundering assertion with which we start; that the great fundamental quality that makes God, and us with him, what we are is creative activity. After this, we can scarcely pretend that there is anything negative, static, or

sedative about the Christian religion. "In the beginning
God created"; from everlasting to everlasting. He is God the
Father and Maker. And, by implication, man is most god-
like and most himself when he is occupied in creation. And
by this statement we assert further that the will and power
to make is an absolute value, the ultimate good-in-itself,
self-justified and self-explanatory.

How far can we check this assertion as it concerns ourselves? The men who create with their minds and those who
create (not merely labor) with their hands will, I think,
agree that their periods of creative activity are those in
which they feel right with themselves and the world. And
those who bring life into the world will tell you the same
thing. There is a psychological theory that artistic creation
is merely a compensation for the frustration of sexual creativeness; but it is more probable that the making of life is
only one manifestation of the universal urge to create. Our
worst trouble today is our feeble hold on creation. To sit
down and let ourselves be spoon-fed with the ready-made
is to lose our grip on our only true life and our only real
selves.

*And in the only-begotten Son of God, by whom all things
were made. He was incarnate; crucified, dead and buried; and
rose again.* The second statement warns us what to expect
when the creative energy is manifested in a world subject to
the forces of destruction. It makes things and manifests itself in time and matter, and can no other because it is
begotten of the creative will. So doing, it suffers through
the opposition of other wills, as well as through the dead
resistance of inertia. (There is no room here to discuss
whether will is really free; if we did not, in fact, believe it to
be free, we could neither act nor live.)

The creative will presses on to its end, regardless of what
it may suffer by the way. It does not choose suffering, but it
will not avoid it, and must expect it. We say that it is love,
and sacrifices itself for what it loves; and this is true, provided we understand what we mean by sacrifice. Sacrifice is

what it looks like to other people, but to that-which-loves I think it does not appear so. When one really cares, the self is forgotten, and the sacrifice becomes only a part of the activity. Ask yourself: if there is something you supremely want to do, do you count as self-sacrifice the difficulties encountered or the other possible activities cast aside? You do not. The time when you deliberately say, "I must sacrifice this, that, or the other" is when you do not supremely desire the end in view. At such times you are doing your duty, and that is admirable, but it is not love. But as soon as your duty becomes your love the self-sacrifice is taken for granted, and, whatever the world calls it, you call it so no longer.

Moreover, defeat cannot hold the creative will; it can pass through the grave and rise again. If it cannot go by the path of cooperation, it will go by the path of death and victory. But it does us no credit if we force it to go that way. It is our business to recognize it when it appears and lead it into the city with hosannas. If we betray it or do nothing to assist it, we may earn the unenviable distinction of going down in history with Judas and Pontius Pilate.

I believe in the Holy Ghost, the lord and life-giver. In this odd and difficult phrase, the Christian affirms that the life in him proceeds from the eternal creativeness; and that therefore so far as he is moved by that creativeness, and so far only, he is truly alive. The word *ghost* is difficult to us; the alternative word *spirit* is in some ways more difficult still, for it carries with it still more complicated mental associations. The Greek word is *pneuma*, breath: "I believe in the breath of life." And indeed, when we are asked, "What do you value more than life?" the answer can only be, "Life—the right kind of life, the creative and god-like life." And life, of any kind, can be had only if we are ready to lose life altogether—a plain observation of fact that we acknowledge every time a child is born, or, indeed, whenever we plunge into a stream of traffic in the hope of attaining a more desirable life on the other side.

And I believe in one Church and baptism, in the resurrection of the body and life everlasting. The final clauses define what Christians believe about man and matter. First, that all those who believe in the creative life are members of one another and make up the present body in which that life is manifest. They accept for themselves everything that was affirmed of creative life incarnate, including the love and, if necessary, the crucifixion, death, and victory. Looking at what happened to that life, they will expect to be saved, not from danger and suffering, but in danger and suffering. And the resurrection of the body means more, I think, than we are accustomed to suppose. It means that, whatever happens, there can be no end to the manifestation of creative life. Whether the life makes its old body again, or an improved body, or a totally new body, it will and must create, since that is its true nature.

"This is the Christian faith, which except a man believe faithfully he cannot be saved." The harsh and much-disputed statement begins to look like a blunt statement of fact, for how can anyone make anything of life if there is no belief in life? If we truly desire a creative life for ourselves and other people, it is our task to rebuild the world along creative lines, but we must be sure that we desire it enough.

Creed or Chaos?

And when he is come, he will reprove the world of sin, and of righteousness, and of judgment; Of sin, because they believe not in me; Of righteousness, because I go to the Father, and ye see me no more; Of judgment, because the prince of this world is judged.
—John 16:8–11.

IT IS WORSE THAN USELESS for Christians to talk about the importance of Christian morality unless they are prepared to take their stand upon the fundamentals of Christian theology. It is a lie to say that dogma does not matter; it matters enormously. It is fatal to let people suppose that Christianity is only a mode of feeling; it is vitally necessary to insist that it is first and foremost a rational explanation of the universe. It is hopeless to offer Christianity as a vaguely idealistic aspiration of a simple and consoling kind; it is, on the contrary, a hard, tough, exacting, and complex doctrine,

34

steeped in a drastic and uncompromising realism. And it is fatal to imagine that everybody knows quite well what Christianity is and needs only a little encouragement to practice it. The brutal fact is that in this Christian country not one person in a hundred has the faintest notion what the Church teaches about God or man or society or the person of Jesus Christ.

If you think I am exaggerating, ask the army chaplains. Apart from a possible one percent of intelligent and instructed Christians, there are three kinds of people we have to deal with. There are the frank and open heathen, whose notions of Christianity are a dreadful jumble of rags and tags of Bible anecdotes and clotted mythological nonsense. There are the ignorant Christians, who combine a mild, gentle-Jesus sentimentality with vaguely humanistic ethics—most of these are Arian heretics.* Finally, there are the more-or-less instructed churchgoers, who know all the arguments about divorce and auricular confession and communion in two kinds, but are about as well equipped to do battle on fundamentals against a Marxian atheist or a Wellsian agnostic as a boy with a peashooter facing a fan-fire of machine guns. Theologically, this country is at present in a state of utter chaos, established in the name of religious toleration, and rapidly degenerating into the flight from reason and the death of hope. We are not happy in this condition, and there are signs of a very great eagerness, especially among the younger people, to find a creed to which they can give wholehearted adherence.

This is the Church's opportunity, if she chooses to take it. So far as the people's readiness to listen goes, she has not been in so strong a position for at least two centuries. The rival philosophies of humanism, enlightened self-interest, and mechanical progress have broken down badly; the antagonism of science has proved to be far more apparent than real; and the happy-go-lucky doctrine of *laissez-faire* is

---

*Or possibly Adoptionists; they do not formulate their theories with any great precision.—D.L.S.

completely discredited. But no good whatever will be done by a retreat into personal piety or by mere exhortation to a recall to prayer. The thing that is in danger is the whole structure of society, and it is necessary to persuade thinking men and women of the vital and intimate connection between the structure of society and the theological doctrines of Christianity.

The task is not made easier by the obstinate refusal of a great body of nominal Christians, both lay and clerical, to face the theological question. "Take away theology and give us some nice religion" has been a popular slogan for so long that we are likely to accept it, without inquiring whether religion without theology has any meaning. And however unpopular I may make myself, I shall and will affirm that the reason why the churches are discredited today is not that they are too bigoted about theology, but that they have run away from theology. The Church of Rome alone has retained her prestige because she puts theology in the foreground of her teaching. Some of us may perhaps think it a rather unimaginative and confined theology, but that is not the point. The point is that the Church of Rome is a theological society, in a sense in which the Church of England, taken as a whole, is not, and that because of this insistence of theology, she is a body disciplined, honored, and sociologically important.

I should like to do two things. First, to point out that if we really want a Christian society, we must teach Christianity, and that it is absolutely impossible to teach Christianity without teaching Christian dogma. Secondly, to put before you a list of half a dozen or so main doctrinal points that the world most especially needs to have drummed into its ears at this moment—doctrines forgotten or misinterpreted but which (if they are true as the Church maintains them to be) are cornerstones in that rational structure of human society that is the alternative to world chaos.

I will begin with this matter of the inevitability of dogma, if Christianity is to be anything more than a little, mild, wishful thinking about ethical behavior.

Writing in *The Spectator*, Dr. Selbie, former Principal of Mansfield College, discussed the subject of "The Army and the Churches." In the course of this article there occurs a passage that exposes the root cause of the failure of the churches to influence the life of the common people.

. . . the rise of the new dogmatism, whether in its Calvinist or Thomist form, constitutes a fresh and serious threat to Christian unity. The tragedy is that *all this, however interesting to theologians, is hopelessly irrelevant to the life and thought of the average man*, who is more puzzled than ever by the disunion of the Churches, and by the theological and ecclesiastical differences on which it is based.

Now I am perfectly ready to agree that disputes between the churches constitute a menace to Christendom. And I will admit that I am not quite sure what is meant by the new dogmatism; it might, I suppose, mean the appearance of new dogmas among the followers of St. Thomas and Calvin, respectively. But I rather fancy it means a fresh attention to, and reassertion of, old dogma, and that when Dr. Selbie says that all this is irrelevant to the life and thought of the average man, he is deliberately saying that Christian dogma, as such, is irrelevant.

But if Christian dogma is irrelevant to life, to what, in Heaven's name, is it relevant?—since religious dogma is in fact nothing but a statement of doctrines concerning the nature of life and the universe. If Christian ministers really believe it is only an intellectual game for theologians and has no bearing upon human life, it is no wonder that their congregations are ignorant, bored, and bewildered. And, indeed, in the very next paragraph, Dr. Selbie recognizes the relation of Christian dogma to life:

. . . peace can come about only through a practical application of Christian principles and values. But this must have behind it *something more than a reaction against* that *pagan humanism* that has been found wanting.

The "something more" is dogma, and cannot be anything else, for between humanism and Christianity and between paganism and theism there is no distinction whatever except a distinction of dogma. That you cannot have Christian principles without Christ is becoming increasingly clear because their validity as principles depends on Christ's authority; and as we have seen, the totalitarian states, having ceased to believe in Christ's authority, are logically quite justified in repudiating Christian principles. If the average man is required to believe in Christ and accept His authority for Christian principles, it is surely relevant to inquire who or what Christ is, and why His authority should be accepted. But the question, "What think ye of Christ?" lands the average man at once in the very knottiest kind of dogmatic riddle. It is quite useless to say that it doesn't matter particularly who or what Christ was or by what authority he did those things, and that even if he was only a man, he was a very nice man and we ought to live by his principles; for that is merely humanism, and if the average man in Germany chooses to think that Hitler is a nicer sort of man with still more attractive principles, the Christian humanist has no answer to make.

It is not true at all that dogma is hopelessly irrelevant to the life and thought of the average man. What is true is that ministers of the Christian religion often assert that it is, present it for consideration as though it were, and, in fact, by their faulty exposition of it make it so. The central dogma of the Incarnation is that by which relevance stands or falls. If Christ were only man, then he is entirely irrelevant to any thought about God; if he is only God, then he is entirely irrelevant to any experience of human life. It is, in the strictest sense, necessary to the salvation of relevance that a man should believe rightly the Incarnation of Our Lord, Jesus Christ. Unless he believes rightly, there is not the faintest reason why he should believe at all. And in that case, it is wholly irrelevant to chatter about Christian principles.

If the average man is going to be interested in Christ at all, it is the dogma that will provide the interest. The trouble is that, in nine cases out of ten, he has never been offered the dogma. What he has been offered is a set of technical theological terms that nobody has taken the trouble to translate into language relevant to ordinary life.

". . . Jesus Christ, the Son of God, is God and man." What does this suggest, except that God the Creator (the irritable, old gentleman with the beard) in some mysterious manner fathered upon the Virgin Mary something amphibious, neither one thing nor t'other, like a merman? And, like human sons, wholly distinct from and (with some excuse) probably antagonistic to the father? And what, in any case, has this remarkable hybrid to do with John Doe or Jane Doe? This attitude of mind is that called by theologians Nestorianism, or perhaps a debased form of Arianism. But we really cannot just give it a technical label and brush it aside as something irrelevant to the thought of the average man. The average man produced it. It is, in fact, an immediate and unsophisticated expression of the thought of the average man. And at the risk of plunging him into the abominable heresy of the Patripassians or the Theopaschites, we must unite with Athanasius to assure John and Jane Doe that the God who lived and died in the world was the same God who made the world, and that, therefore, God himself has the best possible reasons for understanding and sympathizing with John and Jane's personal troubles.

"But," John Doe and Jane Doe will instantly object that, "it can't have mattered very much to him if he was God. A god can't really suffer like you and me. Besides, the parson says we are to try and be like Christ; but that's all nonsense—we can't be God, and it's silly to ask us to try." This able exposition of the Eutychian heresy can scarcely be dismissed as merely "interesting to theologians"; it appears to interest John and Jane to the point of irritation. Willy-nilly, we are forced to involve ourselves further in dogmatic theology and insist that Christ is perfect God and perfect man.

At this point, language will trip us up. The average man is not to be restrained from thinking that "perfect God" implies a comparison with gods less perfect, and that "perfect man" means "the best kind of man you can possibly have." While both these propositions are quite true, they are not precisely what we want to convey. It will perhaps be better to say, "altogether God and altogether man"—God and man at the same time, in every respect and completely; God from eternity to eternity and from the womb to the grave, a man also from the womb to the grave and now.

"That," replies John Doe, "is all very well, but it leaves me cold. Because, if He was God all the time, he must have known that his sufferings and death and so on wouldn't last, and he could have stopped them by a miracle if he had liked, so his pretending to be an ordinary man was nothing but playacting." And Jane Doe adds, "You can't call a person 'altogether man' if He was God and didn't want to do anything wrong. It was easy enough for Him to be good, but it's not at all the same thing for me. How about all that temptation stuff? Playacting again. It doesn't help me to live what you call a Christian life."

John and Jane are now on the way to becoming convinced Apollinarians, a fact which, however interesting to theologians, has a distinct relevance also to the lives of those average men, since they propose, on the strength of it, to dismiss Christian principles as impracticable. There is no help for it. We must insist upon Christ's possession of a reasonable soul as well as human flesh; we must admit the human limitations of knowledge and intellect; we must take a hint from Christ himself and suggest that miracles belong to the Son of Man as well as to the Son of God; we must postulate a human will liable to temptation; and we must be quite firm about "equal to the Father as touching his Godhead and inferior to the Father as touching his manhood." Complicated as the theology is, the average man has walked straight into the heart of the Athanasian Creed, and we are bound to follow.

Teachers and preachers never, I think, make it sufficiently clear that dogmas are not a set of arbitrary regulations invented *a priori* by a committee of theologians enjoying a bout of all-in dialectical wrestling. Most of them were hammered out under pressure of urgent practical necessity to provide an answer to heresy. And heresy is, as I have tried to show, largely the expression of opinion of the untutored average man, trying to grapple with the problems of the universe at the point where they begin to interfere with daily life and thought. To me, engaged in my diabolical occupation of going to and fro in the world and walking up and down in it, conversations and correspondence bring daily a magnificent crop of all the standard heresies. I am extremely well familiar with them as practical examples of the life and thought of the average man, though I had to hunt through the encyclopedia to fit them with their proper theological titles for the purposes of this address. For the answers I need not go so far; they are compendiously set forth in the creeds.

But an interesting fact is this: that nine out of ten of my heretics are exceedingly surprised to discover that the creeds contain any statements that bear a practical and comprehensible meaning. If I tell them it is an article of faith that the same God who made the world endured the suffering of the world, they ask in perfect good faith what connection there is between that statement and the story of Jesus. If I draw their attention to the dogma that the same Jesus who was the divine love was also the light of light, the divine wisdom, they are surprised. Some of them thank me very heartily for this entirely novel and original interpretation of Scripture, which they never heard of before and suppose me to have invented. Others say irritably that they don't like to think that wisdom and religion have anything to do with each other, and that I should do much better to cut out the wisdom and reason and intelligence and stick to a simple gospel of love. But whether they are pleased or annoyed, they are interested; and the thing that interests them, whether or not they suppose it to be my invention, is the resolute assertion of the dogma.

As regards Dr. Selbie's complaint that insistence on dogma only affronts people and throws into relief the internecine quarrels of Christendom, may I say two things? First, I believe it to be a grave mistake to present Christianity as something charming and popular with no offense in it. Seeing that Christ went about the world giving the most violent offense to all kinds of people, it would seem absurd to expect that the doctrine of his person can be so presented as to offend nobody. We cannot blink at the fact that gentle Jesus, meek and mild, was so stiff in his opinions and so inflammatory in his language that he was thrown out of church, stoned, hunted from place to place, and finally gibbeted as a firebrand and a public danger. Whatever his peace was, it was not the peace of an amiable indifference; and he said in so many words that what he brought with him was fire and sword. That being so, nobody need be too much surprised or disconcerted at finding that a determined preaching of Christian dogma may sometimes result in a few angry letters of protest or a difference of opinion on the parish council.

The other thing is this: that I find by experience there is a very large measure of agreement among Christian denominations on all doctrine that is really ecumenical. A rigidly Catholic interpretation of the creeds, for example—including the Athanasian Creed—will find support both in Rome and in Geneva. Objections will come chiefly from the heathen, and from a noisy but not very representative bunch of heretical parsons who once in their youth read Robertson or Conybeare and have never got over it. But what is urgently necessary is that certain fundamentals should be restated in terms that make their meaning—and indeed, the mere fact that they have a meaning—clear to the ordinary, uninstructed heathen to whom technical theological language has become a dead letter.

May I now mention some of the dogmas concerning

which I find there are most ignorance and misunderstanding and about which I believe the modern world most urgently needs to be told? Out of a very considerable number I have selected seven as being what I may call key positions, namely, God, man, sin, judgment, matter, work, and society. They are, of course, all closely bound together—Christian doctrine is not a set of rules, but one vast interlocking rational structure—but there are particular aspects of these seven subjects that seem to me to need special emphasis at the moment.

(1) *God.* At the risk of appearing quite insolently obvious, I shall say that if the Church is to make any impression on the modern mind she will have to preach Christ and the cross.

Of late years, the Church has not succeeded very well in preaching Christ; she has preached Jesus, which is not quite the same thing. I find that the ordinary man simply does not grasp at all the idea that Jesus Christ and God the Creator are held to be literally the same person. They believe Catholic doctrine to be that God the Father made the world and that Jesus Christ redeemed mankind, and that these two characters are quite separate personalities. The phrasing of the Nicene Creed is here a little unfortunate—it is easy to read it as: "being of one substance with the-Father-by-whom-all-things-were-made." The church catechism—again rather unfortunately—emphasizes the distinction: "God the Father, who hath made me and all the world, God the Son, who hath redeemed me and all mankind." The distinction of the persons within unity of the substance is philosophically quite proper, and familiar enough to any creative artist; but the majority of people are not creative artists, and they have it very firmly fixed in their heads that the person who bore the sins of the world was not the eternal creative life of the world, but an entirely different person, who was in fact the victim of God the Creator. It is dangerous to emphasize one aspect of a doctrine at the expense of the other, but at this present moment the danger that anybody will confound the persons is so remote as to be negligible. What everybody does is to divide the substance—with the result that the whole Jesus history becomes an unmeaning anecdote of the brutality of God to man.

It is only with the confident assertion of the creative divinity of the Son that the doctrine of the Incarnation becomes a real revelation of the structure of the world. And here Christianity has its enormous advantage over every other religion in the world. It is the *only* religion that gives value to evil and suffering. It affirms—not, like Christian Science, that evil has no real existence, nor yet, like Buddhism, that good consists in a refusal to experience evil—but that perfection is attained through the active and positive effort to wrench a real good out of a real evil.

I will not now go into the very difficult question of the nature of evil and the reality of not being, though the modern physicists seem to be giving us a very valuable lead about that particular philosophic dilemma. But it seems to me most important that, in face of present world conditions, the doctrines of the reality of evil and the value of suffering should be kept in the very front line of Christian affirmation. I mean, it is not enough to say that religion produces virtues and personal consolations side by side with the very obvious evils and pains that afflict mankind, but that God is alive and at work within the evil and the suffering, perpetually transforming them by the positive energy which he had with the Father before the world was made.

(2) *Man.* A young and intelligent priest remarked to me the other day that he thought one of the greatest sources of strength in Christianity today lay in the profoundly pessimistic view it took of human nature. There is a great deal in what he says. The people who are most discouraged and made despondent by the barbarity and stupidity of human behavior at this time are those who think highly of *homo sapiens* as a product of evolution, and who still cling to an optimistic belief in the civilizing influence of progress and

enlightenment. To them, the appalling outbursts of bestial ferocity in the totalitarian states, and the obstinate self-ishness and stupid greed of capitalist society, are not merely shocking and alarming. For them, these things are the utter negation of everything in which they have be-lieved. It is as though the bottom had dropped out of their universe. The whole thing looks like a denial of all reason, and they feel as if they and the world had gone mad together.

Now for the Christian, this is not so. He is as deeply shocked and grieved as anybody else, but he is not as-tonished. He has never thought very highly of human na-ture left to itself. He has been accustomed to the idea that there is a deep interior dislocation in the very center of human personality, and that you can never, as they say, "make people good by an Act of Parliament," just because laws are man-made and therefore partake of the imperfect and self-contradictory nature of man. Humanly speaking, it is not true at all that "truly to know the good is to do the good"; it is far truer to say with St. Paul that "the evil I would not, that I do"; so that the mere increase of knowl-edge is of very little help in the struggle to outlaw evil. The delusion of the mechanical perfectibility of mankind through a combined process of scientific knowledge and unconscious evolution has been responsible for a great deal of heartbreak. It is, at bottom, far more pessimistic than Christian pessimism because, if science and progress break down, there is nothing to fall back upon. Humanism is self-contained—it provides for man no resources outside him-self. The Christian dogma of the double nature in man—which asserts that man is disintegrated and necessarily im-perfect in himself and all his works, yet closely related by a real unity of substance with an eternal perfection within and beyond him—makes the present parlous state of human society seem both less hopeless and less irrational. I say "the present parlous state"—but that is to limit it too much. A man told me the other day: "I have a little boy of a year old. When the war broke out, I was very much distressed about him because I found I was taking it for granted that life ought to be better and easier for him than it had been for my generation. Then I realized that I had no right to take this for granted at all—that the fight between good and evil must be the same for him as it had always been, and then I ceased to feel so much distressed."

As Lord David Cecil has said: "The jargon of the philosophy of progress taught us to think that the savage and primitive state of man is behind us, we still talk of the present 'return to barbarism.' But barbarism is not behind us, it is beneath us." And in the same article he observes: "Christianity has compelled the mind of man, not because it is the most cheering view of human existence, but because it is truest to the facts." I think this is true; and it seems to me quite disastrous that the idea should have got about that Christianity is an other-worldly, unreal, idealistic kind of religion that suggests that if we are good we shall be happy—or if not, it will all be made up to us in the next existence. On the contrary, it is fiercely and even harshly realistic, insisting that the kingdom of heaven can never be attained in this world except by unceasing toil and struggle and vigilance: that, in fact, we cannot be good and cannot be happy, but that there are certain eternal achievements that make even happiness look like trash. It has been said, I think by Berdyaev, that nothing can prevent the human soul from preferring creativeness to happiness. In this lies man's substantial likeness to the Divine Christ, who in this world suffers and creates continually, being incarnate in the bonds of matter.

(3) *Sin*. This doctrine of man leads naturally to the doctrine of sin. One of the really surprising things about the present bewilderment of humanity is that the Christian Church now finds herself called upon to proclaim the old and hated doctrine of sin as a gospel of cheer and encouragement. The final tendency of the modern philosophies—hailed in their day as a release from the burden of

sinfulness—has been to bind man hard and fast in the chains of an iron determinism. The influences of heredity and environment, of glandular makeup and the control exercised by the unconscious, of economic necessity and the mechanics of biological development, have all been invoked to assure man that he is not responsible for his misfortunes and therefore not to be held guilty. Evil has been represented as something imposed upon him from without, not made by him from within. The dreadful conclusion follows inevitably, that as he is not responsible for evil, he cannot alter it; even though evolution and progress may offer some alleviation in the future, there is no hope for you and me, here and now. I well remember how an aunt of mine, brought up in an old-fashioned liberalism, protested angrily against having continually to call herself a miserable sinner when reciting the Litany. Today, if we could really be persuaded that we are miserable sinners—that the trouble is not outside us but inside us, and that therefore, by the grace of God, we can do something to put it right—we should receive that message as the most hopeful and heartening thing that can be imagined.

Needless to say, the whole doctrine of original sin will have to be restated in terms that the ordinary modern man, brought up on biology and Freudian psychology, can understand. These sciences have done an enormous amount to expose the nature and mechanism of man's inner dislocation and ought to be powerful weapons in the hand of the Church. It is a thousand pities that the Church should ever have allowed these weapons to be turned against her.

(4) *Judgment*. Much the same thing is true of the doctrine of judgment. The word *punishment* for sin has become so corrupted that it ought never to be used. But once we have established the true doctrine of man's nature, the true nature of judgment becomes startlingly clear and rational. It is the inevitable consequence of man's attempt to regulate life and society on a system that runs counter to the facts of his own nature. In the physical sphere, typhus and cholera are

a judgment on dirty living and not because God shows an arbitrary favoritism to nice, clean people, but because of an essential element in the physical structure of the universe. In the state, the brutal denial of freedom to the individual will issue in a judgment of blood because man is so made that oppression is more intolerable to him than death. The avaricious greed that prompts men to cut down forests for the speedy making of money brings down a judgment of flood and famine because the sin of avarice in the spiritual sphere runs counter to the physical law of nature. We must not say that such behavior is wrong because it does not pay, but rather that it does not pay because it is wrong. As T. S. Eliot says: "A wrong attitude toward nature implies, somewhere, a wrong attitude toward God, and the consequence is an inevitable doom."

(5) *Matter.* At this point we shall find ourselves compelled to lay down the Christian doctrine concerning the material universe; and it is here, I think, that we shall have our best opportunity to explain the meaning of sacramentalism. The common man labors under a delusion that, for the Christian, matter is evil and the body is evil. For this misapprehension, St. Paul must bear some blame, St. Augustine of Hippo a great deal more, and Calvin a very great deal. But so long as the Church continues to teach the manhood of God and to celebrate the sacraments of the Eucharist and of marriage, no living man should dare to say that matter and body are not sacred to her. She must insist strongly that the whole material universe is an expression and incarnation of the creative energy of God, as a book or a picture is the material expression of the creative soul of the artist. For that reason, all good and creative handling of the material universe is holy and beautiful, and all abuse of the material universe is a crucifixion of the body of Christ. The whole question of the right use to be made of art, of the intellect, and of the material resources of the world is bound up in this. Because of this, the exploitation of man or of matter for commercial uses stands condemned, together

with all debasement of the arts and perversions of the intellect. If matter and the physical nature of man are evil, or if they are of no importance except as they serve an economic system, then there is nothing to restrain us from abusing them as we choose—nothing except the absolute certainty that any such abuse will eventually come up against the unalterable law and issue in judgment and destruction. In these as in all other matters, we cannot escape the law; we have only the choice of fulfilling it freely by the way of grace or willy-nilly by the way of judgment.

(6) *Work.* The unsacramental attitude of modern society to man and matter is probably closely connected with its unsacramental attitude to work. The Church is a good deal to blame for having connived at this. From the eighteenth century onwards, she has tended to acquiesce in what I may call the industrious apprentice view of the matter: "Work hard and be thrifty, and God will bless you with a contented mind and a competence." This is nothing but enlightened self-interest in its vulgarest form and plays directly into the hands of the monopolist and the financier. Nothing has so deeply discredited the Christian Church as her squalid submission to the economic theory of society. The burning question of the Christian attitude to money is being so eagerly debated nowadays that it is scarcely necessary to do more than remind ourselves that the present unrest, both in Russia and in Central Europe, is an immediate judgment upon a financial system that has subordinated man to economics, and that no mere readjustment of economic machinery will have any lasting effect if it keeps man a prisoner inside the machine.

This is the burning question; but I believe there is a still more important and fundamental question waiting to be dealt with, and that is, what men in a Christian society ought to think and feel about work. Curiously enough, apart from the passage in Genesis that suggests that work is a hardship and a judgment on sin, Christian doctrine is not very explicit about work. I believe, however, that there is a

Christian doctrine of work, very closely related to the doctrines of the creative energy of God and the divine image in man. The modern tendency seems to be to identify work with gainful employment; and this is, I maintain, the essential heresy at the back of the great economic fallacy that allows wheat and coffee to be burned and fish to be used for manure while whole populations stand in need of food. The fallacy is that work is not the expression of man's creative energy in the service of society, but only something he does in order to obtain money and leisure.

A very able surgeon put it to me like this: "What is happening," he said, "is that nobody works for the sake of getting the thing done. The result of the work is a by-product; the aim of the work is to make money to do something else. Doctors practice medicine not primarily to relieve suffering, but to make a living—the cure of the patient is something that happens on the way. Lawyers accept briefs not because they have a passion for justice, but because the law is the profession that enables them to live."

"The reason," he added, "why men often find themselves happy and satisfied in the army is that for the first time in their lives they find themselves doing something not for the sake of the pay, which is miserable, but for the sake of getting the thing done."

I will only add to this one thing that seems to me very symptomatic. I was shown a "scheme for a Christian society" drawn up by a number of young and earnest Roman Catholics. It contained a number of clauses dealing with work and employment—minimum wages, hours of labor, treatment of employees, housing, and so on—all very proper and Christian. But it offered no machinery whatever for ensuring that the work itself should be properly done. In its lack of a sacramental attitude to work, that is, it was as empty as a set of trade-union regulations. We may remember that a medieval guild did insist, not only on the employer's duty to his workmen, but also on the laborer's duty to his work.

If man's fulfilment of his nature is to be found in the full expression of his divine creativeness, then we urgently need a Christian doctrine of work, which shall provide, not only for proper conditions of employment, but also that the work shall be such as a man may do with his whole heart, and that he shall do it for the very work's sake. But we cannot expect a sacramental attitude to work, while many people are forced, by our evil standard of values, to do work that is a spiritual degradation—a long series of financial trickeries, for example, or the manufacture of vulgar and useless trivialities.

(7) *Society*. Lastly, a word or two about the Christian doctrine of society—not about its translation into political terms, but about its dogmatic basis. It rests on the doctrine of what God is and what man is, and it is impossible to have a Christian doctrine of society except as a corollary to Christian dogma about the place of man in the universe. This is, or should be, obvious. The one point to which I should like to draw attention is the Christian doctrine of the moral law. The attempts to abolish wars and wickedness by the moral law is doomed to failure because of the fact of sinfulness. Law, like every other product of human activity, shares the integral human imperfection; it is, in the old Calvinistic phrase, "of the nature of sin." That is to say, all legality, if erected into an absolute value, contains within itself the seeds of judgment and catastrophe. The law is necessary, but only, as it were, as a protective fence against the forces of evil, behind which the divine activity of grace may do its redeeming work. We can, for example, never make a positive peace or a positive righteousness by enactments against offenders; law is always prohibitive, negative, and corrupted by the interior contradictions of man's divided nature; it belongs to the category of judgment. That is why an intelligent understanding about sin is necessary to preserve the world from putting an unjustified confidence in the efficacy of the moral law taken by itself. It will never drive our Beelzebub; it cannot because it is only human and not divine.

Nevertheless, the law must be rightly understood, or it is

not possible to make the world understand the meaning of grace. There is only one real law—the law of the universe; it may be fulfilled either by way of judgment or by the way of grace, but it must be fulfilled one way or the other. If men will not understand the meaning of judgment, they will never come to understand the meaning of grace. If they hear not Moses or the prophets, neither will they be persuaded, though one rose from the dead.

A Vote of Thanks to Cyrus

I OWE A CERTAIN DEBT to Cyrus the Persian. I made his acquaintance fairly early, for he lived between the pages of a children's magazine, in a series entitled *Tales from Herodotus*, or something of that kind. There was a picture of him being brought up by the herdsman of King Astyages, dressed in a short tunic very like the garment worn by the young Theseus or Perseus in the illustrations to Kingsley's *Heroes*. He belonged quite definitely to classicial times; did he not overcome Croesus, that rich king of whom Solon had said, "Call no man happy until he is dead"? The story was half fairy tale—"his mother dreamed," "the oracle spoke"—but half history too: he commanded his soldiers to divert the course of the Euphrates, so that they might march into Babylon along the riverbed; that sounded like practical warfare. Cyrus was pigeonholed in my mind with the Greeks and Romans.

So for a long time he remained. And then, one day, I realized, with a shock as of sacrilege, that on that famous expedition he had marched clean out of our Herodotus and slap into the Bible. *Mene, mene, tekel uppharsin*—the palace wall had blazed with the exploits of Cyrus, and Belshazzar's feast had broken up in disorder under the stern and warning eye of the prophet Daniel.

But Daniel and Belshazzar did not live in the classics at all. They lived in the Church, with Adam and Abraham and Elijah, and were dressed like Bible characters, especially Daniel. And here was God—not Zeus or Apollo or any of the Olympian crowd, but the fierce and disheveled old gentleman from Mount Sinai—bursting into Greek history in a most uncharacteristic way and taking an interest in events and people that seemed altogether outside His province. It was disconcerting.

And there was Esther. She lived in a book called *Stories from the Old Testament*, and had done very well for God's chosen people by her diplomatic approach to King Ahasuerus. A good Old-Testament-sounding name, Ahasuerus, reminding one of Ahab and Ahaz and Ahaziah. I cannot remember in what out-of-the-way primer of general knowledge I came across the astonishing equation, thrown out casually in a passing phrase, "Ahasuerus (or Xerxes)." Xerxes!—but one knew all about Xerxes. He was not just classics, but real history; it was against Xerxes that the Greeks had made their desperate and heroic stand at Thermopylae. There was none of the fairy-tale atmosphere of Cyrus about him—no dreams, no oracles, no faithful herdsman—only the noise and dust of armies tramping through the hard outlines and clear colors of a Grecian landscape, where the sun always shone so much more vividly than it did in the Bible.

I think it was chiefly Cyrus and Ahasuerus who prodded me into the belated conviction that history was all of a piece, and that the Bible was part of it. One might have expected Jesus to provide the link between two worlds—the

Caesars were classical history all right. But Jesus was a special case. One used a particular tone of voice in speaking of him, and he dressed neither like Bible nor like classics—he dressed like Jesus, in a fashion closely imitated (down to the halo) by his disciples. If he belonged anywhere, it was to Rome, in spite of strenuous prophetic efforts to identify him with the story of the Bible Jews. Indeed, the Jews themselves had undergone a mysterious change in the blank pages between the Testaments: in the Old, they were good people; in the New, they were bad people—it seemed doubtful whether they really were the same people. Nevertheless, Old or New, all these people lived in Church and were Bible characters—they were not real in the sense that King Alfred was a real person; still less could their conduct be judged by standards that applied to one's own contemporaries.

Most children, I suppose, begin by keeping different bits of history in watertight compartments, of which Bible is the tightest and most impenetrable. But some people seem never to grow out of this habit—possibly because of never having really met Cyrus and Ahasuerus (or Xerxes). Bible critics in particular appear to be persons of very leisurely mental growth. Take, for example, the notorious dispute about the Gospel according to St. John.

Into the details of that dispute I do not propose to go. I only want to point out that the arguments used are such as no critic would ever dream of applying to a modern book of memoirs written by one real person about another. The defects imputed to St. John would be virtues in Mr. Jones, and the values and authenticity of Mr. Jones's contribution to literature would be proved by the same arguments that are used to undermine the authenticity of St. John.

Suppose, for example, Mr. Bernard Shaw were . . . to [write] a volume of reminiscences about Mr. William Archer; would anybody object that the account must be received with suspicion because most of Archer's other contemporaries were dead, or because the style of G.B.S. was very unlike that of a *Times* obituary notice, or because the book contained a great many intimate conversations not recorded in previous memoirs and left out a number of facts that could easily be ascertained by reference to the *Dictionary of National Biography?* Or if Mr. Shaw (being a less vigorous octogenarian than he happily [was]) had dictated part of his material to a respectable clergyman, who had himself added a special note to say that Shaw was the real author and that readers might rely on the accuracy of the memoirs since, after all, Shaw was a close friend of Archer and ought to know. Should we feel that these two worthy men were thereby revealed as self-confessed liars, and dismiss their joint work as a valueless fabrication? Probably not; but then Mr. Shaw is a real person, and lives, not in the Bible, but in Westminster. The time has not come to doubt him. He is already a legend, but not yet a myth; two thousand years hence, perhaps—.

Let us pretend for a moment that Jesus is a real person who died within living memory, and that John is a real author, producing a real book; what sort of announcement shall we look for in the literary page of an ordinary newspaper? Let us put together a brief review, altering some of the names a little to prevent that Bible feeling.

Memoirs of Jesus Christ. By John Bar-Zebedee; edited by the Rev. John Elder, Vicar of St. Faith's, Ephesus. (Kirk, 1978.)

The general public has had to wait a long time for the intimate personal impressions of a great preacher, though the substance of them has for many years been familiarly known in Church circles. The friends of Mr. Bar-Zebedee have frequently urged the octogenarian divine to commit his early memories to paper; this he has now done, with the assistance and under the careful editorship of the Vicar of St. Faith's. The book fulfils a long-felt want.

Very little actually has been put in print about the striking personality who exercised so great an influence upon the last generation. The little anonymous collecting of "Sayings" by "Q" is now, of course, out of print and unobtainable. This is the less regrettable in that the greater part of it has been embodied in Mr. J. Mark's brief obituary study and in the subsequent biographies of Mr. Matthews and Mr. Lucas (who, unhappily, was unable to complete his companion volume of the *Acts of the Apostles*). But hitherto, all these reports have been compiled at secondhand. Now for the first time comes the testimony of a close friend of Jesus, and, as we should expect, it offers a wealth of fresh material.

With great good judgment, Mr. Bar-Zebedee has refrained from going over old ground, except for the purpose of tidying up the chronology that, in previous accounts, was conspicuously lacking. Thus, he makes it plain that Jesus paid at least two visits to Jerusalem during the three years of His ministry—a circumstance that clears up a number of confusing points in the narrative of His arrest; and the two examinations in the ecclesiastical courts are at last clearly distinguished. Many new episodes are related; in particular, it has now become possible to reveal the facts about the mysterious affair at Bethany, hitherto discreetly veiled out of consideration for the surviving members of the Lazarus family, whom rumor had subjected to much vulgar curiosity and political embarrassment.

But the most interesting and important portions of the book are those devoted to Christ's lectures in the temple and the theological and philosophical instructions given privately to his followers. These, naturally, differ considerably in matter and manner from the open-air "talks" delivered before a mixed audience, and shed a flood of new light, both on the massive intellectual equipment of the preacher and on the truly astonishing nature of his claim to authority. Mr. Bar-Zebedee interprets and comments upon these remarkable discourses with considerable learning and with the intimate understanding of one familiar with his master's habits of thought.

Finally, the author of these memoirs reveals himself as that delightful *rara avis*, a "born writer." He commands a fine economy and precision in the use of dialogue; his character sketches (as in the delicate comedy of the blind beggar at the Pool of Siloam) are little masterpieces of quiet humor, while his descriptions of the meal in the upper room, the visit of Simon Bar-Jonah and himself to the sepulcher, and the last uncanny encounter by the Lake of Tiberias are distinguished by an atmospheric quality that places this account of the Nazarene in a category apart.

How reasonable it all sounds, in the journalese jargon to which we have grown accustomed! And how much more readily we may accept discrepancies and additions when once we have rid ourselves of that notion "the earlier, the purer," which, however plausible in the case of folklore, is entirely irrelevant when it comes to real biography. Indeed, the first life of any celebrity is nowadays accepted as an interim document. For considered appreciation we must wait until many contemporaries have gone to where rumor cannot distress them, until grief and passion have died down, until emotion can be remembered in tranquility.

It is rather unfortunate that the higher criticism was first undertaken at a time when all textual criticism tended to be destructive—when the body of Homer was being torn into fragments, the Arthurian romance reduced to its Celtic elements, and the authority of manuscripts established by a mechanical system of verbal agreements. The great secular scholars have already recanted and adopted the slogan of the great archaeologist Didron: "Preserve all you can; restore seldom; never reconstruct." When it came to the Bible, the spirit of destruction was the more gleefully iconoclastic because of the conservative extravagances of the verbal inspiration theory. But the root of the trouble is to be found, I suspect (as usual), in the collapse of dogma. Christ, even for Christians, is not quite really real—not altogether human—and the taint of unreality has spread to his disciples and friends and to his biographers; they are not "real" writers, but just "Bible" writers. John and Matthew and Luke and Mark, some or all of them, disagree about the occasion on which a parable was told or an epigram uttered. One or all must be a liar or untrustworthy because Christ (not being quite real) must have made every remark once and once only. He could not, of course, like a real teacher, have used the same illustration twice, or found it necessary to hammer the same point home twenty times over, as one does when addressing audiences of real people and not of Bible characters.

Nor (one is led to imagine) did Christ ever use any ordinary behavior that is not expressly recorded of him. "We are twice told that he wept, but never that he smiled"—the inference being that he never did smile. Similarly, no doubt, we may infer that he never said, "Please" or "Thank you." But perhaps these common courtesies were left unrecorded precisely because they were common, whereas the tears were (so to speak) "news." True, we have lately got into the habit of headlining common courtesies; the newspaper that published the review of St. John's memoirs would probably have announced on a previous occasion:

PROPHET SMILES

The Prophet of Nazareth smiled graciously yesterday morning on inviting himself to lunch with little Mr. Zacchaeus, a tax collector, who had climbed into a sycamore to watch him pass.

St. Luke, with a better sense of style, merely records that: He looked up and saw him, and said unto him, Zacchaeus, make haste and come down; for today I must abide in thy house. And he made haste and came down and received Him joyfully.

Politeness would suggest that one does not commandeer other people's hospitality with a morose scowl, and that if one is received joyfully, it is usually because one has behaved pleasantly. But these considerations would, of course, apply only to real people.

"Altogether man, with a rational mind and human body—." It is just as well that from time to time Cyrus should march out of Herodotus into the Bible for the synthesis of history and the confutation of history.

The Dates in
The Red-Headed League

AMONG THE CURIOUS CHRONOLOGICAL PROBLEMS encountered by the Sherlock Holmes student, one of the most delicate and fascinating is that of the dates in *The Red-Headed League*. Its difficulties have been most ably set forth by Mr. H. W. Bell in his scholarly and comprehensive study, *Sherlock Holmes and Dr. Watson*. This work—the first and only attempt to place all the cases in chronological order—must inevitably form the basis of all future Holmes-Watson exegesis, and the following statement of the problem is summarized from its pages:

1. Watson says that Jabez Wilson's visit to Baker Street took place on a Saturday in the autumn of 1890. Later on, the day is fixed, by the notice on the door of the League's premises, as October 9. But October 9, 1890, was a Thursday.

2. The advertisement shown to Holmes on this occasion is stated by Watson to have appeared in the *Morning Chronicle* of

April 27, "just two months ago." This is incompatible with all the other dates.

3. Jabez Wilson says that the advertisement appeared "this day eight weeks," which, reckoning back from October 9, would bring it to Thursday, August 14.

4. Wilson also says that the League paid him £4 every Saturday for eight weeks, and that this "cost them two-and-thirty pounds." It is hardly conceivable that Wilson should be mistaken about the money he received. But on the last Saturday "October 9"), the office of the League was closed, and he got no pay. If, therefore, he worked only for eight weeks, he should have received only £28 in all.

Let us now see what we can make of these contradictions. The year 1890 is determined by the original date of publication in the *Strand Magazine* for August, 1891. "(("One day in the autumn of last year") and by the notice on the League door ("The Red-Headed League is dissolved. October 9, 1890"). The day of the week on which Wilson visited Holmes is also fixed, not merely by Holmes's own statements ("today is Saturday"—"today being Saturday rather complicates matters"), but also by the fact that, as Mr. Bell points out, "the choice of Saturday was an essential part of the bankrobbers' plot." The visit to Baker Street, the investigation at Wilson's establishment, and the final capture of the criminals all take place within twenty-four hours (Saturday morning* to the early hours of Sunday), so that we are restricted to a Saturday in the autumn of 1890. Since the date April 27 is an obvious error, which could not by any stretch of the imagination be called "a day in the autumn," there is no reason to reject the month of October mentioned in the notice. We are therefore obliged to choose between the four Saturdays in October, 1890, which fell on the 4, 11, 18, and 25, respectively.

---

*Mr. Bell says "early afternoon"; but Wilson's visit, Holmes's fifty minutes of reflection, and the journey to the City all took place before lunch. Wilson probably arrived about eleven o'clock, coming immediately from Pope's Court, which he had reached at 10 A.M.

Mr. Bell, thinking that Dr. Watson may have misread his own figure 4 as a 9, selects October 4. I emphatically agree that this is the correct date, though I differ from Mr. Bell as to the precise way in which the mistake came about. In my opinion, the crucial points of the problem are (a) the surprising error April 27, and (b) the discrepancy about the money, neither of which anomalies is accounted for in Mr. Bell's commentary. In the following notes I shall hope to show exactly how *a* occurred and to prove that *b* was no error at all, and thus to establish the date by two independent and mutually supporting lines of reasoning.

1. The date October 4 for Wilson's visit to Holmes is *a priori* the most likely, since, as Mr. Bell remarks, Watson is hardly likely to have mistaken any one of the double figures, 11, 18, or 25 for the single figure 9.

2. The advertisement in the *Morning Chronicle* directed the applicants to attend at 7 Pope's Court "on Monday." It was evidently on the very Monday specified in the advertisement that Vincent Spaulding showed the paper to Wilson, since they "put the shutters up" and started for Pope's Court immediately.

3. The wording of the advertisement at first sight suggests that it appeared in the previous Saturday's issue, and this suggestion is supported by Wilson's remark that it appeared "this day *eight* weeks." On examination, however, this will not hold water. If the advertisement appeared on the Saturday, why did Spaulding (who lived on the premises) not show it to Wilson at once? Why should he be reading Saturday's paper on Monday morning? The inference is that the advertisement actually appeared on the Monday. The wording may have been due to carelessness, or the advertisement may have been intended to appear on the Saturday and have been crowded out or arrived too late for insertion on that day.

4. This view is strongly supported by Watson's remark that the advertisement appeared "just two *months* ago." This, if accurate, brings us back to Monday, August 4. Wilson, no doubt, made the common error of reckoning a month as four weeks, whereas Watson was going correctly by the calendar.

5. Duncan Ross asked Wilson if he could "be ready tomorrow," and he accordingly started work the day following the interview,

viz. Tuesday, August 5. On the Saturday immediately succeeding, he was paid £4 "for my week's work." Actually, he had worked only five days, but the salary would, no doubt, be reckoned as from the time of his engagement on the Monday, and, in fact, it is clear from the text that this was so.

6. Wilson thus received in all eight payments of £4. *viz.* on August 9, 16, 23, and 30, and September 6, 13, 20, and 27, before the League was dissolved on the morning of the *ninth* Saturday, October 4; these payments making up the correct total of £32.

7. The only difficulties that now remain are the two incorrect dates given in the text: (a) April 27 as the date of the advertisement, and (b) October 9 as the date of the dissolution of the League.

(a) This is patently absurd and suggests the error of a not-too-intelligent compositor at work upon a crabbed manuscript. Watson was a doctor, and his writing was therefore probably illegible at the best of times; moreover, he may have written his dates in a contracted form and used, in addition, a *J* pen in a poor state of repair. The adjoined pair of figures shows how easily August 4 might be mistaken, under these conditions, for April 27. In this way, the very error itself provides independent testimony that August 4 was the actual date of the advertisement, since it is difficult to see how any of the other dates in August (11, 18, 25)* could have been mistaken for 27, while the Saturday dates have already been shown to be impossible. But if August 4 were the date

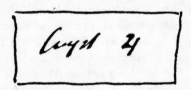

(Fig. 1. *Dr. Watson's writing of August 4 (Augst.4).* Note the formation of the *g* (hoopless), the illshaped *s*, and the uncrossed *t;* also the preliminary flourish to the left-hand stroke of the 4.

*Any one of these dates would throw the date of the dissolution of the League forward to a double-figure date (October 11, 18, 25), which could not be readily mistaken for a 9. August 25 is open to the further objection that Watson (as is clearly proved by Mr. Bell in an interesting study of *The Sign of Four*) wrote his 5 rather like a 6, without the crossbar, so that it certainly could not have resembled a 7.

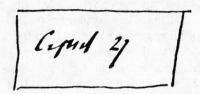

Fig. 2. *Dr. Watson's writing of April 27.* Note the *pr* without loop and the undotted *i*.

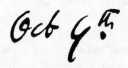

Fig. 3. Ross's suggested method of writing October 4.

of the advertisement, then October 4 must have been the date of Wilson's visit to Holmes; thus the two conclusions are mutually checked and confirmed. No other system of dating accounts either for the error April 27 or for the £32, whereas the present hypothesis accounts reasonaby for both and is the only one that will do so.

(b) If we accept this explanation of April 27, we are confronted with a slight difficulty about the second error: "October 9 for October 4" in the notice pinned on the League door. Could Watson write the figure 4 in two such dissimilar ways that it could be misread, on the one occasion as 27 and on another occasion as 9? It seems possible that, in this instance, Watson himself carelessly misread the handwriting of Duncan Ross on the notice card. Ross may have written his 4 in some such form as shown in Fig. 3, and Watson, hurriedly espying the inscription, either then or later, when he came to compile his story, may have written down what he thought he saw, without troubling to verify the date by the calendar.

It is in any case abundantly clear that the good doctor did not at any time carefully revise his proofs, and it may be (as Mr. T. S. Blakeney suggests in *Sherlock Holmes: Fact or Fiction?*) that he was especially vague and distrait when writing this story, owing to "the (presumed) death of Holmes shortly before, which evidently hit Watson hard." Had he read his proofs with any attention, he could not possibly have passed the blatant absurdity of April 27.*

Having now shown that October 4 and August 4 are almost certainly the correct dates for Wilson's visits to Holmes and to Pope's Court respectively, we find ourselves face to face with a very remarkable corollary—namely, that the Monday on which the advertisement appeared in the *Morning Chronicle* and on which Wilson entered upon his engagement with the Red-Headed League, was August Bank Holiday. This appears, at a first glance, to be most improbable. However, in Holmes's own words, "I ought to know by this time that when a fact appears to be opposed to a long train of deductions, it invariably proves to be capable of bearing some other interpretation." And, in fact, when we examine the text in detail, we shall find the strongest corroborative evidence in favor of Bank Holiday.

Let us begin by examining the nature of Jabez Wilson's business and the geography of Saxe-Coburg Square (or Coburg Square; there seems to be some doubt as to the precise title, due also, no doubt, to Watson's slipshod method of jotting down his notes).

The first thing we observe is that Wilson describes his establishment as "a small pawnbroker's business." Now, pawnbroking is usually carried on in connection with a shop of some kind, having a window in which unredeemed pledges are displayed for sale. But there is no mention of either shop or window† in connection with Jabez Wilson's

---

*Students may object that Mr. Bell has discovered another occasion (*The Man with the Twisted Lip*) on which Watson read his own 4 as a 9 (Bell, p. 66). But I am inclined to think that here Mr. Bell's second suggestion may be the correct one, and that Watson simply wrote Ju. 19," forgetting that this abbreviation might stand either for June or for July.

†It is true that the *Strand Magazine* artist depicts the establishment with a window that appears to be intended for a shop window, but no goods are displayed there. In any case, the evidence of the illustrations is only to be accepted with caution. See Mr. Bell's section on *The Musgrave Ritual* (p. 14).

pawnbroking, and it is, in fact, quite evident from the text that nothing of the kind existed. On p. 42 Holmes says, "Today is Saturday," and, after a brief interval of contemplation, turns to Watson with the words, "Put on your hat and come." It is before lunch (p. 43), and therefore all the shops would be open, and certainly were open, for we read on p. 44 of "the immense stream of commerce" and the footpaths "black with the hurrying swarm of pedestrians." This was after the visit to Wilson's, so that we may conclude that, if Wilson had had a shop, it should have been open when Holmes and Watson called.

This being so, if Holmes wanted to see the shop assistant, Vincent Spaulding, in a casual way, without arousing suspicion, what should we expect him to do? Surely to walk straight in and inquire [about] the price of some object in the window. (True, in such a case, the knees of Spaulding's trousers, which Holmes particularly wanted to examine, might have been concealed by the counter, but that difficulty could readily have been overcome by requesting him to bring the object forward into the light of the doorway.) But it seems clear that no such opportunity presented itself. The place was only "announced" by "three gilt balls and a brown board." There were no shop and no window, and Holmes was thus obliged to fall back upon knocking at the door of the house and, on having it opened to him, putting forward an unconvincing inquiry about the way to the Strand, which could have been put with far more propriety at the tobacconist's, the little newspaper shop, or the Vegetarian Restaurant.

So far, so good. There was no shop; and we must suppose that the business was a moneylending business and nothing more, unredeemed pledges being presumably disposed of by private arrangement with other secondhand establishments.

Let us now go back to the events of Monday, August 4, the day on which Wilson and Spaulding answered the advertisement.

We are told that, on this occasion, Vincent Spaulding "came down into the office." This, to begin with, supports the conclusion that the business was carried on in an office and not in a shop. Where, then, did Spaulding come "down" from? Certainly not from the shop, if such had existed (for any shop or place of public business would be on the ground floor), unless we suppose the "office" to have been in the basement, which seems scarcely reasonable. If, then, Spaulding came "down" to the office, it was either from a bedroom or living room on an upper floor, or else from some upper room used for the storage of goods. If he came from a living room or (*a fortiori*) from a bedroom, then he was idling while his employer worked, and, with so exceptionally diligent a young man, how could that have happened at any time other than a public holiday? (I shall come presently to the nature of Jabez Wilson's work in the office.) If, on the other hand, Spaulding came "down" from a storeroom, it is quite possible that he was engaged in putting away and inventorying the goods deposited there—a very suitable occupation for a day on which no regular business was being transacted. Actually, I am inclined to think that he was thus employed,* since on p. 35 Wilson states that Spaulding "was very glad to have a holiday," thus suggesting that he would, in the ordinary course of events, have expected to work on that particular day.

Jabez Wilson, in the office, was undoubtedly at work— and upon what? It appears very likely that both he and Spaulding were engaged in storing, valuing and otherwise dealing with pledges deposited on the previous Saturday, and booking up the various transactions completed on that day. Thursday and Friday, as we know, were normally Wilson's busiest days, but Saturday, being payday, is the day on which pledges are most frequently redeemed, and

---

*At the moment when he came down, he was presumed to have been reading the paper, but this need only mean that he had knocked off work for a few minutes. Perhaps it was the regular time for his "elevenses." He would not, of course, get the paper till Wilson had finished with it.

pawnbrokers always keep open to a late hour on Saturdays. This means a good deal of business would be left to be carried over, on Monday, from the daybook to the ledger. In addition, if the Monday were a Bank Holiday, there would also be a number of thriftless people who had actually pawned goods on the Saturday so as to get extra money for their weekend pleasuring. Thus we get a mental picture of Spaulding engaged (or supposed to be engaged) in stock-taking upstairs, while his employer is at work on the books in the office, both taking advantage of the public holiday to set their house in order. It is also quite conceivable that they would not be averse from doing a little moneylending even on a Bank Holiday morning. What was there to prevent the man who had squandered his wages in the public house on the Saturday and Sunday from sending his wife round to knock discreetly at the front door on Monday, bringing the family Bible or the flatirons in a modest paper parcel?

But now we come to a very important point. When Spaulding had shown Jabez Wilson the paper, he was instructed to "put up the shutters for the day and come right away"; after which Wilson adds, "so we shut the business up." Immediately we ask ourselves: If there were no shop window, to what shutters does this refer? Why should any shutters be put up at all? If this were an ordinary weekday, with the "girl of fourteen" at home and working about the house, what imaginable reason could there be for putting up the shutters, which (in the absence of a shop) could only be the shutters of the "office" or the dwelling rooms? The point is puzzling, in any case, but the most reasonable answer seems to be this: That it was Bank Holiday, that the girl had been given the day off, and that the shutters were put up on the ground floor, first to indicate to any caller that there was nobody to answer the door and, secondly, as a measure of protection for the money in the office safe, which could not, of course, have been paid in to the bank either on the Saturday evening, the Sunday, or the Bank Holiday morning. In short, the shutters were put up because the house was empty, and the expression "we shut the business up" probably merely means that the work upon the books, etc., was discontinued.

The next passage to be considered is the description of the journey to Pope's Court. It is noticeable that no mention is made anywhere of open shops or of the ordinary city traffic. On the contrary, it is distinctly asserted that "Fleet Street was choked" with red-headed folk, and that Pope's Court was packed "like a coster's orange-barrow." This was in 1890, not in 1934. Even today it would be difficult to find enough permanently unemployed red-headed men in London* to "choke" Fleet Street on a working day; in 1890, it would have been impossible. Therefore, if all these men were able to leave their work to answer an advertisement, it must have been because Bank Holiday had already released them. And can we suppose that so serious a dislocation of the traffic as the "choking" of Fleet Street would imply could have been permitted on a working day without police interference? Evidently there was no attempt at the formation of an orderly queue outside the League premises, since Spaulding was permitted to "push, pull and butt" his way through the crowd; yet we hear of no protest from the occupiers of other premises in Pope's Court. It is evident that no business was being carried on that day in the city; the day was a Monday; therefore the day was Bank Holiday Monday. This unusual date was, doubtless, expressly chosen so that neither Wilson nor Spaulding should have any pressing reason for staying in Saxe-Coburg Square. We must remember that it was important, from the conspirators' point of view, that both men should be free to attend at Pope's Court, not merely to avoid delay and error in getting hold of the right Jabez Wilson, but also so that Spauld-

*The advertisement had only appeared that morning, and there was no time for applicants to come in from the provinces.

ing* should be on hand to influence his employer's decision by offering to attend to the business in his absence.

It is, no doubt, odd that Wilson should not have mentioned to Holmes that the interview took place on Bank Holiday; but in his flustered state of mind the fact had probably slipped his memory; nor was there any reason why he should attach special importance to it. It may, perhaps, be a small corroborative point that he waited until the morning following the interview before effecting the purchase of a penny bottle of ink, a quill pen, and seven sheets of foolscap. True, he was in low spirits on the Monday evening, but, on the other hand, he had returned from Pope's Court in a state of joyful excitement; and Spaulding might well have suggested the immediate purchase of the stationery had any shops been open at the time. I do not, however, insist upon this. The most interesting and suggestive point in the narrative is, I submit, the absence of a shop window combined with the putting-up of the shutters. It will be noticed, by the way, that the shutters were "put up for the day," although (until he saw the crowds) Wilson could have had no reason to suppose that the interview would occupy more than a couple of hours at most. Evidently he had determined to make a day of it in any case; and this adds further weight to the argument for Bank Holiday.

NOTE ON DR. WATSON'S HANDWRITING

The only document we possess, purporting to be in the handwriting of Dr. Watson, is the sketch-map that illustrates the adventure of *The Priory School*.† It bears his name in block letters at the right-hand bottom corner and presents at first sight an aspect of authenticity. The wording

---

*Spaulding would, indeed, miss a few hours of valuable time from his tunneling work under the empty bank, but this would be considered of minor importance, compared with the necessity of carrying through the plot to get Wilson out of the way.

†*Strand Magazine*, February 1904.

is clear, and the letters, on the whole, neatly formed, though five out of the ten small *i*'s are undotted, the small *r* is loopless and tends to degenerate into a single stroke, the capital *E* resembles a *C*, and there are variations in the forms of the capitals *R* and *T*. In any case, whoever executed the wording would, of course, be taking particular pains to make it legible and suitable for reproduction as a line block, and it probably is very unlike the same person's hand when writing ordinary MS or notes.

But is the writing necessarily that of Dr. Watson? In *The Naval Treaty* we find a sketch-plan in exactly the same handwriting, purporting to have been drawn by Percy Phelps. In *The Golden Pince-nez* the identical handwriting again makes its appearance, masquerading this time as that of Stanley Hopkins.

It is possible, of course, that Watson himself redrew the two last-mentioned sketches for the blockmaker, though, since he evidently had access to Holmes's collection of original documents (e.g. the letter reproduced in *The Reigate Squires*), there is no obvious reason why he should have done so. It may be urged that at the time of *The Naval Treaty* (1888), he was married and not living in Baker Street; but this does not apply to *The Golden Pince-nez*, which belongs to 1891, the year of Holmes's return.

The probability is that all three of the plans—hurriedly executed on scraps of paper—reached the blockmaker in a crumpled and dirty condition unsuitable for reproduction, and were redrawn by him from the originals. Or, since the same artist illustrated the whole series of stories, from the *Adventures* to the *Return*, he may have done the redrawing.

The letter in *The Reigate Squires* is in a different category. The exact reproduction of the original handwriting was essential, and, although we know that it was badly crumpled during Holmes's struggle with Alec Cunningham, it was, of course, carefully ironed out and preserved as an important piece of evidence in the case; the blockmaker had to do his best with it.

It is a very curious thing that the handwriting on the blotting paper in *The Missing Three-Quarter* should also bear a suspicious resemblance to that of this ubiquitous calligrapher. It is supposed, on this occasion, to be the autograph of Godfrey Staunton, written on a telegraph form with "a broad-pointed quill pen," and blotted with "thin" post-office blotting paper. For a document produced under these conditions, it is remarkably legible, and the ink has spread very little.

Finally, in the definitive ("Omnibus") edition of 1928, the signature *John H. Watson* has been omitted from the map of the Priory School. This cannot be without significance. Watson doubtless felt its presence to be misleading and had it excised from the block as a tacit admission that neither sketch nor writing was from his own hand.

Toward a Christian Esthetic*

I HAVE BEEN ASKED to speak about the arts in [England]—
their roots in Christianity, their present condition, and the
means by which (if we find that they are not flourishing as
they should) their mutilated limbs and withering branches
may be restored by regrafting into the main trunk of Christian tradition.

*It will be immediately obvious how deeply this paper is indebted to
R. G. Collingwood's *Principles of Art*, particularly as regards the disentan-
gling of art proper (expression and imagination) from the pseudoarts of
amusement and magic. The only contribution I have made of my own
(exclusive of incidental errors) has been to suggest, however tentatively, a
method of establishing the principles of art proper upon that Trinitarian
doctrine of the nature of creative mind that does, I think, really underlie
them. On this foundation it might perhaps be possible to develop a Christian aesthetic, which, finding its source and sanction in the theological
center, would be at once more characteristically Christian and of more universal application than any aesthetic whose contact with Christianity is
made only at the ethical circumference.—D.L.S.

This task is of quite peculiar difficulty, and I may not be able to carry it out in exactly the terms that have been proposed to me. And that for a rather strange reason. In such things as politics, finance, sociology, and so on, there really are a philosophy and a Christian tradition; we do know more or less what the Church has said and thought about them, how they are related to Christian dogma, and what they are supposed to do in a Christian country.

But oddly enough, we have no Christian esthetic—no Christian philosophy of the arts. The Church as a body has never made up her mind about the arts, and it is hardly too much to say that she has never tried. She has, of course, from time to time puritanically denounced the arts as irreligious and mischievous, or tried to exploit the arts as a means to the teaching of religion and morals—but I shall hope to show you that both these attitudes are false and degrading and are founded upon a completely mistaken idea of what art is supposed to be and do. And there have, of course, been plenty of writers on esthetics who happened to be Christians, but they seldom made any consistent attempt to relate their esthetic to the central Christian dogmas. Indeed, so far as European esthetic is concerned, one feels that it would probably have developed along precisely the same lines had there never been an Incarnation to reveal the nature of God—that is to say, the nature of all truth. But that is fantastic. It we commit ourselves to saying that the Christian revelation discovers to us the nature of all truth, then it must discover to us the nature of the truth about art among other things. It is absurd to go placidly along explaining art in terms of a pagan esthetic and taking no notice whatever of the complete revolution of our ideas about the nature of things that occurred, or should have occurred, after the first Pentecost. I will go so far as to maintain that the extraordinary confusion of our minds about the nature and function of art is principally due to the fact that for nearly two thousand years we have been trying to reconcile a pagan, or at any rate a Unitarian, esthetic with a Christian—that is, a Trinitarian and Incarnational—theology. Even that makes us out too intelligent. We have not tried to reconcile them. We have merely allowed them to exist side by side in our minds; and where the conflict between them became too noisy to be overlooked, we have tried to silence the clamor by main force, either by brutally subjugating art to religion, or by shutting them up in separate prison cells and forbidding them to hold any communication with each other.

Now, before we go any further, I want to make it quite clear that what I am talking about now is esthetic (the philosophy of art) and not about art itself as practiced by the artists. The great artists carry on with their work on the lines God has laid down for them, quite unaffected by the esthetic worked out for them by philosophers. Sometimes, of course, artists themselves dabble in esthetic, and what they have to say is very interesting, but often very misleading. If they really are great and true artists, they make their poem (or whatever it is) first, and then set about reconciling it with the fashionable esthetic of their time; they do not produce their work to conform to their notions of esthetic— or, if they do, they are so much-the-less artists, and the work suffers. Secondly, what artists chatter about to the world and to one another is not as a rule their art but the technique of their art. They will tell you, as critics, how it is they produce certain effects (the poet will talk about assonance, alliteration, and meter; the painter about perspective, balance, and how he mixes his colors, etc.)—and from that we may get the misleading impression that the technique is the art, or that the aim of art is to produce some sort of effect. But this is not so. We cannot go for a march unless we have learned, through long practice, how to control the muscles of our legs; but it is not true to say that the muscular control is the march. And while it is a fact that certain tricks produce effects—such as Tennyson's use of vowels and consonants to produce the effect of a sleepy murmuring in "The moan of doves in immemorial elms," or of metallic clashing in "The bare black cliff clanged round him"—it is not true that the poem is merely a set of physical, or even of emotional, effects. What a work of art really is and does we shall come to later. For the moment I want only to stress the difference between esthetic and art and to make it clear that a great artist will produce great art, even though the esthetic of the time may be hopelessly inadequate to explain it.

For the origins of European esthetic we shall, of course, turn to Greece; and we are at once brought up against the two famous chapters in which Plato discusses the arts and decides that certain kinds of art, and in particular certain kinds of poetry, ought to be banished from the perfect state. Not all poetry—people often talk as though Plato had said this, but he did not; certain kinds he wished to keep, and this makes his attitude all the more puzzling because, though he tells us quite clearly why he disapproves of the rejected kinds, he never explains what it is that makes the other kinds valuable. He never gets down to considering, constructively, what true art is or what it does. He tells us only about what are (in his opinion) the bad results of certain kinds of art—nor does he ever tackle the question whether the bad moral results of which he complains may not be due to a falseness in the art, i.e., to the work's being pseudoart or inartistic art. He seems to say that certain forms of art are inherently evil in themselves. His whole handling of the thing seems to us very strange, confused, and contradictory; yet his esthetic has dominated all our critical thinking for many centuries and has influenced, in particular, the attitude of the Church more than the Church perhaps knows. So it is necessary that we should look at Plato's argument. Many of his conclusions are true—though often, I think, he reaches them from the wrong premises. Some of them are, I think, demonstrably false. But especially, his whole grasp of the subject is inadequate. That is not Plato's fault. He was one of the greatest thinkers of all time, but he was a pagan; and I am becoming convinced that no pagan philosopher could produce an adequate esthetic, simply for lack of a right theology. In this respect, the least in the kingdom of heaven is greater than John the Baptist.

What does Plato say?

He begins by talking about stories and myths, and after dismissing as beneath consideration the stories and poems that are obviously badly written, he goes on to reject those that are untrue, or that attribute evil and disgusting behavior to the gods, or that tend to inculcate bad and vulgar passions or antisocial behavior in the audience. After this (which sounds very much like what moralists and the clergy are always saying nowadays) he leaves the subject matter and goes on to certain forms of poetry and art—those forms that involve *mimesis*—the mimetic arts. Now *mimesis* can be translated as imitation or representation; and we can at once see that certain forms of art are more mimetic than others. Drama, painting, and sculpture are, on the whole, mimetic—some natural object or action is represented or imitated (though we may find exceptions in modernist and surrealist paintings that seem to represent nothing in heaven or earth). Music, on the other hand, is not mimetic—nothing is imitated from the natural world, unless we count certain effects such as the noise of drums in a martial piece, or trills and arpeggios representing the song of birds or the falling of water, down to the squeaks, brayings, twitterings, and whistlings of cinema organs. In the third book of the *Republic*, Plato says he will allow the mimetic arts, provided that the imitation or representation is of something morally edifying, that sets a good example; but he would banish altogether the representation of unworthy objects, such as national heroes wallowing about in floods of tears, and people getting drunk, or using foul language. He thinks this kind of thing bad for the actors and also for the audience. Nor (which seems odd to us) are actors to imitate anything vulgar or base, such as artisans plying their trades, galley slaves or bos'ns; nor must there be any trivial nonsense about stage effects and farmyard imitations. Nothing is to be acted or shown except what is worthy to be imitated, the noble actions of wise men—a gallery of good examples.

We may feel that Plato's theater would be rather on the austere side. But in the tenth book he hardens his heart still further. He decides to banish all mimetic art, all representation of every kind—and that for two reasons.

The first reason is that imitation is a kind of cheat. An artist who knows nothing about carpentering may yet paint a carpenter, so that if the picture is set up at a distance, children and stupid people may be deceived into thinking that it really is a carpenter. Moreover, in any case, the realities of things exist only in heaven in an ideal and archetypal form; the visible world is only a pale reflection or bad imitation of the heavenly realities; and the work of art is only a cheating imitation of the visible world. Therefore, representational art is merely an imitation of an imitation—a deceptive trick that tickles and entertains while turning men's minds away from the contemplation of the eternal realities.

At this point some of you will begin to fidget and say, "Hi! Stop! Surely there is a difference between mimicry intended to deceive and representation. I admit that there are such things as tin biscuit boxes got up to look like the works of Charles Dickens, which may deceive the unwary, and that very simple-minded people in theaters have been known to hiss the villain or leap on the stage to rescue the heroine—but as a rule we know perfectly well that the imitation is only imitation and not meant to take anyone in. And surely there's a difference between farmyard imitations and John Gielgud playing Hamlet. And besides—even if you get an exact representation of something—say a documentary film about a war, or an exact verbal reproduction of a scene at the Old Bailey—that's not the same thing as *Coriolanus* or the trial scene in *The Merchant of Venice*; the work of art has something different, something more—

poetry or a sort of a something . . ." and here you will begin to wave your hands about vaguely.

You are, of course, perfectly right. But let us for the moment just make a note of how Plato's conception of art is influenced by his theology—the visible world imitating, copying, reflecting a world of eternal changeless forms already existent elsewhere; and the artist, conceived of as a sort of craftsman or artisan engaged in copying or imitating something that exists already in the visible world.

Now let us take [Plato's] second reason for banishing all representational art. He says that even where the action represented is in itself good and noble, the effect on the audience is bad because it leads them to dissipate the emotions and energies that ought to be used for tackling the problems of life. The feelings of courage, resolution, pity, indignation, and so on are worked up in the spectators by the mimic passions on the stage (or in pictures or music) and then frittered away in a debauch of emotion over these unreal shadows, leaving the mind empty and slack, with no appetite except for fresh sensations of an equally artificial sort.

Now, that is a real indictment against a particular kind of art, which we ought to take seriously. In the jargon of modern psychology, Plato is saying that art of this kind leads to phantasy and daydreaming. Aristotle, coming about fifty years after Plato, defended this kind of art. He said that undesirable passions, such as pity and terror, were in this way sublimated—you worked them off in the theater, where they could do no harm. If, he means, you feel an inner urge to murder your wife, you go and see *Othello* or read a good, gory thriller, and satisfy your blood lust that way, and if we had the past part of his *Poetics*, which dealt with comedy, we should probably find it suggested in the same way that an excess of sexual emotion can be worked off by going to a good, dirty farce or vulgar music hall and blowing the whole thing away in a loud, bawdy laugh.

Now, people still argue as to whether Plato or Aristotle was right about this. But there are one or two things I want you to notice. The first is that what Plato is really concerned with banishing from his perfect state is the kind of art that aims at mere entertainment—the art that dissipates energy instead of directing it into some useful channel. And though Aristotle defends art for entertainment, it is still the same kind of art he is thinking about.

The second thing is that both Plato and Aristotle—but especially Plato—are concerned with the moral effect of art. Plato would allow representational art so long as he thought that it had the effect of canalizing the energies and directing them to virtuous action. He banishes it, on further consideration, only because he has come to the conclusion that *no* representational art of any kind—not even the loftiest tragedy—is successful in bracing the moral constitution. He does not tell us very clearly what poetry he will keep, or why, except that it is to be of what we should call a lyrical kind, and, presumably, bracing and tonic in sentiment, and directly inculcating the love of the good, the beautiful, and the true.

Thirdly: Plato lived at the beginning, and Aristotle in the middle, of the era that saw the collapse and corruption of the great Greek civilization. Plato sees the rot setting in and cries out like a prophet to his people to repent while there is yet time. He sees that the theater audience is in fact looking to the theater for nothing but amusement and entertainment, that their energies are, in fact, frittering themselves away in spurious emotion—sob stuff and sensation, and senseless laughter, phantasy and daydreaming, and admiration for the merely smart and slick and clever and amusing. And there is an ominous likeness between his age and ours. We too have audiences and critics and newspapers assessing every play and book and novel in terms of its entertainment value, and a whole generation of young men and women who dream over novels and wallow in daydreaming at the cinema, and who seemed to be in a fair way of doping themselves into complete irresponsibility over the conduct of life until war came, as it did to Greece, to jerk them back to reality. Greek civilization was destroyed; ours is not yet destroyed. But it may be well to remember Plato's warning: "If you receive the pleasure-seasoned muse, pleasure and pain will be kings in your city instead of law and agreed principles."

And there is something else in Plato that seems to strike a familiar note. We seem to know the voice that urges artists to produce works of art with a high moral tone—propaganda works, directed to improving young people's minds and rousing them to a sense of their duties, doing them good, in fact. And at the same time, we find—among artists and critics alike—a tendency to repudiate representational art, in favor of something more austere, primitive, and symbolic, as though the trouble lay there.

It is as though, in the decline of Greece, and in what is known as the decline of the West, both Plato and we agreed in finding something wrong with the arts—a kind of mutual infection, by which the slick, sentimental, hedonistic art corrupts its audience, and the pleasure-loving, emotional audience in turn corrupts the arts by demanding of them nothing but entertainment value. And the same sort of remedy is proposed in both cases—first, to get rid of representationalism—which, it is hoped, will take away the pleasure and entertainment and so cure the audience's itch for amusement; secondly, to concentrate on works that provide a direct stimulus to right thinking and right action. What we have really got here is a sort of division of art into two kinds: entertainment art, which dissipates the energies of the audience and pours them down the drain; and another kind of art that canalizes energy into a sort of millstream to turn the wheel of action—and this we may perhaps call spellbinding art. But do these two functions comprise the whole of art? Or are they art at all? Are they perhaps only accidental effects of art, or false art—something masquerading under the name of art—or menial tasks to which we enslave art? Is the real nature and end of art something quite different from either? Is the real trouble something wrong with our esthetic, so that we do not know what we ought to look for in art, or how to recognize it when we see it, or how to distinguish the real thing from the spurious imitation?

Suppose we turn from Plato to the actual poets he was writing about—to Aeschylus, for instance, the great writer of tragedies. Drama, certainly, is a representational art, and therefore, according to Plato, pleasure art, entertainment art, emotional and relaxing art, sensational art. Let us read the *Agamemnon*. Certainly it is the representation by actors of something—and of something pretty sensational: the murder of a husband by an adulterous wife. But it is scarcely sensational entertainment in the sense that a thriller novel on the same subject is sensational entertainment. A daydreaming, pleasure-loving audience would hardly call it entertainment at all. It is certainly not relaxing. And I doubt whether it either dissipates our passions in Plato's sense or sublimates them in Aristotle's sense, any more than it canalizes them for any particular action, though it may trouble and stir us and plunge us into the mystery of things. We might extract some moral lessons from it; but if we ask ourselves whether the poet wrote that play in order to improve our minds, something inside us will, I think, say no. Aeschylus was trying to tell us something, but nothing quite so simple as that. He is saying something—something important—something enormous. And here we shall be suddenly struck with the inadequacy of the strictures against representational art.

"This," we shall say, "is not the copy or imitation of something bigger and more real than itself. It is bigger and more real than the real-life action that it represents. That a false wife should murder a husband—that might be a paragraph in the *News of the World* or a thriller to read in the train—but when it is shown to us like this, by a great poet, it is as though we went behind the triviality of the actual event to the cosmic significance behind it. And, what is more, this is not a representation of the actual event at all; if a BBC reporter had been present at the murder with a television set and microphone, what we heard and saw would have been nothing like this. This play is not anything that ever happened in this world—it is something happening in the mind of Aeschylus, and it had never happened before."

Now here, I believe, we are getting to something —something that Plato's heathen philosophy was not adequate to explain, but which we can begin to explain by the light of Christian theology. Very likely the heathen poet could not have explained it either. If he had made the attempt, he too would have been entangled in the terms of his philosophy. But we are concerned, not with what he might have said, but with what he did. Being a true poet, he was true in his work—that is, his art was that point of truth in him that was true to the external truth, and only to be interpreted in terms of eternal truth.

The true work of art, then, is something new; it is not primarily the copy or representation of anything. It may involve representation, but that is not what makes it a work of art. It is not manufactured to specification, as an engineer works to a plan—though it may involve compliance with the accepted rules for dramatic presentation and may also contain verbal "effects" that can be mechanically accounted for. We know very well, when we compare it with so-called works of art that are turned out to pattern, that in this connection neither circumcision availeth anything nor uncircumcision, but a new creature. Something has been created.

This word—this idea of art as creation—is, I believe, the one important contribution that Christianity has made to esthetics. Unfortunately, we are likely to use the words *creation* and *creativeness* very vaguely and loosely because we do not relate them properly to our theology. But it is significant that the Greeks did not have this word in their esthetic at all. They looked on a work of art as a kind of *techne*, a manufacture. Neither, for that matter, was the word in their theology—they did not look on history as the continual act of God fulfilling itself in creation.

How do we say that God creates, and how does this compare with the act of creation by an artist? To begin with, of course, we say that God created the universe "out of nothing"—he was bound by no conditions of any kind. Here there can be no comparison; the human artist is in the universe and bound by its conditions. He can create only within that framework and out of that material that the universe supplies. Admitting that, let us ask in what way God creates. Christian theology replies that God, who is a Trinity, creates by, or through, his Second Person, his Word or Son, who is continually begotten from the First Person, the Father, in an eternal creative activity. And certain theologians have added this very significant comment: the Father, they say, is known only to himself by beholding his image in his Son.

Does that sound very mysterious? We will come back to the human artist and see what it means in terms of his activity. But first, let us take note of a new word that has crept into the argument by way of Christian theology—the word *image*. Suppose, having rejected the words *copy*, *imitation*, and *representation* as inadequate, we substitute the word *image* and say that what the artist is doing is imaging forth something or the other, and connect that with St. Paul's phrase: "God . . . hath spoken to us by his Son, the brightness of this glory and express image of his person." Something which, by being an image, expresses that which it images. Is that getting us a little nearer to something? There is something that is, in the deepest sense of the words, unimaginable, known to itself (and still more, to us) only by the image in which it expresses itself through creation; and, says Christian theology very emphatically, the Son, who is the express image, is not the copy, or imitation, or representation of the Father, nor yet inferior or subsequent to the Father in any way. In the last resort, in the depths of their mysterious being, the unimaginable and the image are one and the same.

Now for our poet. We said, when we were talking of the *Agamemnon*, that this work of art seemed to be something happening in the mind of Aeschylus. We may now say, perhaps, more precisely, that the play is the expression of this interior happening. But what, exactly, was happening?

There is a school of criticism that is always trying to explain, or explain away, a man's works of art by trying to dig out the events of his life and his emotions outside the works themselves, and saying "these are the real Aeschylus, the real Shakespeare, of which the poems are only faint imitations." But any poet will tell you that this is the wrong way to go to work. It is the old, pagan esthetic that explains nothing—or that explains all sorts of things about the work except what makes it a work of art. The poet will say: "My poem is the expression of my experience." But if you then say, "What experience?" he will say, "I can't tell you anything about it except what I have said in the poem—the poem is the experience." The Son and the Father are *one;* the poet himself did not know what his experience was until he created the poem which revealed his own experience to himself.

To save confusion, let us distinguish between an event and an experience. An event is something that happens to one, but one does not necessarily experience it. To take an extreme instance: suppose you are hit on the head and get a concussion and, as often happens, when you come to, you cannot remember the blow. The blow on the head certainly happened to you, but you did not experience it; all you experience is the aftereffects. You only experience a thing when you can express it—however haltingly—to your own mind. You may remember the young man in T. S. Eliot's play, *The Family Reunion*, who says to his relatives:

> You are all people
> To whom nothing has happened, at most a continual
> impact
> Of external events. . . .

He means that they have got through life without ever really experiencing anything because they have never tried to express to themselves the real nature of what has happened to them.

A poet is a man who not only suffers the impact of external events but also experiences them. He puts the experience into words in his own mind, and in so doing recognizes the experience for what it is. To the extent that we can do that, we are all poets. A poet so-called is simply a man like ourselves with an exceptional power of revealing his experience by expressing it, so that not only he, but we ourselves, recognize that experience as our own.

I want to stress the word *recognize*. A poet does not see something—say the full moon—and say: "This is a very beautiful sight; let me set about finding words for the appropriate expression of what people ought to feel about it." That is what the literary artisan does, and it means nothing. What happens is that then, or at some time after, he finds himself saying words in his head and says to himself: "Yes—that is right. That is the experience the full moon was to me. I recognize it in expressing it, and now I know what it was." And so, when it is a case of mental or spiritual experience—sin, grief, joy, sorrow, worship—the thing reveals itself to him in words and so becomes fully experienced for the first time. By thus recognizing it in its expression, he makes it his own—integrates it into himself. He no longer feels himself battered passively by the impact of external events; it is no longer something happening to him, but something happening in him; the reality of the event is communicated to him in activity and power. So that the act of the poet in creation is seen to be threefold—a trinity—experience, expression, and recognition: the unknowable reality in the experience; the image of that reality known in its expression; and power in the recognition; the whole making up the single and indivisible act of a creative mind.

Now, what the poet does for himself, he can also do for us. When he has imaged forth his experience, he can incarnate it, so to speak, in a material body—words, music, painting—the thing we know as a work of art. And since he is a man like the rest of us, we shall expect that our experience will have something in common with his. In the image of his experience, we can recognize the image of some experience of our own—something that had happened to us, but which we had never understood, never formulated or expressed to ourselves, and therefore never known as a real experience. When we read the poem, or see the play or picture, or hear the music, it is as though a light were turned on inside us. We say: "Ah! I recognize that! That is something that I obscurely felt to be going on in and about me, but I didn't know what it was and couldn't express it. But now that the artist has made its image—imaged it forth—for me, I can possess and take hold of it and make it my own and turn it into a source of knowledge and strength." This is the communication of the image in power, by which the third person of the poet's trinity brings us, through the incarnate image, into direct knowledge of the, in itself, unknowable and unimaginable reality. "No man cometh to the Father save by me," said the incarnate image; and he added, "but the spirit of power will lead you into all truth."

This recognition of the truth that we get in the artist's work comes to us as a revelation of new truth. I want to be clear about that. I am not referring to the sort of patronizing recognition we give to a writer by nodding our heads and observing: "Yes, yes, very good, very true—that's just what I'm always saying." I mean the recognition of a truth that tells us something about ourselves that we had not been always saying, something that puts a new knowledge of ourselves within our grasp. It is new, startling, and perhaps shattering, and yet it comes to us with a sense of familiarity. We did not know it before, but the moment the poet has shown it to us, we know that, somehow or other, we had always really known it.

Very well. But, frankly, is that the sort of thing the average British citizen gets, or expects to get, when he goes to the theater or reads a book? No, it is not. In the majority of cases, it is not in the least what he expects, or what he wants. What he looks for is not this creative and Christian kind of art at all. He does not expect or desire to be upset by sudden revelations about himself and the universe. Like the people of Plato's decadent Athens, he has forgotten or repudiated the religious origins of all art. He wants entertainment, or, if he is a little more serious-minded, he wants something with a moral, or to have some spell or incantation put on him to instigate him to virtuous action.

Now, entertainment and moral spellbinding have their uses, but they are not art in the proper sense. They may be the incidental effects of good art, but they may also be the very aim and essence of false art. And if we continue to demand of the arts only these two things, we shall starve and silence the true artist and encourage instead the false artist, who may become a very sinister force indeed.

Let us take the amusement art. What does that give us? Generally speaking, what we demand and get from it is the enjoyment of the emotions that usually accompany experience without having had the experience. It does not reveal us to ourselves; it merely projects on to a mental screen a picture of ourselves as we already fancy ourselves to be—only bigger and brighter. The manufacturer of this kind of entertainment is not by any means interpreting and revealing his own experience to himself and us—he is either indulging his own daydreams, or—still more falsely and venially—he is saying: "What is it the audience think they would like to have experienced? Let us show them that, so that they can wallow in emotion by pretending to have experienced it." This kind of pseudoart is "wish fulfillment" or "escape" literature in the worst sense. It is an escape, not from the "impact of external events" into the citadel of experienced reality, but an escape from reality and experience into a world of merely external events—the progressive externalization of consciousness. For occasional relaxation this is all right; but it can be carried to the point where, not merely art, but the whole universe of phenomena becomes a screen on which we see the magnified projection of our unreal selves as the object of equally unreal emotions. This brings about the complete corruption of the consciousness, which can no longer recognize reality in experience. When things come to this pass, we have a civilization that lives for amusement, a civilization without guts, without experience, and out of touch with reality.

Or take the spellbinding kind of art. This at first sight seems better because it spurs us to action, and it also has its uses. But it too is dangerous in excess because once again it does not reveal reality in experience, but only projects a lying picture of the self. As the amusement art seeks to produce the emotions without the experience, so this pseudoart seeks to produce the behavior without the experience. In the end it is directed to putting the behavior of the audience beneath the will of the spellbinder, and its true name is not art, but art magic. In its vulgarest form it becomes pure propaganda. It can (as we have reason to know) actually succeed in making its audience into the thing it desires to have them. It can really in the end corrupt the consciousness and destroy experience until the inner selves of its victims are wholly externalized and made the puppets and instruments of their own spurious passions. This is why it is dangerous for anybody—even for the Church—to urge artists to produce works of art for the express purpose of doing good to people. Let her by all means encourage artists to express their own Christian experience and communicate it to others. That is the true artist saying: "Look! Recognize your experience in my own." But "edifying art" may only too often be the pseudoartist corruptly saying: "This is what you are supposed to believe and feel and do—and I propose to work you into a state of mind in which you will believe and feel and do as you are told." This pseudoart does not really communicate power to us; it merely exerts power over us.

What is it, then, that these two pseudoarts—the entertaining and the spellbinding—have in common? And how are they related to true art? What they have in common is the falsification of consciousness; and they are to art as the idol is to the image. The Jews were forbidden to make any image for worship because before the revelation of the threefold unity in which image and unimaginable are one, it was only too fatally easy to substitute the idol for the image. The Christian revelation set free all the images by showing that the true image subsisted within the Godhead Itself. It was neither copy, nor imitation, nor representation, nor inferior, not subsequent, but the brightness of the glory, and the express image of the person—the very mirror in which reality knows itself and communicates itself in power.

But the danger still exists, and it always will recur whenever the Christian doctrine of the image is forgotten. In our esthetic, that doctrine has never been fully used or understood, and in consequence our whole attitude to the artistic expression of reality has become confused, idolatrous, and pagan. We see the arts degenerating into mere entertainment that corrupts and relaxes our civilization, and we try in alarm to correct this by demanding a more moralizing and bracing kind of art. But this is only setting up one idol in place of the other. Or we see that art is becoming idolatrous, and we suppose that we can put matters right by getting rid of the representational element in it. But what is wrong is not the representation itself, but the fact that what we are looking at, and what we are looking for, are not the image but an idol. Little children, keep yourselves from idols.

It has become a commonplace to say that the arts are in a bad way. We are in fact largely given over to the entertainers and the spellbinders; and because we do not understand that these two functions do not represent the true nature of art, the true artists are, as it were, excommunicate and have no audience. But here there is not, I think, so much a relapse from a Christian esthetic as a failure ever to find and examine a real Christian esthetic based on dogma and not on ethics. This may not be a bad thing. We have at least a new line of country to explore that has not been trampled on and built over and fought over by countless generations of quarrelsome critics. What we have to start from is the Trinitarian doctrine of creative mind and the light that that doctrine throws on the true nature of images.

The great thing, I am sure, is not to be nervous about God—not to try and shut out the Lord Immanuel from any sphere of truth. Art is not he—we must not substitute art for God; yet this also is he for it is one of his images and therefore reveals his nature. Here we see in a mirror darkly—we behold only the images; elsewhere we shall see face to face, in the place where image and reality are one.

Creative Mind

THE QUARREL BETWEEN the sciences and the humanities is chiefly a quarrel of words. And when I say that, I do not mean to suggest that it is a quarrel about nothing. Both parties are setting out to explore reality, each by its own method. But they have only one set of tools between them. And because they use these tools very differently—because they cannot even agree together about the nature and purpose of the tools—the accounts that they present to the world as the result of their explorations are likely to appear mutually unintelligible and violently antagonistic. You would scarcely think they could both be examining the same reality.

Let me say at once that the scientists are working under peculiar difficulties and deserve our deepest sympathy. For the words, the tools, that the scientist is obliged to use were forged by the other and have few or none of the qualities that the scientist desires in an instrument of precision. The modern scientist is chiefly interested in measurable quantities and is sometimes likely to suppose that nothing is quite real unless it can be measured. But to measure, let us say, the length of anything, he requires a yardstick; and his task will not be an easy one if the yardstick, instead of remaining rigid and uniform, develops a nasty trick of expanding, shrinking, bulging, curling about, or throwing out offshoots in different directions. But this is precisely the way in which language behaves. Words alter their meaning in course of time and in various contexts; to change the metaphor a little, they are like magnets charged with power that affect and deflect all the instruments of precision that come within their field of influence. The desperate attempts of scientists to reduce language to a kind of algebraic formula in which the same symbol has always the same meaning resemble the process of trying to force a large and obstreperous cat into a small basket. As fast as you tuck in the head, the tail comes out; when you have at length confined the hind legs, the forepaws come out and scratch; and when, after a painful struggle, you shut down the lid, the dismal wailings of the imprisoned animal suggest that some essential dignity in the creature has been violated and a wrong done to its nature.

Or let us take another image. To make a precise scientific description of reality out of words is like trying to build a rigid structure out of pure quicksilver; it is using language for a purpose that defies the very nature of its being. The whole history of modern scientific terminology is that of a struggle to make language conform to a rule of behavior that is not its own—a struggle, let me suggest, that has in itself something irrational and unscientific about it. . . . Indeed, of late years, scientists have grown more and more inclined to abandon the unequal conflict and to present their discoveries in terms and formulas of their own devising, which are not subject to the peculiar mutability that affects human language. They talk to one another in long strings of mathematical symbols, or in those unpronounceable polysyllabic formulas that enshrine the nature of new chemical combinations, or in diagrams. The only objection to these symbolic notations is that they communicate nothing except to other scientists in the same line of business. Take the instance I used just now, the substance known as quicksilver. This word, invented by the poet who dwells in everyone, means "living silver." Taken in its literal meaning, it tells the world two things about the substance, both of which are false: it suggests that it is something organic, and that it is a form of the metal called silver. But, taken in its poetic meaning, it tells two other things about it, both of which are true: namely, that its shape is changeable like the shape of a living thing, and that its appearance is metallic, white, and shining like that of silver. Thus the word *quicksilver* conveys to the ordinary man, together with a certain measure of scientific falsehood, an equal amount of poetic truth. To the scientist, however, the poetic truth appears, for his special purposes, irrelevant, and the mixture of falsehood definitely objectionable. The word *quicksilver* is of no assistance to him. Nor is the alternative *mercury* any better. It regrettably recalls the superstitions of the alchemists, by which this metal was associated with the god Mercury, and by which the planets were supposed to influence the makeup of the human organism, so that one spoke of a mercurial temperament. Words of this kind merely darken scientific counsel. In the hope of getting rid of these unfortunate verbal associations, the chemist falls back upon giving the stuff, not a name, but a symbol. He writes down the letters Hg and hopes that this time he has finally escaped the influence of the poet. The symbol Hg is (or is intended to be) pure symbol. It does not describe or interpret the substance—it merely stands for the substance; and it has the merit, or the drawback, according to the purpose for which it is used, of conveying absolutely nothing about the substance to anyone who is not previously acquainted with the substance itself.

So far, so good. But in point of fact, the chemist has not got rid of the poet altogether. For one thing, he was careless at the outset on choosing his symbol. The letters Hg are merely the abbreviation of a Greek word, *hydrarguros*, meaning "fluid silver"—a word only one degree less pictur-esque and inaccurate than the English *quick* or *living* silver. Had the chemist been less lazy, less ready to take the line of least resistance, he could, of course, have avoided this asso-ciation by selecting some quite arbitrary symbol. The fact that he did not only shows that there is more of the com-mon man and the common poet felt hanging about the sci-entist than he is always willing to admit.

But the thing goes deeper than that. Even if the symbol Hg were quite arbitrary and meaningless in origin, it will only remain pure scientific symbol so long as the common poet refrains from tinkering about with it. If it should occur to the poet to lay hands upon it and transfer it to his own poetic vocabulary, it will cease to be scientific formula and will again become language, charged with all the emotional associations, all the mutability, and all the vague magnetic power which belong to the nature of language. If the poet, correctly associating the expression Hg with the substance it denotes, chooses to talk of an Hg temperament in the sense of a mercurial temperament, no bitter outcry from the outraged chemist can prevent him, or disentangle the letters Hg from the literary and emotional accretions that will promptly gather about it. Even if a fortuitous alphabetical similarity should cause popular imagination to see a poet-ical resemblance between the fluid adaptability of Hg and the activities of the Home Guard, the scientist will be help-less to prevent it. If this symbol is to remain pure, he must be constantly changing it—or else must be at pains to choose a symbol so abstract and unpronounceable that neither he nor anybody else can ever introduce it into ordinary conversation. For anything that can be used in conversation is language and has to submit to the natural law of language.

It is fascinating to watch the never-ending struggle as language and scientific method develop side by side. The process is always the same. The scientist seizes upon a word originally made by the common poet and endeavors to restrict it to a single, definite meaning that shall be the same in every context. The physicist, for instance, takes a word such as *force* or *energy* and uses it to denote a particular factor in physics that can be mathematically expressed. To his horror, the general public refuses to restrict the word in this manner, and innumerable misunderstandings occur. Not only does the common man continue to use the words in metaphorical meanings which they cannot bear in scientific contexts, he also reads those meanings into the scientist's expositions of physics, deducing from them all kinds of metaphysical conclusions quite foreign to the physicist's intentions. Or, if the scientist does succeed in capturing a word and restricting its meaning, some other word will arrive and take over all the former meanings of the original word, so that the same pair of words may be used in successive centuries to mean totally different things and may even become substituted for each other, without anybody's noticing what has happened.

Let me give one or two examples of this.

In the eighteenth century, the word *reason* was taken hold of by scientists and was used by them to mean something practically identical with the method of reasoning that at that time was scoring so great a triumph in the field of scientific discovery. But that was not the meaning of *reason* to a philosopher of the Middle Ages. To him, *reason* included very much more—for example, the qualities we now call intellect, intuition, and imagination, as well as the faculties of observation and deductive logic. When a medieval theologian called God the Son the Divine Reason, he did not mean that the Creator of the world was an inductive process. He meant something much nearer to what the Russian theologian Berdyaev meant when he said: "God created the world by imagination."

In the Middle Ages, the word *imagination* meant primarily the faculty of producing mental images—something more like what we now mean by visual fancy. But as the word *reason* became more and more identified with scientific method, the word *imagination* had to take over more and more of the work previously done by the word *reason*. The various uses of these words are still found side by side in common speech. When we say contemptuously that a thing is all imagination, we mean that it is mere fancy—an image corresponding to no reality. But when we say that a scheme of—let us say—postwar construction displays real imagination, we mean, not merely that it is seen vivid and complete like an image or picture, but that it shows profound insight and intellectual grasp of the whole subject. The two adjectives *imaginary* and *imaginative* correspond to the older and later use of the word *imagination*. The word *image* itself has different meanings in different contexts. Compare, for instance, its meaning in the phrase "to make a graven image" and in the phrase "God made man in His own image" and then compare both of them with the optician's technical use of the word when he says that the appearance formed on a screen by an optical lens is a true image, whereas that formed in a mirror is not. The optician is using the word in a restricted sense—he is using it, that is, as a technical term—one word, one meaning. When the common man reads a scientific book, he has to learn what is the precise technical use of the terms employed by the scientist. When the scientist reads a work of literature, he has to remember that every word in that book must be interpreted—not absolutely, as though it were a technical term, but relatively to its context.

The possibilities of confusion are very great—especially when one bears in mind that a scientist in one department is himself only a common poet in his use and understanding of the technical vocabulary of another department of science. Theology, for example, is a science with a highly technical vocabulary of its own; and when (for example) a biologist ventures (as he frequently does) into criticism of other people's theology, he is likely to tumble into errors quite as grotesque as those made by popular preachers who adorn their sermons with misapplied scraps of biology. I remember reading with fascination and malignant joy a prolonged argument between a distinguished scientist and a theologian on the subject of transubstantiation. It occupied a great deal of paper and went on for months. But from beginning to end of the correspondence, it never occurred to the scientist to suspect, nor to his opponent to inform him, that the technical theological meaning of the word *substance* was not merely different from its meaning in current contemporary speech, but almost its direct opposite. It could scarcely even be called a quarrel about words—it was a random exchange of words that prevented them from every discovering what the subject was they had undertaken to quarrel about.

Or take again the case of the word *reality*. No word occasions so much ill-directed argument. We are now emerging from a period when people were inclined to use it as though nothing were real unless it could be measured; and some old-fashioned materialists still use it so. But if you go back behind the dictionary meanings—such as "that which has objective existence"—and behind its philosophic history to the derivation of the word, you find that *reality* means "the thing thought." Reality is a concept; and a real object is that which corresponds to the concept. In ordinary conversation we still use the word in this way. When we say "those pearls are not real," we do not mean that they cannot be measured; we mean that the measurement of their makeup does not correspond to the concept *pearl*, that, regarded as pearls, they are nothing more than an appearance; they are quite actual, but they are not real. As *pearls*, in fact, they have no objective existence. Professor Eddington is much troubled by the words *reality* and *existence*; in his *Philosphy of Physical Science* he can find no use or meaning for the word *existence*—unless, he admits, it is taken to mean "that which is present in the thought of God." That, he thinks, is not the meaning usually given to it. But it is, in fact, the precise meaning, and the only meaning, given to it by the theologian.

I have taken up a lot of your time with talk about words—which may seem very far removed from the subject of creative mind. But I have two objects in doing so. The first is simply to warn you that my use of words will not always be your use of words, and that the words of the common poet—the creator in words—must never be interpreted absolutely, but only in relation to their context. They must be considered as fields of force, which disturb and are disturbed by their environment. Secondly, I want to place before you this passage from the works of Richard Hard—an eighteenth-century English divine:

The source of bad criticism, as universally of bad philosophy, is the abuse of terms. A poet they say must follow nature; and by nature, we are to suppose, can only be meant the known and experienced course of affairs in this world. Whereas the poet has a world of his own, where experience has less to do than consistent imagination.

It was the Royal Society who announced in 1687 that they "exacted from their members a close, naked, natural way of speaking . . . bringing all things as near the mathematical plainness as they can." Words, they imply, are not to be metaphorical or allusive or charged with incalculable associations—but to approximate as closely as possible to mathematical symbols: "one word, one meaning." And to this Hard retorts in effect that, for the poet, this use of language is simply not "natural" at all. It is contrary to the nature of language and to the nature of the poet. The poet does not work by the analysis and measurement of observables, but by a "consistent imagination."

Poets create, we may say, by building up new images, new intellectual concepts, new worlds, if you like, to form new consistent wholes, new unities out of diversity. And I should like to submit to you that this is in fact the way in which all creative mind works—in the sciences as everywhere else—in divine as well as in human creation, so far as we can observe and understand divine methods of creation. That is, that within our experience, creation proceeds by the discovery of new conceptual relations between things so as to form them into systems having a consistent wholeness corresponding to an image in the mind, and, consequently, possessing real existence.

Let us take a few instances quite at random. The physicists have been exciting us a good deal lately by horrible revelations about the stuff the visible universe is made of. They tell us that it is not really full of solid things as we suppose, and that it is not really full of the different kinds of things we suppose. Everything (if I understand them rightly) is composed of the same thing—namely (I must go very carefully here for fear of committing them to some too positive statement)—namely, certain items of a more or less electrical nature, moving about (whatever motion may be—or would it be better to say "functioning"?) in a great deal of empty space, whatever that may be. Boiled down to the last proton and neutron, everything in the universe is the same thing. There is no clear-cut dividing line between one thing and another. There is only some kind of related activity and a numerical relation to distinguish the atom of helium from any other of the ninety-two elements, or you and me from the air we breathe. Indeed, there is, in a sense, nothing very much to show where you and I leave off and the rest of the universe begins. When we ponder this too closely, we may begin to wonder whether we possess any reality at all. But (escaping from the hypnotic power of words) we may console ourselves with the thought that the reality of the atom, or of ourselves, consists precisely in the relation that binds us into a recognizable unity. Our behavior corresponds to a mental concept that sees us as a whole. The atom and ourselves are, as it were, created out of an undifferentiated universe by an act of consistent imagination that holds us together as one thing. It does not matter for our purpose whose imagination is supposed to be involved—the important thing for our reality is that we can be thus imaged into existence.

At what point does the creative imagination of the baby begin to select consistent unities out of the atomic material offered to his observation? The psychologists have not yet told us very much about this. We do know, however, from a study of the history of language, that perception of the unity of "this-tree-here" precedes the perception of the unity of "trees-in-general." There has to be a mental gathering together of like images before the creation of a great, all-embracing image of "the tree" in the abstract. The realization that this-thing is in many respects like that-thing leads to a concept of a thing-in-itself: the relation in which this-thing and that-thing and all the other like things are bound into a unity.

At this point we begin to ask whether the word *tree* denotes any objective reality apart from the separate trees that make up the concept. We can measure the individual trees, use them, do things with them; whether we can do anything with tree-in-general, except think about it, is another question. We will not stop to discuss that for the moment— merely noting that the concept *tree* is a great act of creative imagination, which at least enables us to think much more usefully about individual trees. We can reason about the concept "trees-in-the-abstract" as if it were an actual object, and, having thoughts about it, we can apply our conclusions to actual, measurable trees.

Note the words "as if" because the moment we say those words we are coming very near to the thing called poetic creation. Let us take another instance. At some point the primitive savage, at some point the individual infant, having perceived a likeness among certain groups of related atoms, begins to make a further relation between these groups—this time a numerical relation: one tree, two trees, twenty trees, a hundred trees. And from the perception of this relation, [the infant] creates a new concept: number-in-itself.

According to one great mathematician: "God made the integers; all else is the work of man." And, according to many mathematicians, number is, as it were, the fundamental characteristic of the universe. But what *is* number, other than a relation between like things—like groupings of atoms—like unities? We say that we see six eggs (or we said so when eggs were plentiful). Certainly we see egg, egg, egg, egg, egg, egg in a variety of arrangements; but can we see *six*—apart from the eggs? No man hath seen an integer at any time. There has perhaps never been a greater act of the creative imagination than the creation of the concept of number as a thing-in-itself. Yet, with that concept, the mathematician can work, handling pure number as if it possessed independent existence and producing results applicable to things measurable and observable.

I am trying to suggest to you what are the characteristics of creative imagination—creative mind, reason, intellect, or whatever you like to call it. In this rough survey of creative achievement, we may pick out those phrases: the perception of likenesses, the relating of like things to form a new unity, and the words *as if*.

I will now take two instances of a rather different kind of creation—the poet's kind. The poet's imagination creates by [simile or] metaphor. It perceives a likeness between a number of things that at first sight appear to have no measurable relation, and it builds them into a new kind of unity, a new universe, that can be handled with power as if it possessed independent existence, and whose power is operative in the world of things that can be observed and measured.

When I said some time ago that the efforts of the scientist to use language as though it were mathematical symbol resembled those of a man trying to cram a cat into a basket, I was not actually using [simile or] metaphor. But I was pointing out a series of likenesses from which a metaphorical image might be created. The poet will take this process a step further. He will write a line such as that famous line of Shakespeare's about the honeybees:

The singing masons building roofs of gold.

Now, the scientist who wants one word, one meaning, may very properly object to almost every word in this line. He will point out that the word *singing* would be better confined to the noise produced by the vibration of the vocal chords; that bees have no vocal chords; that the noise they make is produced by the vibration of their flight apparatus; and that it has no such emotional significance as the idea of "singing" implies. Further, that bees are not, in the strict sense of the word, masons, and that their manipulation of wax in their mandibles to make honey cells is quite unlike the action of masons in a stonecutter's yard; "building" he might allow; but "roofs" (he will say) is an inaccurate description of a conglomeration of hexagonal cells; while the word *gold* is preposterous, seeing that neither the atomic structure nor even the color of the product in question is correctly indicated by such a misleading word. He will not, that is, recognize the poet's new unity, constructed from a new set of likenesses, because it does not conform to scientific method. It is a different set of likenesses, not verifiable with a yardstick; and the unity is not one that can be separated from the surrounding universe by any tests that his technique can apply.

But if he comes to test it with the technique which he possesses, not as a scientist, but as a common man, he will find that the metaphor behaves exactly like any other unity constructed by the creative imagination: it does establish a likeness; it does behave as a separable whole, and it produces observable effects as if it possessed independent existence. It can, for example, produce that observable effect on observable nerve and blood tissues that is known as making one's heart leap—it may even produce an observable reaction from the tear glands, resulting in a measurable quantity of brackish water. A scientific description of the process of cell formation by the worker bee might produce other observable results, equally important; but it would not produce those.

It will be noticed that the words of that line—"*The singing masons building roofs of gold*"—are far more powerful in combination than they are separately. Yet each word brings with it a little accumulation of power of its own—for each word is itself a separate unity and a separate creative act. "Singing" has the suggestion of a spontaneous expression of joy and physical well-being, and—since the singing creatures are a whole hiveful—it also suggests social rejoicing, a gladness felt in common. "Masons" and "building" bring with them associations of the joy of skilled craftsmanship, the beauty of great buildings, and a further social suggestion, in that buildings are commonly designed to be the homes, or working places, or shrines for worship, of all sorts of people. "Roofs of gold" carries a special reminiscence of the golde. city of the new Jerusalem—together with such romantic 1..mes as the golden city of Manoa and so on; and "gold" has, of course, innumerable rich and glowing suggestions, ranging from the light of the sun to the common association of worldly wealth. All these are welded in one line into the image of the joyful craftsmen singing over their task as they build the golden city; and this, by a metaphor, is identified with the sensation of standing in a sunny garden, hearing the drone of the bees as they pack the honeycomb with sweetness. Two images are fused into a single world of power by a cunning perception of a set of likenesses between unlike things. That is not all: in its context, the line belongs to a passage that welds the fused image again into yet another unity, to present the picture of the perfect state:

> For so work the honeybees,
> Creatures that by a rule in nature teach
> The act of order to a peopled kingdom.

This is not scientist's truth; it is poet's truth, like the truth latent in that unscientific word, *quicksilver*. It is the presentation of a unity among like things, producing a visible, measurable effect as if the unity were itself measurable.

The creation of a whole work of art proceeds along the same lines. A work of fiction, for example, possesses poetic truth, provided that the author has rightly seen which things can be so related as to combine into a convincing unity—provided, as Hard says, the work is an act of consistent imagination. If the imagination is consistent, the work will produce effects as if it were actually true. If it is not consistent, then the effects produced will be the wrong ones—they will not work out properly—any more than Kepler's circular solar system would work out properly in observation because it was wrongly imagined. As soon as Kepler had imagined his system consistently, the calculations came out right; it is, of course, open to the relativist to say that Kepler's system with its central sun and elliptical planetary orbits is no more absolutely true than any other system, and, indeed, that whether the earth goes round the sun or the sun round the earth is merely a question of how you look at it. That may be perfectly true; but it does not affect the issue. To a relativist, no doubt, the Ptolemaic, earth-centered system with its elaborate epicycles, is as relatively true as the Copernican—only, it is much less convenient, much less simple, much less productive of good results in practice; in a word, it is much less powerfully imagined. Similarly, one may say that the most preposterous story in *Peg's Paper* has just as much or little claim to be called scientifically true as *Hamlet*. Neither set of events ever happened in any verifiable or proven sense of the words. If *Hamlet* has a truth that the *Peg's Paper* novelette has not, it is because it is created by a more consistent imagination, and its measurable effects on humanity are richer and more valuable.

For the next instance of consistent imagination, I will ask you to wander with me down a very curious, little bypath.

It was during the last century that the great war was fought between churchmen and men of science over the theory of Evolution. We need not fight afresh every battle in that campaign. The scientists won their victory chiefly, or at any rate largely, with the help of the paleontologists and the biologists. It was made clear that the earlier history of the earth and its inhabitants could be reconstructed from fossil remains surviving in its present, and from vestigial structures remaining in the various plants and animals with which it is now peopled. It was scarcely possible to suppose any longer that God had created each species—to quote the text of *Paradise Lost*—"perfect forms, limb'd, and full grown," except on what seemed the extravagant assumption that, when creating the universe, he had at the same time provided it with the evidence of a purely imaginary past that had never had any actual existence. Now, the first thing to be said about this famous quarrel is that the churchmen need never have been perturbed at all about the method of creation, if they had remembered that the Book of Genesis was a book of poetical truth, and not intended as a scientific handbook of geology. They got into their difficulty, to a large extent, through having unwittingly slipped into accepting the scientist's concept of the use of language, and supposing that a thing could not be true unless it was amenable to quantitative methods of proof. Eventually, and with many slips by the way, they contrived to clamber out of this false position; and today no reasonable theologian is at all perturbed by the idea that creation was effected by evolutionary methods. But, if the theologians had not lost touch with the nature of language; if they had not insensibly fallen into the eighteenth-century conception of the universe as a mechanism and God as the great engineer; if, instead, they had chosen to think of God as a great, imaginative artist—then they might have offered a quite different kind of interpretation of the facts, with rather entertaining consequences. They might, in fact, have seriously put forward the explanation I mentioned just now:

that God had at some moment or other created the universe complete with all the vestiges of an imaginary past.

I have said that this seemed an extravagant assumption; so it does, if one thinks of God as a mechanician. But if one thinks of him as working in the same sort of way as a creative artist, then it no longer seems extravagant, but the most natural thing in the world. It is the way every novel in the world is written.

Every serious novelist starts with some or all of his characters "in perfect form and fully grown," complete with their pasts. Their present is conditioned by a past that exists, not fully on paper, but fully or partially in the creator's imagination. And as he goes on writing the book, he will—especially if it is a long work, like *The Forsyte Saga* or the "Peter Wimsey" series—plant from time to time in the text of the book allusions to that unwritten past. If his imagination is consistent, then all those allusions, all those, so to speak, planted fossils, will tell a story consistent with one another and consistent with the present and future actions of the characters. That is to say, that past, existing only in the mind of the maker, produces a true and measurable effect upon the written part of the book, precisely as though it had, in fact, "taken place" within the work of art itself.

If you have ever amused yourselves by reading some of the works of "spoof" criticism about Sherlock Holmes (e.g., *Baker Street Studies*, or H. W. Bell's *Sherlock Holmes and Dr. Watson*), you will see just how far pseudoscientific method can be used to interpret these fossil remains scattered about the Sherlock Holmes stories, and what ingenuity can be used to force the indications into an apparent historical consistency. As regards the past of his characters, Conan Doyle's imagination was not, in fact, very consistent; there are lapses and contradictions, as well as lacunae. But let us suppose a novelist with a perfectly consistent imagination, who had conceived characters with an absolutely complete and flawless past history; and let us suppose, further, that the fossil remains were being examined by one of the characters, who (since his existence is contained wholly within the covers of the book just as ours is contained wholly within the universe) could not get outside the written book to communicate with the author. (This, I know, is difficult, rather like imagining the inhabitant of two-dimensional space, but it can be done.) Now, such a character would be in precisely the same position as a scientist examining the evidence that the universe affords of its own past. The evidence would all be there, it would all point in the same direction, and its effects would be apparent in the whole action of the story itself (that is, in what, for him, would be "real" history). There is no conceivable set of data, no imaginable line of reasoning, by which he could possibly prove whether or not that past had ever gone through the formality of taking place. On the evidence—the fossil remains, the self-consistency of all the data, and the effects observable in himself and his fellow characters—he would, I think, be forced to conclude that it had taken place. And, whether or no, he would be obliged to go on behaving as if it had taken place. Indeed, he could not by any means behave otherwise because he had been created by his maker as a person with those influences in his past.

I think that if the churchmen had chosen to take up that position, the result would have been entertaining. It would have been a very strong position because it is one that cannot be upset by scientific proof. Probably, theologians would have been deterred by a vague sense that a God who made his universe like this was not being quite truthful. But that would be because of a too limited notion of truth. In what sense is the unwritten past of the characters in a book less true than their behavior in it? Or if a prehistory that never happened exercises on history an effect indistinguishable from the effect it would have made by happening, what real difference is there between happening and not happening? If it is deducible from the evidence, self-consistent, and recognizable in its effects, it is quite real, whether or not it ever was actual.

I am not, of course, giving it as my opinion that the world was made yesterday all of a piece, or even that it first came into being at the point where prehistory stops and history begins. I am only saying that if it had, then, provided the imagination were consistent, no difference of any kind would have been made to anything whatever in the universe. Though, of course, if we were willing to accept such a theory, we might find it easier to deal with some of our problems about time. And, by the way, we should then expect a continuous deposit, as time went on into the future, of fresh evidence about the past. That is, new paleological and other records would be discovered from time to time as the author put them there and directed attention to them— much in the same way as evidential allusions to Peter Wimsey's school days are likely to make their appearance from time to time as the series of his adventures continues. You will notice that paleological discoveries are made from time to time—this proves nothing either way; on either hypothesis they would be bound to occur. All I have tried to do in this piece of fantasy is to show that where you have a consistent imagination at work, the line between scientific and poetic truth may become very hard to draw.

You will probably be tempted, by your habit of mind, to ask—what does all this prove? It does not, in the scientific sense of the word, prove anything. The function of imaginative speech is not to prove, but to create—to discover new similarities and to arrange them to form new unities, to build new self-consistent worlds out of the universe of undifferentiated mind-stuff.

Every activity has its own technique; the mistake is to suppose that the technique of one activity is suitable for all purposes. In scientific reasoning for example, the poet's technique of metaphor and analogy is inappropriate and even dangerous—its use leads to conclusions that are false to science, that build it new unities out of quantitative likenesses, and things that are numerically comparable. The error of the Middle Ages, on the whole, was to use analogical, metaphorical, poetical techniques for the investigation of scientific questions. But increasingly, since the seventeenth century, we have tended to the opposite error—that of using the quantitative methods of science for the investigation of poetic truth. But to build poetic systems of truth, the similarities must be, not quantitative, but qualitative, and the new unity that will emerge will be a world of new values. Here, metaphor and analogy are both appropriate and necessary—for both these processes involve the arranging of things according to some quality that the dissimilars have in common: thus (to go back to my early simile) common language and an infuriated cat, though in quantitative respects very unlike, have in common a certain quality of intractability. And thus, too, the associative values of words, which make them such bad tools for the scientist, make them the right tools for the poet, for they facilitate the establishment of similarities between many widely differing concepts, and so make easy the task of the creative imagination building up its poetic truths.

Perhaps I ought to add a caution about words. I said that words were, metaphorically, fields of force. May I, in my metaphorical, poetical, and unscientific way, press this analogy a little further. It is as dangerous for people unaccustomed to handling words and unacquainted with their technique to tinker about with these heavily charged nuclei of emotional power as it would be for me to burst into a laboratory and play about with a powerful electromagnet or other machine highly charged with electrical force. By my clumsy and ignorant handling, I should probably, at the very least, contrive to damage either the machine or myself; at the worst I might blow up the whole place. Similarly the irresponsible use of highly electric words is very strongly to be deprecated.

At the present time, we have a population that is literate, in the sense that everybody is able to read and write; but, owing to the emphasis placed on scientific and technical training at the expense of the humanities, very few of our people have been taught to understand and handle language as an instrument of power. This means that, in this country alone, forty million innocents or thereabouts are wandering inquisitively about the laboratory, enthusiastically pulling handles and pushing buttons, thereby releasing uncontrollable currents of electric speech, with results that astonish themselves and the world. Nothing is more intoxicating than a sense of power: the demagogue who can sway crowds, the journalist who can push up the sales of his paper to the two-million mark, the playwright who can plunge an audience into an orgy of facile emotion, the parliamentary candidate who is carried to the top of the poll on a flood of meaningless rhetoric, the ranting preacher, the advertising salesman of material or spiritual commodites, are all playing perilously and irresponsibly with the power of words, and are equally dangerous whether they are cynically unscrupulous or (as frequently happens) have fallen under the spell of their own eloquence and become the victims of their own propaganda. For the great majority of those whom they are addressing have no skill in assessing the value of words and are as helpless under verbal attack as were the citizens of Rotterdam against assault from the air. When we first began to realize the way in which the common sense of Europe had been undermined and battered down by Nazi propaganda, we were astonished as well as horrified; yet there was nothing astonishing about it. It was simply another exhibition of ruthless force: the employment of a very powerful weapon by experts who understood it perfectly against people who were not armed to resist it and had never really understood that it was a weapon at all. And the defense against the misuse of words is not flight, nor yet the random setting off of verbal fireworks, but the wary determination to understand the potentialities of language and to use it with resolution and skill.

It is right that the scientists should come to terms with the humanities; for in daily life scientists also are common men, and the flight from language will never avail to carry them out of its field of power. They must learn to handle that instrument, as they handle other instruments, with a full comprehension of what it is, and what it does; and in so doing they will come to recognize it as a source of delight as well as of danger. The language of the imagination can never be inert; as with every other living force, you must learn to handle it or it will handle you. "The question is," said Humpty Dumpty, "which is to be master—that's all."

The Image of God

IN THE BEGINNING God created. He made this and he made that, and he saw that it was good. And he created man in his own image; in the image of God created he him; male and female created he them.

Thus far the author of Genesis. The expression "in his own image" has occasioned a good deal of controversy. Only the most simple-minded people of any age or nation have supposed the image to be a physical one. The innumerable pictures that display the Creator as a hirsute, old gentleman in flowing robes seated on a bank of cloud are recognized to be purely symbolic. The image, whatever the author may have meant by it, is something shared by male and female alike; the aggressive masculinity of the pictorial Jehovah represents power, rationality or what you will; it has no relation to the text I have quoted. Christian doctrine and tradition, indeed, by language and picture, set its face

113

against all sexual symbolism for the divine fertility. Its Trinity is wholly masculine, as all language relating to man as a species is masculine.

The Jews, keenly alive to the perils of pictorial metaphor, forbade the representation of the Person of God in graven images. Nevertheless, human nature and the nature of human language defeated them. No legislation could prevent the making of verbal pictures; God walks in the garden, stretches out his arm, his voice shakes the cedars. His eyelids try the children of men. To forbid the making of pictures about God would be to forbid thinking about God at all, for man is so made that he has no way to think except in pictures. But continually, throughout the history of the Jewish-Christian Church, the voice of warning has been raised against the power of the picture-makers: "God is a spirit," "without body, parts or passions"; He is pure being. "I am that I am."

Man, very obviously, is not a being of this kind: this body, parts, and passions are only too conspicuous in his makeup. How then can he be said to resemble God? Is it his immortal soul, his rationality, his self-consciousness, his free will, or what, that gives him a claim to this rather startling distinction? A case may be argued for all these elements in the complex nature of man. But had the author of Genesis anything particular in his mind when he wrote? It is observable that in the passage leading up to the statement about man, he has given no detailed information about God. Looking at man, he sees in him something essentially divine, but when we turn back to see what he says about the original upon which the "image" of God was modeled, we find only the single assertion, "God created." The characteristic common to God and man is apparently that: the desire and ability to make things.

This, we may say, is a metaphor like other statements about God. So it is, but it is none the worse for that. All language about God must, as St. Thomas Aquinas pointed out, necessarily be analogical. We need not be surprised at this, still less suppose that because it is analogical it is therefore valueless or without any relation to the truth. The fact is that all language about everything is analogical; we think in a series of metaphors. We can explain nothing in terms of itself, but only in terms of other things. Even mathematics can express itself in terms of itself only so long as it deals with an ideal system of pure numbers; the moment it begins to deal with numbers of things it is forced back into the language of analogy. In particular, when we speak about something of which we have no direct experience, we must think by analogy or refrain from thought. It may be perilous, as it must be inadequate, to interpret God by analogy with ourselves, but we are compelled to do so; we have no other means of interpreting anything. Skeptics frequently complain that man has made God in his own image; they should in reason go further (as many of them do) and acknowledge that man has made all existence in his own image. If the tendency to anthropomorphism is a good reason for refusing to think about God, it is an equally good reason for refusing to think about light, or oysters, or battleships. It may quite well be perilous, as it must be inadequate, to interpret the mind of our pet dog by analogy with ourselves; we can by no means enter directly into the nature of a dog; behind the appealing eyes and the wagging tail lies a mystery as inscrutable as the mystery of the Trinity. But that does not prevent us from ascribing to the dog feelings and ideas based on analogy with our own experience; and our behavior to the dog, controlled by this kind of experimental guesswork, produces practical results that are reasonably satisfactory. Similarly the physicist, struggling to interpret the alien structure of the atom, finds himself obliged to consider it sometimes as a "wave" and sometimes as a particle. He knows very well that both these terms are analogical—they are metaphors, "picture-thinking," and, as pictures, they are incompatible and mutually contradictory. But he need not on that account refrain from using them for what they are worth. If he were to wait till he could have immediate experience of the atom, he would have to wait until he was set free from the framework of the universe.* In the meantime, so long as he remembers that language and observation are human functions, partaking at every point of the limitations of humanity, he can get along quite well with them and carry out fruitful researches. To complain that man measures God by his own experience is a waste of time; man measures everything by his own experience; he has no other yardstick.

We have then, various analogies by which we seek to interpret to ourselves the nature of God as it is known to us by experience. Sometimes we speak of him as a king and use metaphors drawn from that analogy. We talk, for instance, of his kingdom, laws, dominion, service, and soldiers. Still more frequently, we speak of him as a father, and think it quite legitimate to argue from the analogy of human fatherhood to the fatherhood of God. This particular picture-thought is one of which Christ was very fond, and it has stamped itself indelibly on the language of Christian worship and doctrine: "God the Father Almighty," "like as a father pitieth his own children," "your Father in heaven careth for you," "the children of God," "the Son of God," "as many as are led by the spirit of God are sons of God." "I will arise and go to my father, "Our Father which are in heaven." In books and sermons we express the relation between God and mankind in terms of human parenthood; we say that, just as a father is kind, careful, unselfish, and forgiving in his dealings with his children, so is God in his dealings with men; that there is a true likeness of nature between God and man as between a father and his sons; and

---

*Research forces us to think far beyond the limits of the imagination. Formulas afford the medium of expressing the new discoveries, but the imagination is incapable of conveying the particular reality to our mind. The confident "it is" is reduced to a hesitating "it appears to be." A process appears to be the action of waves or particles depending on the angle from which it is viewed. Dispense with formulas to express a scientific generalization and only analogy remains.—Huizinga: *In the Shadow of Tomorrow*.

that because we are sons of one Father, we should look on all men as our brothers.

When we use these expressions, we know perfectly well that they are metaphors and analogies; what is more, we know perfectly well where the metaphor begins and ends. We do not suppose for one moment that God procreates children in the same manner as a human father, and we are quite well aware that preachers who use the "father" metaphor intend and expect no such perverse interpretation of their language. Nor (unless we are very stupid indeed) do we go on to deduce from the analogy that we are to imagine God as being a cruel, careless or injudicious father such as way may see from time to time in daily life; still less, that all the activities of a human father may be attributed to God, such as earning money for the support of the family or demanding the first use of the bathroom in the morning. Our own common sense assures us that the metaphor is intended to be drawn from the best kind of father acting within a certain limited sphere of behavior, and is to be applied only to a well-defined number of the divine attributes.

I have put down these very elementary notes on the limitations of metaphor because it is well to remind ourselves before we begin of the way in which metaphorical language—that is to say, all language—is properly used. It is an expression of experience and of the relation of one experience to the other. Further, its meaning is realized only in experience. We frequently say, "Until I had that experience, I never knew what the word *fear* (or love, or anger, or whatever it is) meant." The language, which had been merely pictorial, is transmuted into experience, and we then have immediate knowledge of the reality behind the picture.

The words of creeds come before our eyes and ears as pictures; we do not apprehend them as statements of experience; it is only when our own experience is brought into relation with the experience of the men who framed the creeds that we are able to say: "I recognize that for a statement of experience; I know now what the words mean."

The analogical statements of experience that I want to examine are those used by the Christian creeds about God the Creator.

And first of all, is the phrase "God the Creator" metaphorical in the same sense that "God the Father" is clearly metaphorical? At first sight, it does not appear to be so. We know what a human father is, but what is a human creator? We are very well aware that man cannot create in the absolute sense in which we understand the word when we apply it to God. We say that "He made the world out of nothing," but we cannot ourselves make anything out of nothing. We can only rearrange the unalterable and indestructible units of matter in the universe and build them up into new forms. We might reasonably say that in the "father" metaphor we are arguing from the known to the unknown; whereas, in the "creator" metaphor, we are arguing from the unknown to the unknowable.

But to say this is to overlook the metaphorical nature of all language. We use the word *create* to convey an extension and amplification of something that we do know, and we limit the application of the metaphor precisely as we limit the application of the metaphor of fatherhood. We know a father and picture to ourselves an ideal Father; similarly, we know a human maker and picture to ourselves an ideal Maker. If the word *Maker* does not mean something related to our human experience of making, then it has no meaning at all. We extend it to the concept of a Maker who can make something out of nothing; we limit it to exclude the concept of employing material tools. It is analogical language simply because it is human language, and it is related to human experience for the same reason.

This particular metaphor has been much less studied than the metaphor of "the Father." This is partly because the image of divine fatherhood has been particularly consecrated by Christ's use of it; partly because most of us have a very narrow experience of the act of creation. It is true that everybody is a maker in the simplest meaning of the term. We spend our lives putting matter together in new patterns and so creating forms that were not there before. This is so intimate and universal a function of nature that we scarcely ever think about it. In a sense, even this kind of creation is creation out of nothing. Though we cannot create matter, we continually, by rearrangement, create new and unique entities. A million buttons, stamped out by machine, though they may be exactly alike, are not the *same* button; with each separate act of making, an entity has appeared in the world that was not there before. Nevertheless, we perceive that this is only a very poor and restricted kind of creation. We acknowledge a richer experience in the making of an individual and original work. By a metaphor vulgar but corresponding to a genuine experience, we speak of a model hat or gown as a creation: it is unique, not merely by its entity but by its individuality. Again, by another natural metaphor, we may call a perfectly prepared beefsteak pudding a work of art; and in these words we acknowledge an analogy with what we instinctively feel to be a still more satisfying kind of creation.

It is the artist who, more than other men, is able to create something out of nothing. A whole artistic work is immeasurably more than the sum of its parts.

But here is the finger of God, a flash of the will that can,
Existent behind all laws, that made them, and lo, they are!
And I know not if, save in this, such gift be allowed to man,
That out of three sounds he frame, not a fourth sound, but
a star.

Consider it well: each tone of our scale in itself is nought;
It is everywhere in the world—loud, soft, and all is said:
Give it to me to use! I mix it with two in my thought;
And, there! Ye have heard and seen: consider and bow the head!
—Robert Browning, "Abt Vogler"

"I mix it with two in my thought"; this is the statement of the fact of universal experience that the work of art has real existence apart from its translation into material form. Without the thought, though the material parts already exist, the form does not and cannot. The creation is not a product of the matter and is not simply a rearrangement of the matter. The amount of matter in the universe is limited, and its possible rearrangements, though the sum of them would amount to astronomical figures, is also limited. But no such limitation of numbers applies to the creation of works of art. The poet is not obliged, as it were, to destroy the material of a Hamlet in order to create a Falstaff, as a carpenter must destroy a tree form to create a table form. The components of the material world are fixed; those of the world of imagination increase by a continuous and irreversible process, without any destruction or rearrangement of what went before. This represents the nearest approach we experience to creation out of nothing, and we conceive of the act of absolute creation as being an act analogous to that of the creative artist. Thus Berdyaev is able to say: "God created the world by imagination."

This experience of the creative imagination in the common man or woman and in the artist is the only thing we have to go upon in entertaining and formulating the concept of creation. Outside our own experience of procreation and creation, we can form no notion of how anything comes into being. The expressions "God the Father" and "God the Creator" are thus seen to belong to the same category—that is, of analogies based on human experience and limited or extended by a similar mental process in either case.

If all this is true, then it is to the creative artists that we should naturally turn for an opinion of what is meant by those creedal formulas that deal with the nature of the creative mind. Actually, we seldom seem to consult them in the matter. Poets have, indeed, often communicated in their own mode of expression truths identical with the theologians' truths; but just because of the difference in the modes of expression, we often fail to see the identity of the statements. The artist does not recognize that the phrases of the creeds purport to be observations of fact about the creative mind as such, including his own; while the theologian, limiting the application of the phrases to the divine Maker, neglects to inquire of the artists what light he can throw upon them from his own immediate apprehension of truth. The confusion is as though two men were to argue fiercely whether there was a river in a certain district or whether, on the contrary, there was a measurable volume of H_2O moving in a particular direction with an ascertainable velocity, neither having any suspicion that they were describing the same phenomenon.

Our minds are not infinite; and as the volume of the world's knowledge increases, we tend more and more to confine ourselves, each to his special sphere of interest and to the specialized metaphor belonging to it. The analytic bias of the last three centuries has immensely encouraged this tendency, and it is now very difficult for the artist to speak the language of the theologian or the scientist the language of either. But the attempt must be made; and there are signs everywhere that the human mind is once more beginning to move toward a synthesis of experience.

Problem Picture

SO FAR we have been enquiring into the correspondence between the Christian creeds and the experience of the artist on the subject of the creative mind, and we have seen that there is, in fact, a striking agreement between them.

Now, how does all this concern the common man?

It has become abundantly clear of late years that something has gone seriously wrong with our conception of humanity and of humanity's proper attitude to the universe. We have begun to suspect that the purely analytical approach to phenomena is leading us only further and further into the abyss of disintegration and randomness, and that it is becoming urgently necessary to construct a synthesis of life. It is dimly apprehended that the creative artist does, somehow or other, specialize in construction, and also that the Christian religion does, in some way that is not altogether clear to us, claim to bring us into a right relation with a God whose attribute is creativeness. Accordingly, exhorted on all sides to become creative and constructive, the common man may reasonably turn to these two authorities in the hope that they may shed some light, first, on what creativeness is, and, secondly, on its significance for the common man and his affairs.

Now we may approach this matter in two ways—from either end, so to speak. We may start from the artist himself, by observing that he has, in some way or other, got hold of a method of dealing with phenomena that is fruitful and satisfying to the needs of his personality. We may examine the workings of his mind when it is creatively engaged and discover what is its intrinsic nature. Having done so, we may arrive at some conclusion about the nature of creative mind as such. And at this point we may set our conclusions over against those dogmatic pronouncements that the church has made about the Creator, and discover that between the two there is a difference only of technical phraseology, and between the mind of the maker and the Mind of his Maker, a difference, not of category, but only of quality and degree.

Or we may begin with the creeds alternatively and ask what meaning for us, if any, is contained in this extraordinary set of formulas about Trinity-in-Unity, about the eternal-uncreate-incomprehensible incarnate in space-time-matter, about the begotten Word and the Ghost proceeding, and about the orthodox God-manhood so finickingly insisted upon and so obstinately maintained amid a dusty melee of mutually contradictory heresies. We may take the statements to pieces and translate them into the terms of an artistic analogy, only to discover that there then emerges a picture of the human artist at work—a picture exact to the minutest detail, familiar at every point and corroborated in every feature by day-to-day experience. When we have done this, we may consider how strange and unexpected this must appear if we hold it to be accidental. Obviously, it is not accidental. We may, of course, conclude that it is yet another instance of the rooted anthropomorphism of theologians. In seeking to establish the nature of the God they did not know, the fathers of the Church began by examining the artist they did know, and constructed their portrait of divinity upon that human model. Historically, of course, it is clear that they did not do this intentionally; nothing, I imagine, would be further from their conscious minds than to erect the poet into a Godhead. But they may have done it unconsciously, proceeding from the human analogy, as human reasoning must. The theory is perfectly tenable. Let us, however, take note that if we hold this theory, we cannot, at the same time, hold that Trinitarian doctrine, as formulated, is obscure, a priorist, and unrelated to human experience since we are committed to supposing that it is a plain *a posteriori* induction *from* human experience.

On the other hand, we may conclude that the doctrine derives from a purely religious experience of God, as revealed in Christ and interpreted by abstract philosophic reasoning about the nature of the absolute. In that case, we cannot call it irrational, however intricate and theoretical it may appear, since we have said it is a product of the reason. But if this theory, erected upon reason and religious experience, turns out to be capable of practical application in a totally different sphere of human experience, then we are forced to conclude also that the religious experience of Christianity is no isolated phenomenon; it has, to say the least of it, parallels elsewhere within the universe.

Now, when Isaac Newton observed a certain relationship and likeness between the behavior of the falling apple and that of the circling planets, it might be said with equal plausibility either that he argued by analogy from the apple to a theory of astronomy, or that while evolving a theory of astronomical mathematics he suddenly perceived its application to the apple. But it would scarcely be exact to say that, in the former case, he absurdly supposed the planets to be but apples of a larger growth, with seeds in them; or that, in the latter case, he had spun out a purely abstract piece of isolated cerebration that, oddly enough, turned out to be true about apples, though the movements of the planets themselves had no existence outside Newton's mathematics. Newton, being a rational man, concluded that the two kinds of behavior resembled each other—not because the planets had copied the apples or the apples copied the planets, but because both were examples of the working of one and the same principle. If you took a cross section of the physical universe at the point marked "solar system" and again at the point marked "apple," the same pattern was exhibited; and the natural and proper conclusion was that this pattern was part of a universal structure, which ran through the world of visible phenomena as the grain runs through wood. Similarly, we may take a cross section of the spiritual universe at the point marked "Christian theology" and at the point marked "art," and find at both precisely the same pattern of the creative mind; it is open to us to draw a similar conclusion.

But if we do—if we conclude that creative mind is in fact the very grain of the spiritual universe—we cannot arbitrarily stop our investigations with the man who happens to work in stone, or paint, or music, or letters. We shall have to ask ourselves whether the same pattern is not also exhibited in the spiritual structure of every man and woman. And, if it is, whether, by confining the average man and woman to uncreative activities and an uncreative outlook, we are not doing violence to the very structure of our being. If so, it is a serious matter, since we have seen already the unhappy results of handling any material in a way that runs counter to the natural law of its structure.

It will at once be asked what is meant by asking the common man to deal with life creatively. We do not expect him to turn all his experience into masterpieces in ink or stone. His need is to express himself, in agriculture or manufactures, in politics or finance, or in the construction of an ordered society. If he is required to be an artist in living, the only image suggested by the phrase is that of a well-to-do person such as Oscar Wilde, stretched in a leisured manner upon a sofa and aesthetically contemplating the lilies of the field. The average man cannot afford this. Also, he supposes that the artist exercises complete mastery over his material. But the average man does not feel himself to be a complete master of life (which is his material). Far from it. To the average man, life presents itself, not as material malleable to his hand, but as a series of *problems* of extreme difficulty, which he has to *solve* with the means at his disposal. And he is distressed to find that the more means he can dispose of—such as machine power, rapid transport, and general civilized amenities, the more his problems grow in hardness and complexity. This is particularly disconcerting to him, because he has been frequently told that the increase of scientific knowledge would give him the mastery over nature—which ought, surely, to imply mastery over life.

Perhaps the first thing that he can learn from the artist is that the only way of mastering one's material is to abandon the whole conception of mastery and to co-operate with it in love: whosoever will be a lord of life, let him be its servant. If he tries to wrest life out of its true nature, it will revenge itself in judgment, as the work revenges itself upon the domineering artist.

The second thing is, that the words *problem* and *solution*, as commonly used, belong to the analytic approach to phenomena and not to the creative. Though it has become a commonplace of platform rhetoric that we can "solve our problems" only by dealing with them "in a creative way," those phrases betray either that the speaker has repeated a popular cliche without bothering to think what it means, or that he is quite ignorant of the nature of creativeness.

From our brief study of the human maker's way of creation, it should be fairly clear that the creator does not set out from a set of data, and proceed, like a crossword solver or a student of elementary algebra, to deduce from them a result that shall be final, predictable, complete, and the only one possible. The concept of problem and solution is as meaningless, applied to the act of creation, as it is when applied to the act of procreation. To add John to Mary in a procreative process does not produce a solution of John and Mary's combined problem; it produces George or Susan, who (in addition to being a complicating factor in the life of his or her parents) possesses an independent personality with an entirely new set of problems. Even if, in the manner of the sentimental novel of the nineties, we allow the touch of baby hands to loosen some of the knots into which John and Mary had tied themselves, the solution (meaning George or Susan) is not the only one possible, nor is it final, predictable, or complete.

Again, there is no strictly mathematical or detective-story sense in which it can be said that the works of a poet are the solution of the age in which he lived; indeed, it is seldom at all clear which of these two factors is the result of the other. Much breath and ink are continually expended in the effort to find art, under the impression that this also is a problem awaiting a final, predictable, complete, and sole possible solution. The most one can say is that between the poet and his age, there is an intimate connection of mutual influence, highly complex and various, and working in all directions of time and space.

Yet the common man, obsessed by the practice of a mathematical and scientific period, is nevertheless obscurely aware that the enigmatic figure, the creative artist, possesses some power of interpretation that he has not, some access to the hidden things behind that baffling curtain of phenomena which he cannot penetrate. Sometimes he merely resents this, as men do often resent an inexplicable superiority. Sometimes he dismisses it: "He is a dreamer; let us leave him. Pass." But at other times—especially when the disharmonies of contemporary existence force themselves on his attention with an urgency that cannot be ignored—he will lay hold of the artist and demand to be let into his secret. "Here, you!" he will cry. "You have some trick, some password, some magic formula that unlocks the puzzle of the universe. Apply it for us. Give us the solution of the problems of civilization."

This, though excusable, is scarcely fair, since the artist does not see life as a problem to be solved, but as a medium for creation. He is asked to settle the common man's affairs for him; but he is well aware that creation settles nothing. The thing that is settled is finished and dead, and his concern is not with death but with life: "that ye may have life and have it more abundantly." True, the artist can, out of his own experience, tell the common man a great deal about the fulfillment of man's nature in living; but he can produce only the most unsatisfactory kind of reply if he is persistently asked the wrong question. And an incapacity for asking the right question has grown, in our time and country, to the proportions of an endemic disease.

The desire of being persuaded that all human experience may be presented in terms of a problem having a predictable, final, complete, and sole possible solution accounts, to a great extent, for the late extraordinary popularity of detective fiction. This, we feel, is the concept of life that we want the artist to show us. It is significant that readers should so often welcome the detective story as a way of escape from the problems of existence. It "takes their minds off their troubles." Of course it does; for it softly persuades them that love and hatred, poverty and unemployment, finance and international politics are problems capable of being dealt with and solved in the same manner as the death in the library. The beautiful finality with which the curtain rings down on the close of the investigation conceals from the reader that no part of the problem has been solved except that part that was presented in problematic terms. The murderer's motive has been detected, but nothing at all has been said about the healing of his murderous soul. Indeed, a major technical necessity of the writing is to prevent this aspect of the matter from ever presenting itself to the reader's mind. (For if we know too much about the murderer's soul beforehand, we shall anticipate the solution; and if we sympathize with him too much after discovery, we shall resent his exposure and condemnation. If sympathy cannot be avoided, the author is at pains either to let the criminal escape or to arrange for his suicide, and so transfer the whole awkward business to a higher tribunal, whose decisions are not openly promulgated.)

Since, as I have already explained, I am more intimately acquainted with my own works than with other people's, may I illustrate this point from the novel *Gaudy Night*. This contains three parallel problems, one solved, one partially solved, and the third insoluble. All three are related to the same theme, which is the father-idea of the book.

The first problem is presented in purely problematical terms: "Who caused the disturbances as Shrewsbury College and why?" This is solved, within the terms in which it was set, by the predictable, final, complete, and sole possible answer: "The culprit was the maid Annie; and her motive was revenge for an act of justice meted out against her husband by a certain academic woman in the interests of professional integrity."

The second problem is not really a problem at all; it is a human perplexity. "How are Peter and Harriet to retrieve their relationship from a false and emotional situation into which it has been forced by a series of faults on both sides?" Here, by an exercise on both sides of a strict, intellectual integrity, that situation is so modified that they are enabled to enter into a new relationship, presenting fresh situations with the prospect of further errors and misunderstandings. This "solution" is neither final nor complete; and though it is both predictable and necessary under the law of the book's nature as an artistic structure, it is neither so far as the general law of nature is concerned.

The third problem (if one likes to call it so) is presented, both to the reader and to the academic woman who carried out the act of justice on Annie's husband, in terms of a confrontation of values: Is professional integrity so important that its preservation must override every consideration of the emotional and material consequences? To this moral problem no solution is offered, except in terms of situation and character. Argument on both sides is presented; but judgment is pronounced only in the form: Here are this life and that life, these standards and those standards, these people and those people, locked in a conflict that cannot but be catastrophic. Wherever the quality of experience is enriched, there is life. The only judgment this book can offer you is the book itself.

The enriching (and also catastrophic) quality of integrity is thus the father-idea of the book, providing the mechanics of the detective problem the catalyst that precipitates the instability of the emotional situation, and also a theme that unites the microcosm of the book to the macrocosm of the universe. I have dealt with this story at rather egotistical length because of a criticism made by one intelligent reader, also a writer of detective fiction. He said, "Why do you allow the academic woman to have any doubts that she pursued the right course with Annie's husband? She seems to think she may have been wrong. Doesn't that conflict with your whole thesis?"

What is obvious here is the firmly implanted notion that all human situations are problems like detective problems, capable of a single, necessary, and categorical solution, which must be wholly right, while all others are wholly wrong. But this they cannot be since human situations are subject to the law of human nature, whose evil is at all times rooted in its good, and whose good can only redeem, but not abolish, its evil. The good that emerges from a conflict of values cannot arise from the total condemnation or destruction of one set of values, but only from the building of a new value, sustained, like an arch, by the tension of the original two. We do not, that is, merely examine the data to disentangle something that was in them already: we use them to construct something that was not there before: neither circumcision nor uncircumcision, but a new creature.

The artist's new creature is not a moral judgment but his work of living art. If the common man asks the artist for help in producing moral judgments or practical solutions, the only answer he can get is something like this: You must learn to handle practical situations as I handle the material of my book: you must take them and use them to make a new thing. As A. D. Lindsay puts it in *The Two Moralities*:

In the morality of my station and duties (i.e., of the moral code) the station presents us with the duty, and we say yes or no, "I will" or "I will not." We choose between obeying or disobeying a given command. In the morality of challenge or grace, the situation says, "Here is a mess, a crying evil, a need! What can you do about it?" We are asked not to say "Yes" or "No" or "I will" or "I will not," but to be inventive, to create, to discover something new. The difference between ordinary people and saints is not that saints fulfil the plain duties that ordinary men neglect. The things saints do have not usually occurred to ordinary people at all. . . . "Gracious" conduct is somehow like the work of an artist. It needs imagination and spontaneity. It is not a choice between presented alternatives but the creation of something new.

The distinction between the artist and the man who is not an artist thus lies in the fact that the artist is living in the way of grace, so far as his vocation is concerned. He is not necessarily an artist in handling his personal life, but (since life is the material of his work) he has at least got thus far, that he is using life to make something new. Because of this, the pains and sorrows of this troublesome world can never, for him, be wholly meaningless and useless, as they are to the man who dumbly endures them and can (as he complains with only too much truth) make nothing of them. If, therefore, we are to deal with our problems in a creative way, we must deal with them along the artist's lines: not expecting to solve them by a detective trick, but to make something of them, even when they are, strictly speaking, insoluble.

I do not say that it is impossible to view all human activity, even the activity of the artist, in terms of problem and solution. But I say that, however we use the words, they are wholly inadequate to the reality they are meant to express. We can think of Shakespeare, setting himself to solve the problem of *Hamlet:* that is, the problem of producing a reasonably box-office play from the recalcitrant material bequeathed to him by earlier dramatists. Or we can think of him solving incidental problems of production—e.g., how to arrange his scenes so as to give those actors who were doubling two parts time to change, without introducing padding into the dialogue. We can think of him solving the problem of Hamlet's character: how to reconcile, plausibly, his delay in revenging his father with his swiftness in disposing of Rosencrantz and Guildenstern. But when we have solved all the *Hamlet* problems that puzzle the critics, we are no nearer to laying hold on the essential thing—the idea and the energy that make *Hamlet* a living power. *Hamlet* is something more than the sum of its problems. We can see St. Paul's Cathedral purely in terms of the problems solved by the architect—the calculations of stress and strain imposed by the requirements of the site. But there is nothing there that will tell us why men were willing to risk death to save St. Paul's from destruction; or why the bomb that crashed through its roof was felt by millions like a blow over the heart.

All human achievements can be looked on as problems solved—particularly in retrospect, because, if the work has been well done, the result will then appear inevitable. It seems as though this was the only right way, predestined and inevitable from the start. So it is the right way, in the sense that it is the way that agrees with the maker's father-idea. But there was no inevitability about the idea itself.

It is here that we begin to see how the careless use of the words *problem* and *solution* can betray us into habits of thought that are not merely inadequate but false. It leads us to consider all vital activities in terms of a particular kind of problem, namely, the kind we associate with elementary mathematics and detective fiction. These latter are problems that really can be solved in a very strict and limited sense, and I think the words *problem* and *solution* should be reserved for these special cases. Applied indiscriminately, they are fast becoming a deadly danger. They falsify our apprehension of life as disastrously as they falsify our apprehension of art. At the cost of a little recapitulation, I should like to make this quite clear.

There are four characteristics of the mathematical or detective problem that are absent from the life problem; but because we are accustomed to find them in the one, we look for them in the other, and experience a sense of frustration and resentment when we do not find them.

(1) *The detective problem is always soluble.* It is, in fact, constructed for the express purpose of being solved, and when the solution is found, the problem no longer exists. A detective or mathematical problem that could not be solved by any means at all, would simply not be what we understand by a problem in this sense. But it is unwise to suppose that all human experiences present problems of this kind. There is one vast human experience that confronts us so formidably that we cannot pretend to overlook it. There is no solution to death. There is no means whatever whereby you or I, by taking thought, can solve this difficulty in such a manner that it no longer exists. From very early days, alchemists have sought for the elixir of life, so reluctant is man to concede that there can be any problem incapable of solution. And of late we note a growing resentment and exasperation in the face of death. We do not so much fear the pains of dying, as feel affronted by the notion that anything in this world should be inevitable. Our efforts are not directed, like those of the saint or the poet, to make something creative out of the idea of death, but rather to seeing whether we cannot somehow evade, abolish, and, in fact, solve the problem of death. The spiritual and mental energy that we expend upon resenting the inevitability of death is as much wasted as that which we from time to time

have expended on attempts to solve the problem of perpetual motion.

Further, this irrational preoccupation curiously hampers us in dealing with such a practical question as that of the possibility of war. It encourages us to look on the evil of war as consisting, first and foremost, in the fact that it kills a great many people. If we concentrate on this, instead of thinking of it in terms of the havoc it plays with the lives and souls of the survivors, we shall direct all our efforts to evading war at all costs, rather than to dealing intelligently with the conditions of life that cause wars and are caused by wars. This, in fact, is precisely what we did in 1919–1939.

We did not, of course, really believe that, if only we could evade war, we should evade death altogether. We only talked and behaved as though we thought so. Death is less noticeable when it occurs privately and piecemeal. In time of peace we can pretend, almost successfully, that it is only a regrettable accident, which ought to have been avoided. If a wealthy old gentleman of ninety-two suddenly falls dead of heart failure, the papers headline the event: "Tragic Death of Millionaire"; and we feel quite astonished and indignant that anybody so rich should be cut off in his prime. With all that money available for research, science should have been able to solve the problem of death for him. If we do not think this, then why use the word *tragic* about a death so clean, painless, and mature? (Do not say that the headline is too foolish to be true: I saw it with my own eyes.)

We said last time [World War I] that we hated war because it killed the young and strong before their time. But we are just as angry this time to see the old and the infirm perish with the rest. No man can die more than once; but great disasters, great pestilences, and above all great wars cram our eyes and ears with the detested knowledge that life intends to kill us.

Because of that, we would not risk war, for right or justice, or even in the hope of preserving peace. We threw down our arms, crying, "No More War!", and so delivered up Europe.

Yet we know perfectly well that the paradox "he that will lose his life shall save it" is a plain and practical fact. Unless we are willing to risk death by jumping from a burning house, we shall most certainly be burned to death. Indeed, had not the will of our physical nature been ready to accept death, we could never have been born.

The problem of death is not susceptible of detective-story solution. The only two things we can do with death are, first, to postpone it, which is only a partial solution, and, secondly, to transfer the whole set of values connected with death to another sphere of action—that is, from time to eternity.

This brings us to consider the next two characteristics of the detective problem.

(2) *The detective problem is completely soluble.* No loose ends or unsatisfactory enigmas are left anywhere. The solution provides for everything, and every question that is asked is answered. We are not left with a balance of probabilities in favor of one conclusion or another; nor does the fixing of the crime on the butler involve the detective in fresh enigmas connected with the cook. Such uncertainties may appear to arise in the course of the story, but they are all cleared up in the end by the discovering of the complete solution. It should not be necessary to point out here that this happy result proceeds from the simple fact that the author has been careful not to ask the questions that the solution will not answer.

Now, our tendency to look for this kind of complete solution without lacunae or compensatory drawbacks badly distorts our view of a number of activities in real life. Medicine is a good example. We are inclined to think of health in terms of disease and cure. Here, on the one hand, is (we think) one definite disease, and there, on the other hand, should be the one, definite, and complete cure. Apply the cure to the disease, and the result ought to be an exact solution to the problem presented. If the physician cannot name the disease on sight and immediately produce the prescribed cure, we feel resentful that the man does not know his business.

In the same way, there used to be a firmly rooted belief that to every poison there existed the antidote—a benevolent drug that would exactly reverse, each by each, the effects of the original poison and restore the body to the *status quo ante*. There are in fact, I believe, only two drugs that are complementary in this way, atropine and physostigmine (incidentally, neither of them is benevolent—both are deadly poisons). With other drugs that are used to counteract each other, the reversal of the effects is only partial, or is rather a counteraction of the symptoms than a healing of the mischief done to the organs. In most cases, the usefulness of the curative drug is only to hold off or mitigate the effects of the poison until the body can summon its physical resources to cure itself. In certain instances, one disease can be got rid of only at the cost of contracting another, as in the malaria treatment of syphilis. Or the treatment demanded by—let us say—a diseased condition of the lungs may be impossible for one particular patient because his constitution could not stand its violent effects upon the heart.

We have, perhaps, abandoned the superstitious belief in antidotes; but we continue to hug the delusion that all ill health is caused by some single, definite disease for which there ought to be a single, definite, and complete cure without unfortunate aftereffects. We think of our illness as a kind of crossword of which the answer is known to somebody: the complete solution must be there, somewhere; it is the doctor's business to discover and apply it.

But the physician is not solving a crossword: he is performing a delicate, adventurous, and experimental creative act, of which the patient's body is the material and to which the creative cooperation of the patient's will is necessary. He is not rediscovering a state of health, temporarily obscured: he is remaking it, or, rather, helping it to remake itself. This may indeed be looked upon as a problem, but it is not the same kind of problem as that presented by those in the algebra book: "If a cistern is filled by piles A and B in 25 and 32 minutes, respectively"; and the answer is not likely to be so precise or to cover all the conditions so satisfactorily.

The patient's best way to health and peace of mind is to enter with understanding into the nature of the physician's task. If he does so, he will not only be better placed to cooperate creatively with him, but he will also be relieved from the mental misery of impatience and frustration.

We may note, at the moment of writing, a similar kind of misconception about the problem of the night bomber. The agony of our impatience with these horrid intrusions is only increased by imagining that the solution already exists somewhere or other and that nothing but the criminal folly and sloth of the authorities prevent it from being immediately discovered and applied. We shall feel better about the business if we scrap the whole misleading notion and think instead, "Now a new thing has to be made that has never been made before." It is not to detectives that we have to look for help, but to inventors—to the men of creative ideas. And by this time we know something of the way in which creative work is done.

"We are at work now upon various devices," says some harassed spokesman; and the imagination sees "us" industriously assembling the device, as though it had been delivered in parts from a celestial workshop and had only to be fitted together according to the book of instructions and put into use the same evening. That is not creation's method. There is the wayward, the unpredictable, the not-to-be-commanded idea, which may make its presence felt in the mind after long hours of fruitless thought and work, or suddenly after no thought at all, or after a long, fallow period of unconsciousness, during which the conscious has been otherwise employed, but always in a day and an hour that we know not. There is the long, bitter, baffled struggle of the energy, calculating, designing, experimenting, eliminating error, resisting the slide into randomness; the first manifestation of the idea in a model made with hands; the renewed labor of the activity, testing, improving, unbuilding error to rebuild nearer to the idea; the new model made with hands and rechecked, retested; the labor of a manifold activity in the shops to multiply the image of the idea and distribute it in space; the communication of the idea in power to the men who have to understand and use the device. After all of which, if the idea is a true and powerful idea, it can at length produce its final manifestation in power, and bring, as we say, results. And even then, the result may not be a single and complete answer to the problem because this problem is not like a cipher, which carries within itself the material for its own decoding. Very likely there may be no one conclusive answer to the night bomber.

Another kind of inconclusive problem presents itself when we desire to enjoy, simultaneously and completely, two mutually incompatible things such, for example, as liberty and order, or liberty and equality. I have discussed these elsewhere,* and will add here only the brief reminder that individual liberty is compatible with social order only if the individual freely consents to restrictions on his personal liberty; and that if every man is free to develop all his powers equally to the utmost, there can be no sort of equality between the weak and the strong. Again, there is the hopeless dilemma that confronts every attempt to establish a kingdom of God on earth: "Goodness, armed with power, is corrupted; and pure love without power is destroyed" (Reinhold Neibuhr, *Beyond Tragedy*). Such problems cannot be solved mathematically; there is no single solution that is wholly right. Either there must be compromise, or the situ-

* In chapter 2 of *Begin Here*.

ation must be considered again in other terms, for in the terms in which it is set, the problem is insoluble. This brings us to our third point.

(3) *The detective problem is solved in the same terms in which it is set.* Here is one of the most striking differences between the detective problem and the work of the creative imagination. The detective problem is deliberately set in such a manner that it can be solved without stepping outside its terms of reference. This is part of its nature as a literary form, and the symmetry of this result constitutes a great part of its charm. Does not an initiate member of the Detection Club swear to observe this entirely arbitrary rule?

PRESIDENT: Do you promise that your detectives shall well and truly detect the crimes presented to them, using those wits which it shall please you to bestow upon them and not placing reliance upon, nor making use of, divine revelation, feminine intuition, mumbo jumbo, jiggery-pokery, coincidence or the act of God?
CANDIDATE: I do.

But life is no candidate for the Detection Club. It makes unabashed use of all the forbidden aids (not excepting mumbo jumbo and jiggery-pokery) and frequently sets its problems in terms that must be altered if the problem is to be solved at all.

Take, for example, the problem of unemployment. Have we perhaps so far failed to solve it because of the terms in which we have chosen to set it? In the terms in which it is set, it is an economic problem, concerned with such matters as the proper balance between labor and capital, hours and wages, property and financial returns. When tackled along these lines, it disconcerts us by producing as offshoots all manner of confusing and contradictory questions such as should wages be adjusted to the time worked, or to the amount and quality of the work done, or to the needs of the worker? At this point, we begin to notice irrelevancies and discrepancies, as though our detective story had stepped outside its allotted terms of reference. We notice also that the problem of unemployment limits us to the consideration of employment only; it does not allow us even to consider the work itself—whether it is worth doing or not, or whether the workman is to find satisfaction in the work, or only in the fact of being employed and receiving his pay envelope. We may then ask ourselves, should a man work in order to get enough money to enable him to cease from working, or should he desire only such payment as will enable him to live in order to carry on his work? If the former is true, then blessed are the rich, for they are the flower of a leisured civilization; but, if the latter is true, then blessed is the worker who gets no more than a living wage.

When we have got so far, we may begin to suspect that the problem of unemployment is not soluble in the terms in which it is set, and that what we ought to be asking is a totally different set of questions about work and money. Why, for example, does the actor so eagerly live to work, while the factory worker, though often far better paid, reluctantly works to live? How much money would men need, beyond the subsistence that enables them to continue working, if the world (that is, you and I) admired work more than wealth? Does the fact that he is employed fully compensate a man for the fact that his work is trivial, unnecessary, or positively harmful to society: the manufacture of imbecile and ugly ornaments, for instance, or the deliberate throat-cutting between rival manufacturers of the same commodity? Ought we, in fact, to consider whether work is worth doing before we encourage it for the sake of employment? In deciding whether man should be employed at a high wage in the production of debased and debasing cinema films or at a lower wage in the building of roads and houses, ought we to think at all about the comparative worth and necessity of bad films and good houses? Has the fact that enthusiastic crowds cheer and scream around professional footballers, while offering no enthusiastic greetings to longshoremen, anything to do with the wages offered to footballers and longshoremen, respectively?

When we have ceased to think of work and money in the purely economic terms implied by the problem of unemployment, then we are on our way to thinking in terms of creative citizenship, for we shall be beginning to make something with our minds. Instead of solving a problem, we shall be creating a new way of life.

"Whose, therefore, shall she be in the resurrection? for the seven had her to wife." In the terms in which you set it, the problem is unanswerable; but in the kingdom of heaven, those terms do not apply. You have asked the question in a form that is much too limited; the solution must be brought in from outside your sphere of reference altogether.

(4) *The detective problem is finite.* When it is solved, there is an end of it or, as George Joseph Smith casually observed concerning the brides he had drowned in their baths, "When they are dead, they are done with." The detective problem summons us to the energetic exercise of our wits precisely in order that, when we have read the last page, we may sit back in our chairs and cease thinking. So does the crossword. So does the chess problem. So does the problem about A, B, and C building a wall. The struggle is over and finished with, and now we may legitimately, if we like, cease upon the midnight with no pain. The problem leaves us feeling like that because it is deliberately designed to do so. Because we can, in this world, achieve so little, and so little perfectly, we are prepared to pay good money in order to acquire a vicarious sensation of achievement. The detective novelist knows this, and so do the setters of puzzles. And a schoolboy, triumphantly scoring a line beneath his finished homework, is thankful that he need not, in the manner so disquietingly outlined by Professor Leacock, enquire into the subsequent history of A, B, and C.

But this is the measure, not of the likeness between problems in detection and problems in life, but of the unlikeness. For the converse is also true, when they are done with, they are dead. Consider how, in the last twenty years, we have endeavored to deal with the problem of peace and security, and whether we do not still secretly hug the delusion that it is possible to deal with it as a problem. We really persuaded ourselves that peace was something that could be achieved by a device, by a set of regulations, by a League of Nations, or some other form of constitution, that would solve the whole matter once and for all. We continue to delude ourselves into the belief that when the war is over we shall this time discover the trick, the magic formula, that will stop the sun in heaven, arrest the course of events, make further exertion unnecessary. Last time we failed to achieve this end—and why? Chiefly because we supposed it to be achievable. Because we looked at peace and security as a problem to be solved and not as a work to be made.

Now the artist does not behave like this. He may finish a book, as we may finish a war or set up the machinery of a League, and he may think it is very good and allow his energy a brief sabbath of repose. But he knows very well that this is only a pause in the unending labor of creation. He does not subscribe to the heresy that confounds his energy with his Idea, and the Son's brief sabbath in time with the perpetual sabbaths of the Trinity in heaven. For the thing he has made is a living thing, and it is not sterile. It continually proliferates new themes and new fancies, and new occasions for thought and action. Each chapter concluded is only a day's end in the course of the book; each book concluded is only a year's end in the course of a life's pilgrimage. Or, if you like the metaphor better, it is a still, cut out and thrown off from the endless living picture that his creative mind reels out. It is a picture in itself, but it leads only from the picture behind it to the picture in front of it, as part of a connected process.

This the artist knows, though the knowledge may not always stand in the forefront of his consciousness. At the day's end or the year's end, he may tell himself: the work is done. But he knows in his heart that it is not, and that the passion of making will seize him again the following day and drive him to construct a fresh world. And though he may imagine for the moment that this fresh world is wholly unconnected with the world he has just finished, yet, if he looks back along the sequence of his creatures, he will find that each was in some way the outcome and fulfilment of the rest—and that all his worlds belong to the one universe that is the image of his own Idea. I know it is no accident that *Gaudy Night,* coming toward the end of a long development in detective fiction, should be a manifestation of precisely the same theme as the play *The Zeal of Thy House,* which followed it and was the first of a series of creatures embodying a Christian theology. They are variations upon a hymn to the master maker; and now, after nearly twenty years, I can hear in *Whose Body?* the notes of that tune sounding unmistakably under the tripping melody of a very different descant; and further back still, I hear it again, in a youthful set of stanzas in *Catholic Tales:*

> I make the wonderful carven beams
> Of cedar and of oak
> To build King Solomon's house of dreams
> With many a hammer stroke,
> And the gilded, wide-winged cherubims.

> I have no thought in my heart but this:
> How bright will be my bower
> When all is finished; My joy it is
> To see each perfect flower
> Curve itself up to the tool's harsh kiss.

> How shall I end the thing I planned?
> Such knots are in the wood!
> With quivering limbs I stoop and stand,
> My sweat runs down like blood—
> I have driven the chisel through My hand.

I should not write it quite like that today—at least, I hope. I should avoid the bright bower and the quivering limbs and the exclamation mark in the last verse. But the end is clearly there in the beginning. It would not be quite exact to say that the wheel has come full circle, or even, in the image that the time-students have made fashionable, that the spiral has made another turn over its starting point. The idea was from the beginning in every corner of the universe that it contains and eternally begets its manifestations. There is never any point in time that can conclude or comprehend the idea. The problem is never so solved that it is abolished; but each time it is restated, a new thing is made and signed with the formula "Q.E.F."*

The desire to solve a living problem by a definitive and sterile conclusion is natural enough; it is part of the material will to death. It is bred in the bones of the most enlightened and progressive of mankind, who hate it when they see it in others, not realizing that what appears to them to be a detestable stranger is in fact their own face in a mirror.

The man who uses violent invective against those who seek to uphold the *status quo* or cling to an outworn tradition, is justified in doing so only if he himself contemplates no fixed point of achievement ahead. If he thinks within himself, after the war, or after the revolution, or "after the federation of Europe," or after the triumph of the proletariat, the problem will be solved, then he is no better than they are. And he is horribly deluding both himself and others—the blind leading the blind into a blind alley. In fact, by saying or thinking any such thing, he is establishing precisely the conditions that make any approach to achievement impossible.

When we examine these four characteristics of the detective problem, we begin to see why it is so easy to look upon all the phenomena of life in terms of problem and solution, and also why the solution is so seldom satisfactory, even when we think we have reached it. For in order to persuade ourselves that we can solve life, we have only to define it in terms that admit of solution. Unless we do this, not only the

---

*Quod erat faciendum: Latin for "which was to be done."—[ed.]

solution but the problem itself is unintelligible. Take any phenomenon you like. Take a rose. How will you proceed to solve a rose? You can cultivate roses, smell them, gather and wear them, make them into perfume or potpourri, paint them or write poetry about them; these are all creative activities. But can you solve roses? Has that expression any meaning? Only if you first define the rose in terms that presuppose the answer. You can say, If the rose is regarded as an arrangement of certain chemical components, then the chemical formula for the rose is x. Or you can say, If the rose is regarded geometrically as a complex system of plane surfaces, then the formula for this rose is so-and-so. Or you can say, If the rose is regarded as an example of the Mendelian heredity of color variations, then the method for cultivating blue roses is as follows.

But none of these answers is going to solve the rose; and if the first is complete and final for the chemist, it remains altogether inadequate for the woman putting roses into a vase; and if the second may give some assistance to the painter, it leaves the gardener dissatisfied; while the third is probably undiscoverable, and, even if it were not, would do nothing to help the perfumer. Yet the perfumer, the gardener, the woman, and the painter, being occupied with the rose itself and not with its solution, can all present the world with new manifestations of the rose, and by so doing communicate the rose to one another in power.

The danger of speaking about life exclusively in terms of problem and solution is that we are thus tempted to overlook the limitations of this detective game and the very existence of the initial arbitrary rule that makes the playing of it possible. The rule is to exclude from the terms of the problem everything that the solution cannot solve. It is diverting and useful to know that, for the chemist, a man is made up of a few pennyworth of salt, sugar, iron, and what not, together with an intolerable deal of water. But we must not assert that "man is, in fact, nothing but" these things, or suppose that the solution of the pennyworths in the water will produce a complete and final solution of man. For this means that we have forgotten the qualification "for the chemist." That qualification reduces our assertion to the more limited form: "If man is nothing but a chemical, this is his chemical formula"—a very different matter. Somewhat similarly, the popular game of debunking great men usually proceeds by excluding their insoluble greatness from the terms of the problem and presenting a watery solution of the remainder; but this is, by definition, no solution of the man or of his greatness.

It was said by Kronecker, the mathematician: "God made the integers; all else is the work of man." Man can table the integers and arrange them into problems that he can solve in the terms in which they are set. But before the inscrutable mystery of the integers themselves he is helpless, unless he calls upon that tri-unity in himself that is made in the image of God, and can include and create the integers.

This is the vocation of the creative mind in man. The mind in the act of creation is thus not concerned to solve problems within the limits imposed by the terms in which they are set, but to fashion a synthesis that includes the whole dialectics of the situation in a manifestation of power. In other words, the creative artist, as such, deals, not with the working of the syllogism, but with that universal statement that forms its major premise. That is why he is always a disturbing influence; for all logical argument depends upon acceptance of the major premise, and this, by its nature, is not susceptible of logical proof. The hand of the creative artist, laid upon the major premise, rocks the foundations of the world; and he himself can indulge in this perilous occupation only because his mansion is not in the world but in the eternal heavens.

The artist's knowledge of his own creative nature is often unconscious; he pursues his mysterious way of life in a strange innocence. If he were consciously to pluck out the heart of his mystery, he might say something like this:

I find in myself a certain pattern that I acknowledge as the

law of my true nature, and that corresponds to experience
in such a manner that, while my behavior conforms to the
pattern, I can interpret experience in power. I find, further,
that the same pattern inheres in my work as in myself; and
I also find that theologians attribute to God himself precisely that pattern of being that I find in my work and in
me.

I am inclined to believe, therefore, that this pattern directly corresponds to the actual structure of the living universe, and that it exists in other men as well as in myself;
and I conclude that, if other men feel themselves to be powerless in the universe and at odds with it, it is because the
pattern of their lives and works has become distorted and
no longer corresponds to the universal pattern—because
they are, in short, running counter to the law of their nature.

I am confirmed in this belief by the fact that, so far as I
conform to the pattern of human society, I feel myself also
to be powerless and at odds with the universe; while so far
as I conform to the pattern of my true nature, I am at odds
with human society, and it with me. If I am right in thinking that human society is out of harmony with the law of its
proper nature, then my experience again corroborates that
of the theologians, who have also perceived this fundamental dislocation in man.

If you ask me what is this pattern that I recognize as the
true law of my nature, I can suggest only that it is the pattern of the creative mind—an eternal idea, manifested in
material form by an unresting energy, with an outpouring
of power that at once inspires, judges, and communicates
the work; all these three being one and the same in the
mind and one and the same in the work. And this, I observe, is the pattern laid down by the theologians as the
pattern of the being of God.

If all this is true, then the mind of the maker and the
Mind of the Maker are formed on the same pattern, and all
their works are made in their own image.

It is not at all likely that, if you caught the first artist you saw passing and questioned him, he would explain himself in these terms. He is no more accustomed than the rest of us to look for any connection between theology and experience. Nor, as I said at the beginning, do the theologians of today take much trouble to expound their doctrine by way of the human maker's analogy. They are ready to use the "father symbol" to illustrate the likeness and familiarity between God and his children. But the "creator symbol" is used, if at all, to illustrate the deep gulf between God and his creatures. Yet, as Berdyaev says, "The image of the artist and the poet is imprinted more clearly on his works than on his children." Particularly when it comes to the Trinity of the Godhead, the emphasis is always placed on the mystery and uniqueness of the structure—as though it were a kind of blasphemy to recognize with Augustine that this, at least, is to man a homely and intimate thing, familiar as his garter.

The disastrous and widening cleavage between the church and the arts on the one hand and between the state and the arts on the other leaves the common man with the impression that the artist is something of little account, either in this world or the next; and this has had a bad effect on the artist, since it has left him in a curious spiritual isolation. Yet with all his faults, he remains the person who can throw most light on that creative attitude to life to which bewildered leaders of thought are now belatedly exhorting a no less bewildered humanity.

Nor is the creative mind unpractical or aloof from that of the common man. The notion that the artist is a vague, dreamy creature living in retreat from the facts of life is a false one—fostered, as I shrewdly suspect, by those to whose interest it is to keep administrative machinery moving regardless of the end product. At the irruption of the artist into a state department, officialdom stands aghast, not relishing the ruthless realism that goes directly to essentials.

It is for the sacrilegious hand laid on the major premise that the artist is crucified by tyrannies and quietly smothered by bureaucracies. As for the common man, the artist is nearer to him than the man of any other calling, since his vocation is precisely to express the highest common factor of humanity—that image of the creator that distinguishes the man from the beast. If the common man is to enjoy the divinity of his humanity, he can come to it only in virtue and right of his making.

The wisdom of a learned man cometh by opportunity of leisure and he that hath little business shall become wise.

How can he get wisdom that holdeth the plough, and that glorieth in the good, that driveth oxen, and is occupied in their labours, and whose talk is of bullocks?

He giveth his mind to make furrows, and is diligent to give the king fodder.

So every carpenter and workmaster, that laboreth night and day; and they that cut and grave seals, and are diligent to make great variety, and give themselves to counterfeit imagery, and watch to finish a work:

The smith also sitting by the anvil, and considering the iron work, and vapor of the fire wasteth his flesh, and he fighteth with the heat of the furnace: the noise of the hammer and the anvil is ever in his ears, and his eyes look still upon the pattern of the thing that he maketh; he setteth his mind to finish his work, and watcheth to polish it perfectly:

So doth the potter sitting at his work, and turning the wheel about his feet, who is always carefully set at his work, and maketh all his work by number:

He fashioneth the clay with his arm and boweth down its strength before his feet; he applieth himself to lead it over; and he is diligent to make clean the furnace:

All these trust to their hands: and every one is wise in his work.

Without these cannot a city be inhabited: and they shall not dwell where they will, nor go up and down:

They shall not be sought for in public counsel, nor sit high in the congregation: they shall not sit on the judges' seat, nor understand the sentence of judgment; they cannot declare justice and judgment; and they shall not be found where parables are spoken.

But they will maintain the state of the world, and all their desire is in the work of their craft.

—ECCLESIASTICUS 38:24–34

Christian Morality

SETTING ASIDE THE SCANDAL caused by His messianic claims and His reputation as a political firebrand, only two accusations of personal depravity seem to have been brought against Jesus of Nazareth. First, that he was a Sabbath-breaker. Secondly, that he was "a gluttonous man and a winebibber, a friend of publicans and sinners"—or (to draw aside the veil of Elizabethan English that makes it all sound so much more respectable) that he ate too heartily, drank too freely, and kept very disreputable company, including grafters of the lowest type and ladies who were no better than they should be.

For nineteen and a half centuries, the Christian churches have labored, not without success, to remove this unfortunate impression made by their Lord and Master. They have hustled the Magdalens from the communion table, founded total abstinence societies in the name of him who made the water wine, and added improvements of their own, such as various bans and anathemas upon dancing and theatergoing. They have transferred the Sabbath from Saturday to Sunday, and, feeling that the original commandment "thou shalt not work" was rather half hearted, have added to it a new commandment, "thou shalt not play."

Whether these activities are altogether in the spirit of Christ we need not argue. One thing is certain: that they have produced some very curious effects upon our language. They have, for example, succeeded in placing a strangely restricted interpretation on such words as *virtue*, *purity*, and *morality*. There are a great many people now living in the world who firmly believe that Christian morals, as distinct from purely secular morality, consist in three things and three things only: Sunday observance, not getting intoxicated, and not practicing—well, in fact, not practicing immorality. I do not say that the churches themselves would agree with this definition; I say only that this is the impression they have contrived to give the world, and that the remarkable thing about it is its extreme unlikeness to the impression produced by Christ.

Now, I do not suggest that the Church does wrong to pay attention to the regulation of bodily appetites and the proper observance of holidays. What I do suggest is that by overemphasising this side of morality, to the comparative neglect of others, she has not only betrayed her mission but, incidentally, also defeated her own aims even about morality. She has, in fact, made an alliance with Caesar, and Caesar, having used her for his own purposes, has now withdrawn his support—for that is Caesar's pleasant way of behaving. For the last three hundred years or so, Caesar has been concerned to maintain a public order based upon the rights of private property; consequently, he has had a vested interest in morality. Strict morals made for the stability of family life and the orderly devolution of property, and Caesar (namely, the opinion of highly placed and influential people) has been delighted that the Church should do the work of persuading the citizen to behave accordingly. Further, a drunken worker is a bad worker, and thriftless extravagance is bad for business; therefore, Caesar has welcomed the encouragement of the Church for those qualities that make for self-help in industry. As for Sunday observance, the Church could have that if she liked, so long as it did not interfere with trade. To work all round the weekends in diminishing production, the one day in seven was necessary, and what the Church chose to do with it was no affair of Caesar's.

Unhappily, however, this alliance for mutual benefit between Church and Caesar has not lasted. The transfer of property from the private owner to the public trust or limited company enables Caesar to get on very well without personal morals and domestic stability; the conception that the consumer exists for the sake of production has made extravagance and thriftless consumption a commercial necessity; consequently, Caesar no longer sees eye to eye with the Church about these matters and will as soon encourage a prodigal frivolity on Sunday as on any other day of the week. Why not? Business is business. The Church, shocked and horrified, is left feebly protesting against Caesar's desertion, and denouncing a relaxation of moral codes, in which the heedless world is heartily aided and abetted by the state. The easy path of condemning what Caesar condemns or is not concerned to defend has turned out to be like the elusive garden path in *Through the Looking-Glass;* just when one seemed to be getting somewhere, it gave itself a little shake and one found oneself walking in the opposite direction.

Now, if we look at the Gospels with the firm intention to discover the emphasis of Christ's morality, we shall find that it did not lie at all along the lines laid down by the opinion of highly placed and influential people. Disreputable people who knew they were disreputable were gently told to go and sin no more; the really unparliamentary language was reserved for those thrifty, respectable, and sabbatarian citizens who enjoyed Caesar's approval and their own. And the one and only thing that ever seems to have roused the meek and mild Son of God to a display of outright physical violence was precisely the assumption that "business was business." The moneychangers in Jerusalem drove a very thriving trade and made as shrewd a profit as any other set of brokers who traffic in foreign exchange; but the only use Christ had for these financiers was to throw their property down the front steps of the temple.

Perhaps if the Churches had had the courage to lay their emphasis where Christ laid it, we might not have come to this present frame of mind in which it is assumed that the value of all work and the value of all people are to be assessed in terms of economics. We might not so readily take for granted that the production of anything (no matter how useless or dangerous) is justified so long as it issues in increased profits and wages; that so long as a worker is well paid, it does not matter whether his work is worthwhile in itself or good for his soul; that so long as a business deal keeps on the windy side of the law, we need not bother about its ruinous consequences to society or the individual. Or at any rate, now that we have seen the chaos of bloodshed that follows upon economic chaos, we might at least be able to listen with more confidence to the voice of an untainted and undivided Christendom. Doubtless it would have needed courage to turn Dives from the church door along with Mary Magdalen. (Has any prosperously fraudulent banker, I wonder, ever been refused communion on the grounds that he was, in the words of the English Prayerbook, "an open and notorious evil liver"?) But lack of courage, and appeasement in the face of well-organized iniquity, do nothing to avert catastrophe or to secure respect.

In the list of those seven deadly sins that the Church officially recognizes, there is the sin that is sometimes called sloth, and sometimes accidie. The one name is obscure to us; the other is a little misleading. It does not mean lack of hustle; it means the slow sapping of all the faculties by in-difference and by the sensation that life is pointless and meaningless and not worthwhile. It is, in fact, the very thing that has been called the disease of democracy. It is the child of covetousness and the parent of those other two sins that the Church calls lust and gluttony. Covetousness breaks down the standards by which we assess our spiritual values and causes us to look for satisfactions in this world. The next step is the sloth of mind and body, the emptiness of heart, which destroys energy and purpose and issues in that general attitude to the universe that the interwar jazz musicians aptly named the blues. For the cure of the blues, Caesar (who has his own ax to grind) prescribes the dreary frivoling that the Churches and respectable people have agreed to call immorality, and which in these days is as far as possible from the rollicking enjoyment of bodily plea-sures that, rightly considered, are sinful only by their ex-cess. The mournful and medical aspect assumed by immo-rality in the present age is a sure sign that in trying to cure these particular sins we are patching up the symptoms in-stead of tackling the disease at its roots.

To these facts it is only fair to say that the churches are at last waking up. The best Christian minds are making very strenuous efforts to readjust the emphasis and to break the alliance with Caesar. The chief danger is lest the churches, having for so long acquiesced in the exploiting of the many by the few, should now think to adjust the balance by help-ing on the exploitation of the few by the many, instead of attacking the false standards by which everybody, rich and poor alike, has now come to assess the value of life and work. If the churches make this mistake, they will again be merely following the shift of power from one class of the community to the other and deserting the dying Caesar to enlist the support of his successor. A more equal distribu-tion of wealth is a good and desirable thing, but it can scarcely be attained, and cannot certainly be maintained, unless we get rid of the superstition that acquisitiveness is a virtue and that the value of anything is represented in terms of profit and cost.

The churches are justifiably shocked when the glamor of a film actress is assessed by the number of her love affairs and divorces; they are less shocked when the glamor of a man, or of a work of art, is headlined in dollars. They are shocked when unfortunates are reduced to selling their bodies; they are less shocked when journalists are reduced to selling their souls. They are shocked when good food is wasted by riotous living; they are less shocked when good crops are wasted and destroyed because of overproduction and underconsumption. Something has gone wrong with the emphasis; and it is becoming very evident that until that emphasis is readjusted, the economic balance sheet of the world will have to be written in blood.

The Other Six Deadly Sins

PERHAPS THE BITTEREST COMMENTARY on the way in which Christian doctrine has been taught in the last few centuries is the fact that to the majority of people the word *immorality* has come to mean one thing and one thing only. By a hideous irony, our shrinking reprobation of that sin has made us too delicate so much as to name it, so that we have come to use for it the words that were made to cover the whole range of human corruption. A man may be greedy and selfish; spiteful, cruel, jealous, and unjust; violent and brutal; grasping, unscrupulous, and a liar; stubborn and arrogant; stupid, morose, and dead to every noble instinct—and still we are ready to say of him that he is not an immoral man. I am reminded of a young man who once said to me with perfect simplicity: "I did not know there were seven deadly sins; please tell me the names of the other six."

About the sin called *luxuria* or lust, I shall therefore say only three things. First, that it is a sin, and that it ought to be called plainly by its own name, and neither huddled away under a generic term such as immorality, nor confused with love.

Secondly, that up till now the Church, in hunting down this sin, has had the active alliance of Caesar, who has been concerned to maintain family solidarity and the orderly devolution of property in the interests of the state. But now that contract and not status is held to be the basis of society, Caesar need no longer rely on the family to maintain social solidarity; and now that so much property is held anonymously by trusts and joint stock companies, the laws of inheritance lose a great deal of their importance. Consequently, Caesar is now much less interested than he was in the sleeping arrangements of his citizens, and has in this manner cynically denounced his alliance with the Church. This is a warning against putting one's trust in any child of man—particularly in Caesar. If the Church is to continue her campaign against lust, she must do so on her own—that is, on sacramental—grounds; and she will have to do it, if not in defiance of Caesar, at least without his assistance.

Thirdly, there are two main reasons for which people fall into the sin of luxuria. It may be through sheer exuberance of animal spirits, in which case a sharp application of the curb may be all that is needed to bring the body into subjection and remind it of its proper place in the scheme of man's twofold nature. Or—and this commonly happens in periods of disillusionment like our own, when philosophies are bankrupt and life appears without hope—men and women may turn to lust in sheer boredom and discontent, trying to find in it some stimulus that is not provided by the drab discomfort of their mental and physical surroundings. When that is the case, stern rebukes and restrictions are worse than useless. It is as though one were to endeavor to cure anemia by bleeding; it only reduces further an already impoverished vitality. The mournful and medical aspect of twentieth-century pornography and promiscuity strongly suggests that we have reached one of these periods of spiritual depression where people go to bed because they have nothing better to do. In other words, the regrettable moral laxity of which respectable people complain may have its root cause not in luxuria at all, but in some other of the sins of society, and may automatically begin to cure itself when that root cause is removed.

The Church, then, officially recognizes six other capital or basic sins—seven altogether. Of these, three may be roughly called the warm-hearted, or disreputable sins, and the remaining four the cold-hearted or respectable sins. It is interesting to notice that Christ rebuked the three disreputable sins only in mild or general terms, but uttered the most violent vituperations against the respectable ones. Caesar and the Pharisees, on the other hand, strongly dislike anything warm-hearted or disreputable, and set great store by the cold-hearted and respectable sins, which they are in a conspiracy to call virtues. And we may note that, as a result of this unholy alliance between worldly interest and religious opinion, the common man is rather inclined to canonize the warm-hearted sins for himself, and to thank God openly that he is broad-minded, given to a high standard of living and instinct with righteous indignation—not prurient, strait-laced or namby-pamby, or even as this Pharisee. It is difficult to blame the common man very much for this natural reaction against the insistent identification of Christian morality with everything that Christ most fervently abhorred.

The sin of *ira* or wrath is one, perhaps, to which the English as a nation are not greatly addicted, except in a rather specialized form. On the whole we are slow to anger, and dislike violence. We can be brutal and destructive—usually, however, only under provocation; and much of our apparent brutality is due much less to violence of temper than to sheer unimaginative stupidity (a detestable sin in itself, but quite different in nature and origin). On the whole, we are an easygoing, good-humored people, who hate with difficulty and find it almost impossible to cherish rancor or revenge.

This is true, I think, of the English. It is perhaps not quite true of those who profess and call themselves British. The Celts are quarrelsome; they pride themselves that with them it is a word and a blow. They brood upon the memory of ancient wrongs in a way that to the English is incomprehensible: if the English were Irish by temperament, they would still be roused to fury by the name of the Battle of Hastings, instead of summing it up philosophically as "1066 and All That." The Celts cling fiercely to their ancient tribal savageries, and their religious habits are disputatious, polemical, and (in extreme instances, as on the Irish border) disgraced by bloodthirst and a persecuting frenzy. But let the English not be in too great a hurry to congratulate themselves. They have one besetting weakness, by means of which they may very readily be led or lashed into the sin of wrath: they are peculiarly liable to attacks of righteous indignation. While they are in one of these fits, they will fling themselves into a debauch of fury and commit extravagances that are not only evil but also ridiculous.

We all know pretty well the man—or, perhaps still more frequently, the woman—who says that anybody who tortures a helpless animal should be flogged till he shrieks for mercy. The harsh, grating tone and the squinting, vicious countenance accompanying the declaration are enough to warn us that this righteous anger is devilborn and trembling on the verge of mania. But we do not always recognize this ugly form of possession when it cloaks itself under a zeal for efficiency or a lofty resolution to expose scandals—particularly if it expresses itself only in print or in platform verbiage. It is very well known to the more unscrupulous part of the press that nothing pays so well in the newspaper world as the manufacture of schisms and the exploitation of wrath. Turn over the pages of the more popular papers if you want to see how avarice thrives on hatred and the passion of violence. To foment grievance and to set men at variance is the trade by which agitators thrive and journalists make money. A dogfight, a brawl, or a war is always news; if news of that kind is lacking, it pays well to contrive it. The average English mind is a fertile field in which to sow the dragon's teeth of moral indignation, and the fight that follows will be blind, brutal, and merciless.

That is not to say that scandals should not be exposed or that no anger is justified. But you may know the mischief-maker by the warped malignancy of his language as easily as by the warped malignancy of his face and voice. His fury is without restraint and without magnanimity—and it is aimed, not at checking the offense, but at starting a po-grom against the offender. The mischief-maker would rather the evil were not cured at all than that it were cured quietly and without violence. His evil lust of wrath cannot be sated unless somebody is hounded down, beaten, and trampled on, and a savage war dance executed upon the body.

I have said that the English are readily tempted into this kind of debauch. I will add that it is a debauch, and, like other debauches, leaves them with a splitting head, a bad hangover, and a crushing sense of shame. When they do give way to wrath, they make a very degrading exhibition of themselves because wrath is a thing unnatural to them; it affects them like drink or drugs. In the shamefaced mood that follows, they become spiritless, sick at heart, and en-feebled in judgment. I am therefore the more concerned about a highly unpleasant spirit of vindictiveness that is being commended to us at this moment, camouflaged as righteous wrath and a warlike spirit. It is not a warlike spirit at all—at any rate, it is very unlike the spirit in which soldiers make war. The good soldier is on the whole re-markable both for severity in his measures and for measure in his severity. He is as bloodthirsty as his duty requires him to be, and, as a rule, not more. Even in Germany, the difference between the professional and the political fighter is said to be very marked in this respect.

There are, however, certain people here whose martial howls do not suggest the battle cry even of a savage warrior so much as Miss Henrietta Petowker reciting *The Blood-Drinker's Burial* in Mrs. Kenwigs's front parlor. If I say: "Do not listen to them," it is not because there is no room for indignation, but because there is a point at which righteous indignation passes over into the deadly sin of wrath; and once it has passed that point, it is likely, like all other passions, to stagger over into its own opposite, the equally fatal sin of sloth or accidie, of which we shall have something to say presently. Ungovernable rage is the sin of the warm heart and the quick spirit; in such men it is usually very quickly repented of—though before that happens it may have wrought irreparable destruction. We shall have to see to it that the habit of wrath and destruction that war fastens upon us is not carried over into the peace. And above all we must see to it now that our blind rages are not harnessed and driven by those of the cold head and the cold heart—the envious, the avaricious, and the proud.

The third warm-hearted sin is named *gula* in Latin and in English, gluttony. In its vulgarest and most obvious form, we may feel that we are not much tempted to it. Certain other classes of people—not ourselves—do, of course, indulge in this disreputable kind of wallowing. Poor people of coarse and unrefined habits drink too much beer. Rich people, particularly in America and in those luxury hotels that we cannot afford, stuff themselves with food. Young people—especially girls younger than ourselves—drink far too many cocktails and smoke like chimneys. And some very reprehensible people contrive, even in wartime, to make pigs of themselves in defiance of the rationing order—like the young woman who (according to a recent gossip column) contrived to eat five separate lunches in five separate restaurants in the course of a single morning. But on the whole, England in wartime is not a place where the majority of us can very easily destroy our souls with gluttony. We may congratulate ourselves that, if we have not exactly renounced our sins, this particular sin at any rate has renounced us.

Let us seize this breathing space, while we are out of reach of temptation, to look at one very remarkable aspect of the sin of gula. We have all become aware lately of something very disquieting about what we call our economic system. An odd change has come over us since the arrival of the machine age. Whereas formerly it was considered a virtue to be thrifty and content with one's lot, it is now considered to be the mark of a progressive nation that it is filled with hustling, go-getting citizens, intent on raising their standard of living. And this is not interpreted to mean merely that a decent sufficiency of food, clothes, and shelter is attainable by all citizens. It means much more and much less than this. It means that every citizen is encouraged to consider more, and more complicated, luxuries necessary to his well-being. The gluttonous consumption of manufactured goods had become, before the war, the prime civic virtue. And why? Because the machines can produce cheaply only if they produce in vast quantities; because unless the machines can produce cheaply nobody can afford to keep them running; and because, unless they are kept running, millions of citizens will be thrown out of employment, and the community will starve.

We need not stop now to go round and round the vicious circle of production and consumption. We need not remind ourselves of the furious barrage of advertisements by which people are flattered and frightened out of a reasonable contentment into a greedy hankering after goods that they do not really need; nor point out for the thousandth time how every evil passion—snobbery, laziness, vanity, concupiscence, ignorance, greed—is appealed to in these campaigns. Nor how unassuming communities (described as backward countries) have these desires ruthlessly forced upon them by their neighbors in the effort to find an outlet for goods whose market is saturated. And we must not take up too much time in pointing out how, as the necessity to sell goods in quantity becomes more desperate, the people's appreciation of quality is violently discouraged and suppressed. You must not buy goods that last too long, for production cannot be kept going unless the goods wear out, or fall out of fashion, and so can be thrown away and replaced with others.

If a man invents anything that would give lasting satisfaction, his invention must be bought up by the manufacturer so that it may never see the light of day. Nor must the worker be encouraged to take too much interest in the thing he makes; if he did, he might desire to make it as well as it can be made, and that would not pay. It is better that he should work in a soulless indifference, even though such treatment should break his spirit and cause him to hate his work. The difference between the factory hand and the craftsman is that the craftsman lives to do the work he loves; but the factory hand lives by doing the work he despises. The service of the machine will not have it otherwise. We know about all this and must not discuss it now, but I will ask you to remember it.

The point I want to make now is this: that whether or not it is desirable to keep up this fearful whirligig of industrial finance based on gluttonous consumption, it could not be kept up for a single moment without the cooperative gluttony of the consumer. Legislation, the control of wages and profits, the balancing of exports and imports, elaborate schemes for the distribution of surplus commodities, the state ownership of enterprise, complicated systems of social credit, and finally wars and revolutions are all invoked in the hope of breaking down the thing known as the present economic system. Now it may well be that its breakdown would be a terrific disaster and produce a worse chaos than that which went before—we need not argue about it. The point is that, without any legislation whatever, the whole system would come crashing down in a day if every consumer were voluntarily to restrict purchases to the things really needed. "The fact is," said a workingman the other

day at a meeting, "that when we fall for these advertisements we're being had for mugs." So we are. The sin of
gluttony, of greed, of overmuch stuffing of ourselves, is the
sin that has delivered us over into the power of the machine.

In the evil days between the wars, we were confronted
with some ugly contrasts between plenty and poverty.
Those contrasts should be, and must be, reduced. But let us
say frankly that they are not likely to be reduced so long as
the poor admire the rich for the indulgence in precisely that
gluttonous way of living that rivets on the world the chain
of the present economic system, and do their best to imitate
rich men's worst vices. To do that is to play into the hands
of those whose interest it is to keep the system going. You
will notice that, under a war economy, the contrast is being
flattened out; we are being forced to reduce and regulate
our personal consumption of commodities and to revise our
whole notion of what constitutes good citizenship in the financial sense. This is the judgment of this world; when we
will not amend ourselves by grace, we are compelled under
the yoke of law. You will notice also that we are learning
certain things. There seems, for example, to be no noticeable diminution in our health and spirits due to the fact that
we have only the choice of, say, half a dozen dishes in a
restaurant instead of forty.

In the matter of clothing, we are beginning to regain our
respect for stuffs that will wear well; we can no longer be
led away by the specious argument that it is smarter and
more hygienic to wear underlinen and stockings once and
then throw them away than to buy things that will serve us
for years. We are having to learn, painfully, to save food
and material and to salvage waste products; and in learning
to do these things we have found a curious and stimulating
sense of adventure. For it is the great curse of gluttony that
it ends by destroying all sense of the precious, the unique,
the irreplaceable.

But what will happen to us when the war machine ceases

to consume our surplus products for us? Shall we hold fast
to our rediscovered sense of real values and our adventurous attitude of life? If so, we shall revolutionize world economy without any political revolution. Or shall we again
allow our gluttony to become the instrument of an economic
system that is satisfactory to nobody? That system as we
know it thrives upon waste and rubbish heaps. At present
the waste (that is, sheer gluttonous consumption) is being
done for us in the field of war. In peace, if we do not revise
our ideas, we shall ourselves become its instruments. The
rubbish heap will again be piled on our own doorsteps, on
our own backs, in our own bellies. Instead of the wasteful
consumption of trucks and tanks, metal and explosives, we
shall have back the wasteful consumption of wireless sets
and silk stockings, drugs and paper, cheap pottery and cos-
metics—all of the slop and swill that pour down the sewers
over which the palace of gluttony is built.

Gluttony is warm-hearted. It is the excess and perversion
of that free, careless, and generous mood that desires to
enjoy life and to see others enjoy it. But, like lust and
wrath, it is a headless, heedless sin, that puts the good-na-
tured person at the mercy of the cold head and the cold
heart; and these exploit it and bring it to judgment, so that
at length it issues in its own opposite—in that very dearth
in the midst of plenty at which we stand horrified today.

It is especially at the mercy of the sin called *avaritia* or
covetousness. At one time this sin was content to call itself
honest thrift, and under that name was, as they might say
in Aberdeen, "varra weel respectit." The cold-hearted sins
recommend themselves to church and state by the restraints
they lay upon the vulgar and disreputable warm-hearted
sins. The thrifty poor do not swill beer in pubs or indulge
in noisy quarrels in the streets to the annoyance of decent
people. Moreover, they are less likely to become a burden
on the taxpayers. The thrifty well-to-do do not abash their
pious neighbors by lavish indulgence in gula or luxuria—
which are both very expensive sins. Nevertheless, there

used always to be certain reservations about the respect ac-
corded to covertousness. It was an unromantic, unspec-
tacular sin. Unkind people sometimes called it by rude
names, such as parsimony and niggardliness. It was a narrow, creeping, pinched kind of sin; and it was not a good
mixer. It was more popular with Caesar than with Caesar's
subjects; it had no glamor about it.

. It was left for the present age to endow covetousness with
glamor on a big scale and to give it a title that it could carry
like a flag. It occurred to somebody to call it enterprise.
From the moment of that happy inspiration, covetousness
has gone forward and never looked back. It has become a
swaggering, swash-buckling, piratical sin, going about
with its hat cocked over its eye, and with pistols tucked into
the tops of its jackboots. Its war cries are "Business Efficiency!" "Free Competition!" "Get Out or Get Under!"
and "There's Always Room at the Top!" It no longer works
and saves; it launches out into new enterprises; it gambles
and speculates; it thinks in a big way; it takes risks. It can
no longer be troubled to deal in real wealth and so remain
attached to work and the soil. It has set money free from all
such hampering ties; it has interests in every continent; it is
impossible to pin it down to any one place or any concrete
commodity—it is an adventurer, a roving, rollicking free
lance. It looks so jolly and jovial and has such a twinkle in
its cunning eye that nobody can believe that its heart is as
cold and calculating as ever.

Besides, where is its heart? Covetousness is not incar-
nated in individual people, but in business corporations,
joint stock companies, amalgamations, trusts, which have
neither bodies to be kicked, nor souls to be damned—nor
hearts to be appealed to, either. It is very difficult to fasten
on anybody the responsibility for the things that are done
with money. Of course, if covetousness miscalculates and
some big financier comes crashing down, bringing all the
small speculators down with him, we wag self-righteous
heads and feel that we see clearly where the fault lies. But

we do not punish the fraudulent businessman for his frauds, but for his failure.

The Church says covetousness is a deadly sin, but does she really think so? Is she ready to found welfare societies to deal with financial immorality as she does with sexual immorality? Do the officials stationed at church doors in Italy to exclude women with bare arms turn anybody away on the grounds that they are too well dressed to be honest? Do the vigilance committees who complain of suggestive books and plays make any attempt to suppress the literature that suggests that getting on in the world is the chief object in life? Is Dives, like Magdalen, ever refused the sacraments on the grounds that he, like her, is an "open and notorious evil-liver"? Does the Church arrange services, with bright congregational singing, for total abstainers from usury?

The Church's record is not, in these matters, quite as good as it might be. But it is perhaps rather better than that of those who denounce her for her neglect. The Church is not the Vatican, nor the Metropolitans, nor the Bench of Bishops; it is not even the vicar or the curate or the church wardens; the Church is you and I. And are you and I in the least sincere in our pretense that we disapprove of covetousness?

Let us ask ourselves one or two questions. Do we admire and envy rich poeple because they are rich, or because the work by which they made their money is good work? If we hear that Old So-and-so pulled off a pretty smart deal with the town council, are we shocked by the revelation of the cunning graft involved, or do we say admiringly "Old So-and-so's hot stuff—you won't find many flies on him"? When we go to the cinema and see a picture about empty-headed people in luxurious surroundings, do we say, "What drivel!" or do we sit in misty dream, wishing we could give up our daily work and marry into surroundings like that? When we invest our money, do we ask ourselves whether the enterprise represents anything useful, or merely whether it is a safe thing that returns a good dividend? Do we regularly put our money into football pools or dog racing? When we read the newspaper, are our eyes immediately arrested by anything that says "MILLIONS" in large capitals, preceded by the £ or $ sign? Have we ever refused money on the grounds that the work that we had to do for it was something that we could not do honestly or do well? Do we NEVER choose our acquaintances with the idea that they are useful people to know, or keep in with people in the hope that there is something to be got out of them? And so we—this is important—when we blame the mess that the economical world has got into, do we always lay the blame on wicked financiers, wicked profiteers, wicked capitalists, wicked employers, wicked bankers—or do we sometimes ask ourselves how far we have contributed to make the mess?

Just as the sin of gluttony thrives on our little greeds, so the sin of covetousness thrives on our little acts of avarice—on the stupid and irresponsible small shareholder, for example, who is out to get money for nothing. There is a book called *Wall Street Under Oath** that makes entertaining but rather shameful reading. It is an account of the exposure of various great business and banking frauds in the United States at the time of the postwar slump. When we have finished wondering at the barefaced venality, graspingness, and lack of scruple of the notorious financiers who stood in the dock to answer the charge of fraud, we may fruitfully wonder at the incredible avarice and criminal folly of their victims. For no sharepusher could vend his worthless stock if he could not count on meeting, in his prospective victim, an unscrupulous avarice as vicious as his own, but stupider. Every time we expect, as is said, our money to work for us, we are expecting other people to work for us; and when we expect it to bring in more money in a year than honest work could produce in that time, we are expecting it to cheat and steal on our behalf.

* By Louis Pecora.

We are all in it together. I often wonder why Germany was so foolishly impatient as to go to war. If domination were all she wanted, she could have it without shedding a drop of blood by merely waiting long enough and trusting to the avarice of mankind. You may remember the sordid and cynical French businessman on the boat that brought Elie J. Bois to England after the collapse of France. Someone asked him, "Why did France break down like this?" and he answered: "Because she had too many men like me." France was bought; the politicians were bought; the press was bought. Labor was bought, the church was bought, big business was bought, even the army was bought. Not always by open bribes in cash, but by the insidious appeal to security, and business interests and economic power. Nobody would destroy anything or let go of anything; there was always the hope of making a deal with the enemy. Everybody, down to the smallest provincial official and the pettiest, petty shopkeeper, had a vested interest in nonresistance.

Wars are not made by businessmen, who are terrified at the threat of their powers: what businessmen make are surrenders. Nobody prays more fervently than the businessman to be freed from the crushing burden of armaments; the first thing that happens in a war is the freezing of international credits, which the businessman does not like. The same businessman who will view with perfect indifference the senseless destruction of fish and fruit, coffee and corn in peacetime, because it does not pay to distribute them, is preternaturally sensitive about the senseless destruction of property by war. Patience, cunning, and the appeal to avarice could bring the whole world into economic subjection by a slow, interior corruption. We may, perhaps, count ourselves fortunate that Hitler's patience was at length exhausted and that he conjured up the devil of wrath to cast out the devil of covetousness. When Satan casts out Satan, his kingdom does not stand; but we have come to a grievous pass if we have to choose between one devil and another—if the only deliverance from covetousness is the wrath of war, and the only safeguard against war, a peace based on covetousness.

The virtue of which covetousness is the perversion is something more positive and warm-hearted than thrift. It is the love of the real values, of which the material world has only two: the fruits of the earth and the labor of the people. As for the spiritual values, avarice has no use for them; they cannot be assessed in money, and the moment that anyone tries to assess them in money they softly and suddenly vanish away.

We may argue eloquently that honesty is the best policy. Unfortunately, the moment honesty is adopted for the sake of policy it mysteriously ceases to be honesty. We may say that the best art should be recompensed at the highest rate, and no doubt it should; but if the artist lets his work be influenced by considerations of marketing, he will discover that what he is producing is not art. And we may say, with some justice, that an irreligious nation cannot prosper; but if a nation tries to cultivate religion for the sake of regaining prosperity, the resulting brand of religion will be addressed to a very odd God indeed. There is said to be a revival just now of what is called interest in religion. Even governments are inclined to allot broadcasting time to religious propaganda, and to order National Days of Prayer. However admirable these activities may be, one has a haunting feeling that God's acquaintance is being cultivated because he might come in useful. But God is quite shrewd enough to see through that particular kind of commercial fraud.

But we are only halfway through our list of the deadly sins. Hand in hand with covetousness goes its close companion— *invidia* or envy—which hates to see other men happy. The names by which it offers itself to the world's applause are right and justice, and it makes a great parade of these austere virtues. It begins by asking, plausibly, "Why should not I enjoy what others enjoy?" and it ends by demanding, "Why should others enjoy what I may not?"

Envy is the great leveler. If it cannot level things up, it will level them down; and the words constantly in its mouth are "my rights" and "my wrongs." At its best, envy is a climber and a snob; at its worst, it is a destroyer; rather than have anybody happier than itself, it will see us all miserable together.

In love, envy is cruel, jealous, and possessive. My friend and my marriage partner must be wholly wrapped up in me and must find no interests outside me. That is my right. No person, no work, no hobby must rob me of any part of that right. If we cannot be happy together, we will be unhappy together, but there must be no escape into pleasures that I cannot share. If my husband's work means more to him than I do, I will see him ruined rather than preoccupied; if my wife is so abandoned as to enjoy Beethoven or dancing or anything else that I do not appreciate; I will so nag and insult her that she will no longer be able to indulge those tastes with a mind at ease. If my neighbors are able to take pleasure in intellectual interests that are above my head, I will sneer at them and call them by derisive names because they make me feel inferior, and that is a thing I cannot bear. All men have equal rights, and if these people were born with any sort of privilege, I will see to it that that privilege shall be made worthless, if I can, and by any means I can devise. Let justice be done to me, though the heavens fall and the earth be shot to pieces.

If avarice is the sin of the haves against the have-nots, envy is the sin of the have-nots against the haves. If we want to see what they look like on a big scale, we may say that avarice has been the sin of the Anglo-Saxon democracies, and envy the sin of Germany. Both are cruel—the one with a heavy, complacent, and bloodless cruelty; the other with a violent, calculated, and savage cruelty. But Germany only displays in accentuated form an evil of which we have plenty at home.

The difficulty about dealing with envy is precisely that it is the sin of the have-nots, and that, on that account, it can always find support among those who are just and generous minded. Its demands for a place in the sun are highly plausible, and those who detect any egotism in the demand can readily be silenced by accusing them of oppression, inertia, and a readiness to grind the face of the poor. Let us look for a moment at some of the means by which envy holds the world to ransom.

One of its achievements has been to change the former order by which society was based, on status, and substitute a new basis—that of contract. Status means, roughly speaking, that the relations of social units are ordered according to the intrinsic qualities that those units possess by nature. Men and institutions are valued for what they are. Contract means that they are valued, and their relations ordered, in virtue of what bargain they are able to strike. Knowledge, for example, and the man of knowledge can be rated at a market value—prized, that is, not for the sake of knowledge, but for what is called their contribution to society. The family is esteemed, or not esteemed, according as it can show its value as an economic unit. Thus, all inequalities can, theoretically, be reduced to financial and utilitarian terms, and the very notion of intrinsic superiority can be denied and derided. In other words, all pretension to superiority can be debunked.

The years between the wars saw the most ruthless campaign of debunking ever undertaken by nominally civilized nations. Great artists were debunked by disclosures of their private weaknesses; great statesmen, by attributing to them mercenary and petty motives, or by alleging that all their work was meaningless, or done for them by other people. Religion was debunked and shown to consist of a mixture of craven superstition and greed. Courage was debunked, patriotism was debunked, learning and art were debunked, love was debunked, and with it family affection and the virtues of obedience, veneration, and solidarity. Age was debunked by youth, and youth by age. Psychologists stripped bare the pretensions of reason and conscience and self-control, saying that these were only the respectable disguises of unmentionable unconscious impulses. Honor was debunked with peculiar virulence, and good faith, and unselfishness. Everything that could possibly be held to constitute an essential superiority had the garments of honor torn from its back and was cast out into the darkness of derision. Civilization was finally debunked till it had not a rag left to cover its nakedness.

It is well that the hypocrisies that breed like mushrooms in the shadow of great virtues should be discovered and removed, but envy is not the right instrument for that purpose, for it tears down the whole fabric to get at the parasitic growths. Its enemy, in fact, is the virtues themselves. Envy cannot bear to admire or respect; it cannot bear to be grateful. But it is very plausible; it always announces that it works in the name of truth and equity. Sometimes it may be a good thing to debunk envy a little. For example: here is a phrase that we have heard a good deal of late:

"These services (payments, compensations, or what not) ought not to be made a matter of charity. We have a right to demand that they should be borne by the state."

It sounds splendid; but what does it mean?

Now, you and I are the state, and where the bearing of financial burdens is concerned, the taxpayer is the state. The heaviest burden of taxation is, naturally, borne by those who can best afford to pay. When a new burden is imposed, the rich will have to pay most of it.

Of the money expended in charity, the greater part—for obvious reasons—is contributed by the rich. Consequently, if the burden hitherto borne by charity is transferred to the shoulders of the taxpayer, it will inevitably continue to be carried by exactly the same class of people. The only difference is this: that people will no longer pay because they want to—eagerly and for love—but because they must, reluctantly and under pain of fine or imprisonment. The result, roughly speaking, is financially the same; the only difference is the elimination of the two detested virtues of love and gratitude.

I do not say for a moment that certain things should not be the responsibility of the state—that is, of everybody. No doubt those who formerly contributed out of love should be very willing to pay a tax instead. But what I see very clearly is the hatred of the gracious act and the determination that nobody shall be allowed any kind of spontaneous pleasure in well-doing if envy can prevent it. "This ointment might have been sold for much and given to the poor." Then our nostrils would not be offended by any odor of sanctity—the house would not be "filled with the smell of the ointment." It is characteristic that it should have been Judas who debunked that act of charity.*

The sixth deadly sin is named by the Church *acedia* or

---

* It will be noticed that the appeasement of envy is becoming quite an important factor in our domestic war policy. Thus, certain restrictions on hotel and restaurant catering were imposed, admittedly, not because they would make any appreciable difference to the nation's food resources but in the name of equality and sacrifice. So far, so good. Similarly people with large cellars have been debarred from laying in stocks of coal during the summer, although, had this been permitted up to the limit of their allocation, the problem of winter delivery would have been greatly eased for the coal merchants, and the people with small cellars would have stood a better chance of getting their coal regularly. So far, perhaps, not quite so good. The controversy about education has been enlivened by a beautiful three-cornered duel. One party thinks the public boarding school so evil a luxury that it ought not to be inflicted even upon the rich. A second party thinks it so desirable a luxury that it ought to be thrown open to the poor. The levelers-up and the levelers-down are thus embarrassed by a trifling uncertainty as to which is up and which is down; while a third party contends that the whole boarding system bears so harshly on parent and child alike that the poor would not like it if they had it—though they are not sure whether this argues in the poor a laudable love of family life or a lamentable lack of discipline. The only possible comment seems to be that (a) no exercise is so hard and exacting as that of setting a case on its merits (hence the popular dislike of casuistry); (b) it is always easier to level down than to level up; and (c) a distinguished poet [T. S. Eliot] has warned us that:

> The last temptation is the greatest treason:
> To do the right deed for the wrong reason.
> —D.L.S.

sloth. In the world it calls itself tolerance; but in hell it is called despair. It is the accomplice of the other sins and their worst punishment. It is the sin that believes in nothing, cares for nothing, seeks to know nothing, interferes with nothing, enjoys nothing, loves nothing, hates nothing, finds purpose in nothing, lives for nothing, and remains alive only because there is nothing it would die for. We have known it far too well for many years. The only thing perhaps that we have not known about it is that it is a mortal sin.

The war has jerked us pretty sharply into consciousness about this slugabed sin of sloth, and perhaps we need not say too much about it. But two warnings are rather necessary.

First, it is one of the favorite tricks of this sin to dissemble itself under cover of a whiffling activity of body. We think that if we are busily rushing about and doing things, we cannot be suffering from sloth. And besides, violent activity seems to offer an escape from the horrors of sloth. So the other sins hasten to provide a cloak for sloth. Gluttony offers a whirl of dancing, dining, sports, and dashing very fast from place to place to gape at beauty spots, which, when we get to them, we defile with vulgarity and waste. Covetousness rakes us out of bed at an early hour in order that we may put pep and hustle into our business. Envy sets us to gossip and scandal, to writing cantankerous letters to the papers, and to the unearthing of secrets and scavenging of dustbins. Wrath provides (very ingeniously) the argument that the only fitting activity in a world so full of evildoers and evil demons is to curse loudly and incessantly: "Whatever brute and blackguard made the world"; while lust provides that round of dreary promiscuity that passes for bodily vigor. But these are all disguises for the empty heart and the empty brain and the empty soul of acedia.

Let us take particular notice of the empty brain. Here sloth is in a conspiracy with envy to prevent people from thinking. Sloth persuades us that stupidity is not our sin, but our misfortune; while envy, at the same time, persuades us that intelligence is despicable—a dusty, highbrow, and commercially useless thing.

And secondly, the war has jerked us out of sloth; but wars, if they go on very long, induce sloth in the shape of war-weariness and despair of any purpose. We saw its effects in the last peace, when it brought all the sins in its train. There are times when one is tempted to say that the great, sprawling, lethargic sin of sloth is the oldest and greatest of the sins and the parent of all the rest.

But the head and origin of all sin is the basic sin of *superbia* or pride. In one way there is so much to say about pride that one might speak of it for a week and not have done. Yet in another way, all there is to be said about it can be said in a single sentence. It is the sin of trying to be as God. It is the sin that proclaims that man can produce out of his own wits, and his own impulses, and his own imagination the standards by which he lives: that man is fitted to be his own judge. It is pride that turns man's virtues into deadly sins by causing each self-sufficient virtue to issue in its own opposite, and as a grotesque and horrible travesty of itself. The name under which pride walks the world at this moment is the perfectibility of man, or the doctrine of progress; and its specialty is the making of blueprints for utopia and establishing the kingdom of man on earth.

For the devilish strategy of pride is that it attacks us, not on our weak points, but on our strong. It is preeminently the sin of the noble mind—that *corruptio optimi* that works more evil in the world than all the deliberate vices. Because we do not recognize pride when we see it, we stand aghast to see the havoc wrought by the triumphs of human idealism. We meant so well, we thought we were succeeding— and look what has come of our efforts! There is a proverb that says that the way to hell is paved with good intentions. We usually take it as referring to intentions that have been weakly abandoned, but it has a deeper and much subtler meaning. That road is paved with good intentions strongly and obstinately pursued until they become self-sufficing ends in themselves and deified.

> Sin grows with doing good . . .
> Servant of God has chance of greater sin
> And sorrow, than the man who serves a king.
> For those who serve the greater cause may make
>   the cause serve them,
> Still doing right.*

The Greeks feared above all things the state of mind they called *hubris*—the inflated spirits that come with overmuch success. Overweening in men called forth, they thought, the envy of the gods. Their theology may seem to us a little unworthy, but with the phenomenon itself and its effects they were only too well acquainted. Christianity, with a more rational theology, traces hubris back to the root sin of pride, which places man instead of God at the center of gravity and so throws the whole structure of things into the ruin called judgment. Whenever we say, whether in the personal, political, or social sphere,

> I am the master of my fate;
> I am the captain of my soul

we are committing the sin of pride; and the higher the goal at which we aim, the more far reaching will be the subsequent disaster. That is why we ought to distrust all those high ambitions and lofty ideals that make the well-being of humanity their ultimate end. We cannot make ourselves happy by serving ourselves—not even when we call self-service the service of the community, for the community in that context is only an extension of our own ego. Human happiness is a by-product, thrown off in our service of God. And incidentally, let us be very careful how we preach that Christianity is necessary for the building of a free and prosperous postwar world. The proposition is strictly true, but

*T. S. Eliot, *Murder in the Cathedral*.

to put it that way may be misleading, for it sounds as though we proposed to make God an instrument in the service of man. But God is nobody's instrument. If we say that the denial of God was the cause of our present disasters, well and good; it is of the essence of pride to suppose that we can do without God.

But it will not do to let the same sin creep back in a subtler and more virtuous-seeking form by suggesting that the service of God is necessary as a means to the service of man. That is a blasphemous hypocrisy, which would end by degrading God to the status of a heathen fetish, bound to the service of a tribe, and likely to be dumped head-downwards in the water butt if he failed to produce good harvest weather in return for services rendered.

"Cursed be he that trusteth in man," says Reinhold Niebuhr,* "even if he be pious man or, perhaps, particularly if he be pious man." For the besetting temptation of the pious man is to become the proud man: "He spake this parable unto certain which trusted in themselves that they were righteous."

* Reinhold Niebuhr, *Beyond Tragedy*.

Dante and Charles Williams

WHEN EDWARD FITZGERALD scribbled to a friend, "Mrs. Browning is dead; we shall have no more *Aurora Leighs*, thank God!" he was only being flippant in a deplorably tasteless way. But when certain academic persons, "whom by ear and eye he never knew," expressed a similar relief at the passing of Charles Williams, they probably meant rather more by it, and expressed, unintentionally, a very much higher tribute to the dead. A chronic irritation had been removed from the intellectual atmosphere, and they breathed more freely.

Few things are more striking than the change that has taken place during my own lifetime in the attitude of the intelligentsia toward the spokesmen of Christian opinion. When I was a child, bishops expressed doubts about the Resurrection, and were called courageous. When I was a girl, G. K. Chesterton professed belief in the Resurrection, and was called whimsical. When I was at college, thoughtful people expressed belief in the Resurrection "in a spiritual sense," and were called advanced (any other kind of belief was called obsolete, and its professors were held to be simple-minded). When I was middle-aged, a number of lay persons, including some poets and writers of popular fiction, put forward rational arguments for the Resurrection, and were called courageous. Today, any lay apologist for Christianity, who is not a clergyman and whose works are sold and read, is likely to be abused in no uncertain terms as a mountebank, a reactionary, a tool of the Inquisition, a spiritual snob, an intellectual bully, an escapist, an obstructionist, a psychopathic introvert, an insensitive extrovert, and an enemy of society. The charges are not always mutually compatible, but the common animus behind them is unmistakable, and its name is fear. Writers who attack these domineering Christians are called courageous.

The wheel, it would appear, has come full circle. But in fact the situation is very different from what it was in my childhood. Then, the heretical bishops and the laymen whose lead they were in fact following were thought of as attacking a kind of bastille of inert and outworn tyranny; the exponent of contemporary anti-Christian polemic is felt, on the contrary, to be standing in the breach against the threat of an invading, or at least of a revolutionary, army, possibly, as we shall see later, of a gang of jailbreakers. It is true that every effort is made to represent Christian affirmations as a mere attempt to reimpose the cold, dead hand of the past. Phrases such as "dogmatic," "scholastic," "medieval," "unscientific," "mystical obscurantism," "return to the Dark Ages," "conventional orthodoxy," "taboo," "authoritarian," and so on are bandied about freely in a pejorative sense, and often without any very clear notion of their meaning, but the tone of voice is a new one.

It is perhaps significant that, in this country, the peculiar acrimony of the "scientific humanists," as they like, I think, to call themselves, is seldom directed toward the Church of

Rome. There, if anywhere, one would think, the grip of the medieval mortmain should be observable. But it is not so. Only Protestants trouble their heads about Rome. From the harrow of scientific humanism, Mr. Evelyn Waugh and Mr. Graham Greene slip out almost untouched by the teeth. For so long as I remember, Romans have always received special treatment. They believe things because they have to; kindly people are careful not to offend their susceptibilities; anybody who goes over to Rome is philosophically written off, as though he or she had adopted an alien nationality; Romans do as Rome does, and nobody is surprised or aggrieved. The indignation is reserved for a small group of Anglicans, such as Charles Williams, C. S. Lewis (the special "Cambridge" number of *The Twentieth Century* was a monument to the irritant properties of Christian intellectualism in that university), and, of course, T. S. Eliot, whose so-called retreat into Anglicanism has exposed him to critical savagery that sometimes oversteps the limits not only of charity but also of decency. In the critical attacks on these men, there is, quite plainly discernible, a note of hysteria. The accents are not those of a man liberating a dog from a confined and unwholesome kennel; they are those of a child, who, picking up in the garden a dull and inoffensive-looking stone, sees it stretch forth a leg and wink a knowing eye: "Ugh! it's alive!"

Now, it is precisely this power of evoking a very present and demanding life from that which might be supposed decently dead and sterilized that characterizes all Charles Williams's literary criticism, and more especially, his critical interpretation of Dante—to which, I promise you, I will eventually come. His genius moved him to make contact with the essential life in every work he handled; it was this which made him so inspiring a master to his students in London and Oxford, and this which explains the suspicion, and the occasional antagonism, which his whole method arouses in certain academic circles today. For he did, in a measure, run counter to the modern trend in criticism.

Perhaps the clearest way to put the matter briefly is to say that his judgments were as free as any modern man's judgments could be from what we call a "sense of period." It would not be altogether untrue to say that in this respect he was "medieval"—provided we add that "classical" or "Renaissance" would be an equally appropriate epithet. For period-sense is a thing of very recent origin—it scarcely begins to exist before the closing years of the eighteenth century. We may see this very vividly illustrated in the history of theatrical costume. Right down to Garrick's time, nobody thought it odd to play Coriolanus or Macbeth in a periwig, and all the classical heroines in panniers and powdered hair, any more than Shakespeare had boggled about making his Roman conspirators pull their hats about their brows, or giving Brutus a pocket in his gown. No doubt everybody knew that the custom worn in past ages was different from their own—they knew, but they did not feel that it mattered. They felt that the play was dealing with human beings in a human situation—not with historical personages conditioned by a historical environment. And this was a reflection of their whole attitude to the writers of the past—they judged them as though they were contemporaries, bringing their opinions to the bar of absolute, rather than of relative, truth.

The period-sense, and the dynamic philosophy of history to which it belongs, is, of course, an admirable thing, quickening our understanding of the past and displaying all social and historical changes as movements in a great process of becoming. But if it is insisted upon too much, it may defeat itself. It may end by actually destroying all contact, all sympathy between us and our forebears, and even that very awareness of continuity that it ought to foster. If we look upon Dante (for example) as a man totally explicable in terms of a vanished period, we may succeed in forgetting that he is a man like ourselves. If we account for everything that he said by the consideration that, being born when he was, there was nothing else he could very well say, we shall

have provided ourselves with an excellent excuse for not applying what he said to ourselves: it performed a function in
history, and there its interest ends. The period-sense may,
that is, be used as a defense mechanism against any categorical imperative that we may feel to be inconvenient. So
long as we can look upon it as a mere incident in a historical pattern, our resistance remains unaffected.

In this matter, as in so many others, Christianity displays
its usual propensity for making everything as awkward as
possible. It outrages the tidy-minded by occupying a paradoxical position. On the one hand, it made modern science
and the modern views of history possible by insisting that
the pattern of events was not (as the Greek philosophers
thought) static or cyclic, but a progression in time from a
beginning to an end. On the other, it tiresomely maintains
that at every point in the developing temporal process, the
conditioned truths are preferable to an extratemporal standard of absolute truth, before which all souls enjoy complete equality, no aristocratic privilege being attached to the
accident of later birth.

To Williams, this spiritual equality of past and present
was axiomatic; it was part of the coinherence. For him, the
solidarity of human society lay visibly extended, not only in
space, but also in time. He was, of course, aware that
periods had succeeded one another—a book such as *The Descent of the Dove* bears witness to his strong awareness of
historical process—but for him periods constituted no bar-
riers. With precisely the same conviction that a modern
Communist will assert the bond of fraternity between workers in China and workers in Whitechapel, Williams asserted
(or to speak more exactly, took for granted) the bond of fraternity between a poet in the twentieth century and a poet
in the Middle Ages. He was thus never content with knowing under what pressure of social conditions a poet came to
say what he did; he felt that this did not exhaust the subject
or explain the poem away. He always went on to ask, "Did
the poet speak truth? and if so, what ought we to do about

it?" That is why I said that the life he evoked in his critical
judgments was "present and demanding." He vivified the
past; he did not "revivify" it, in the sense of conscien-
tiously reconstructing it against its period decor. He was as
ready as Sophocles or Shakespeare to see the whole drama
of history performed in modern dress.

Thus he came to Dante prepared to hail him across the
negligible gap of six centuries as a fellow-poet, a fellow-
lover, and a fellow-Christian. In the first paragraph of *The
Figure of Beatrice*, he observes, "Dante is one of those poets
who begin their work with what is declared to be an intense personal experience." In that seemingly casual phrase,
he sweeps Dante into the same trawl with all the other odd
fish who swim in the "great sea of being";—"one of those
poets"—"intense personal experience." It is related of
Charles Williams that on one occasion he was having his
hair cut and at the same time lending a sympathetic ear to
the history of the barber's love affair. "When my girl's
about," said the barber, "I'm that happy I don't feel as if I
had an enemy in the world—I'd forgive anybody anything."

"My dear man," cried Charles, leaping up and wringing
the barber's hand enthusiastically, "my dear man, that's exactly what Dante said."

So it was; and no medieval theory of courtly love had to
be invoked to account for it. In the theology of romantic
love the liturgy is all of one tradition.

It was not from Dante that Williams learned the theology
of romantic love; he learned it from his own experience. But
when he encountered it in Dante, he recognized it immediately and knew that Dante and he were living within the
same tradition. I have seen a letter of his (written, I think,
to the late J. D. Sinclair, but I have unfortunately lost the
reference) in which he protests that what he is trying to
impress upon all the learned commentators of Dante is that
"the thing does happen." Whatever symbolism the interpreters, or Dante himself, may build upon it, the basis of the

whole towering structure is the living experienced fact. His own first introduction to the *Commedia* took place, he told me, when he was hurriedly correcting the proofs of Cary's translation for the Oxford University Press, and his immediate reaction was, "But this is true." By this simple affirmation he opened up a road that had been closed for at least a century; or perhaps it was a road that had never before been driven through precisely that part of the forest. For Dante's position has always been curiously isolated. He has been treated as a theologian, as a moralist, as a political satirist, as a manufacturer of "wild Gothick fancies," as a repository of curious historical allusions, and, occasionally, as a mystic of a rather irregular kind, but very seldom as a poet among poets, creating after the manner of his kind "an accurate image of actual experience." Those are Williams's words,* and they define as nearly as possible what he looked for in all poets, and found in Dante as in any other poet. The Pre-Raphaelites had perhaps come nearest to thus including Dante in the free commonwealth of poets; but their attention was almost exclusively directed to the *Vita Nuova*—for the universalizing of the first human vision into the great divine vision of fulfillment their undisciplined minds could find no use. The great nineteenth-century Dantists had the merit of taking the substance of the poem seriously, but their approach tended to be rather too narrowly ethical, and suggestive of an intelligent but critical congregation listening to an instruction from the pulpit. The early twentieth century endeavored, with no very striking success, to divorce the form from the content, and to save Dante's reputation as a poet by considering "the poetry" in abstraction from the religious experience—which they did not recognize as an experience, or at least not as a poetic experience. But Williams's approach, to Dante as to everybody else, was existential. He recognized in the *Comedy*, not merely the *doctrine* of hell, purgatory, and heaven,

Love and Religion in Dante (Dacre Press).

but the *experience* of those states, expressed in the movements of the images—those creatures of true flesh and blood that, like the matter of a sacrament, are that which they symbolize. It is easy to see why, the poem being such as it is, this approach should be found disquieting. If the thing that happened to Dante in thirteenth-century Florence is identical with what happens today to a barber in Fleet Street, then the whole experience might happen to any of us at any time, and nobody can feel safe.

I do not propose to examine in detail the contents of *The Figure of Beatrice*. I should only be repeating much that I have said elsewhere, and in any case the book itself is its own best commentary and should offer no very great difficulty to anybody who is at all familiar with the body of Williams's work as a whole. All his books illuminate one another, for the same master themes govern them all, so that it is impossible to confine any one theme to a single book. For example, his most impressive commentary on Dante's dream of the siren is to be found, not in *The Figure of Beatrice*, but in those chapters of *Descent into Hell* that deal with Mrs. Sammile and the Succubus; and to read that novel along with the chapters on the *Inferno* is to enrich one's understanding of the whole conception of hell, both in Williams and in Dante. The mystical theology of the affirmative way needs to be studied in *The Place of the Lion* and in the *Taliessin* poems, and its imaginative treatment there compared with its more formal exposition in the Dante volume. And so on. It will be enough to mention briefly some of the points at which the minds of the two poets touch each other most closely. To do more would be impossible, for they start up correspondences everywhere, so that it is possible to say that there is scarcely anything explicit in Williams that is not also explicit or implicit in Dante.

Mr. John Heath-Stubbs, in his admirable booklet on Charles Williams, tells us of a lecture delivered by Williams at Oxford, in which he enumerated the "five principal modes of the Romantic experience, or great images, which occur in poetry." They are: the religious experience itself; the image of woman; the image of nature; the image of the city; and the experience of great art. Of these, four at least he found (whether in the sense of discovering or recognizing them) already manifest in Dante. The religious experience itself is the theme of Dante's work, from first to last, beginning with a conversion on the lower plane, followed by loss of faith, backsliding and the vision of hell, and proceeding through a reeducation on the intellectual level to a second conversion of the higher plane, and so to the ascent of vision. The pattern is a familiar one up to a point, its powerful individuality lying in the tenacity with which the validity of the images is affirmed from first to last.

The image of woman is, of course, asserted in Beatrice, about whose person the theology of romantic love is assembled and displayed. I am not sure that Williams, in calling it "the image of woman," was doing full justice to himself or Dante. The image is not of femaleness as such—the *ewig Weibliches* about which Goethe and D. H. Lawrence and others, have made so much to-do. It is a personal relationship of adoration, and Williams himself was the first to insist that the adoration need not be (though in literature it most frequently is) that of a man for a woman. It might, in the exchange of hierarchies, be that of a woman for a man; if, he would say, Beatrice had written her version of the *Commedia,* Dante himself might have figured in it as the "God-bearing image." Or the element of sex might not enter it at all. But in one way or other, the Image is that of the God-bearing person, whose earthly archetype is Mary, and whose heavenly archetype is Christ.

For Dante, the image of the city is personified in Vergil and his Rome. But it exists also for Dante in Florence, as for Williams in London; and also in his dream of the just empire, corresponding to Vergil's dream of that perfected Augustan Empire, of which the reality fell so far short. Finally, it is manifested directly in the heavenly city of the paradise, and also negatively in the perversions of the city of Dis.

The experience of great art is also there—in Vergil, in the great poets encountered at various stages on the way, in Dante's vivid consciousness of his own poetic calling. But its greatest image is the poem itself, to which, as Dante says, "Heaven and earth have set hand." Immanent in him, but also transcending him, his own art is more than himself—like Beatrice, like city and empire, it is a symbol subdued to the greater thing it symbolizes.

The image of nature, which Williams perceived most clearly and powerfully in Wordsworth, is not so distinctly present in Dante. Neither, for that matter, was it very observable in Charles Williams: "In his poetry," says Mr. Heath-Stubbs, "nature as such has hardly any part to play. His poetry lacks particularity of observation." One might say the same of Dante, for though his treatment of animals and especially birds shows some "particularity of observation," it remains true of him as of Williams that his "landscapes are always emblematic of states of mind." We may, if we like, here refresh ourselves with a little "sense of period." Medieval poets are very seldom nature worshippers, in the sense in which we moderns think of nature. Bad roads, difficulties of transport, the uncertainties of a local and primitive agriculture, and relentless exposure at all times to the vagaries of the weather made their relation to mists and mountains, crops and forests, heat, flood and tempest a grim and practical one. The image of the forest, in particular, is always slightly uncanny—Williams was in tune with them when he took that image (Broceliande, the Dark Wood, the Forest of Arden) as a symbol of the subconscious. Medieval man preferred his nature tamed and made orderly in gardens. Even here, his observation was seldom very particular: "red and yellow flowers," the rose, the lily, the violet, the daisy; the oak, the thorn, the beech, the poplar. "Small fowls making melody," with an occasional nightingale, is about as far as most of his poems go. But there is one remarkable exception. If where we are particular they were vague and generalized, yet where we are usually most vague and generalized they were particular, and moreover felt all that numinous awe that we reserve for the terrestrial phenomena of nature. Better than the earth at their feet they knew and loved the visible heavens. They knew the way of the sun among the houses of the zodiac as intimately and lovingly as we know the face of the landscape from our own windows; and they did not, like some modern novelists, carelessly indulge themselves with two full moons in a fortnight. When we talk of nature, we think of land and water, plants, and animals; we have almost forgotten that the heavens too are nature. But the medieval did not, and when Dante is awestruck by nature it is almost always in the face of the turning of the great wheels—the army of unalterable law. The visible heavens are, for him and his like, the image of mathematical order. It is perhaps a little surprising that Williams did not list this image with the others, for mathematical order meant much to him and supplied him with many of his most pregnant poetical images, particularly in the *Taliessin* poems.

The theme of the sanctity of the flesh is, of course, common to both poets, as it in reason ought to be to all those who acknowledge the Incarnation, and as it must necessarily be to all followers of the affirmative way. For that way begins always with the intuitive perception of the divine image in the material creation—not displacing but informing it, as Moses beheld God in the burning bush, "and the bush was not consumed"; and if pursued to the end, it leads to the illuminative vision of the image of the created manhood in the uncreated image of the glory. Dante, beholding in the flesh-and-blood Florentine girl the appearance of the in-godded Beatrice in her unfallen nature, and Pauline Anstruther, brought face to face with her own "body of glory" in the moment when she willingly takes to herself her ancestor's burden of fear, are variations upon this theme of the "holy and glorious flesh—*la santa e gloriosa carne.*"

The doctrine of substitution is not found very explicitly, I think, in Dante; except, of course, insofar as it is implied in the great passage on the atonement in the seventh canto of the *Paradiso,* and I will not therefore deal with it here. Characteristic of both poets is the great attention they give to the "knowledge of good and evil"—that is, the knowledge of the good in its opposite identity of evil. Williams, in his chapter on the *Inferno,* speaks of the soul being "here drawn down the *perverted way of affirmation*"; and in *He Came Down from Heaven* he has brilliantly expounded the legend of the Fall in this sense: "The Adam . . . knew good, they wished to know good and evil. Since there was not—since there was not and never has been and never will be—anything else than the good to know, they knew good as antagonism." Dante, in a series of carefully contrasted images, shows in hell the perverted experience of those goodnesses that are seen exalted in heaven. Paolo and Francesca, Ulysses and Diomede, Ugolino and Ruggieri are, at different levels, the perverted images of that mutuality that is the life of those blessed who make up the body of the eagle in the heaven of justice and "when they think we, say I," because they are members of one another. The angelic glory that, on the cornices of purgatory, is light and song and courtesy, is known in hell only as an appearance of terror and judgment. In *The Place of the Lion*, the eagle, which is here the principle of knowledge, appears to Damaris Tighe as a horrible pterodactyl, stinking of decay because she has perverted the good of knowledge to her own selfish uses. "They know evil; that is, they know the good of fact as repugnant to them." Even so, the Lady Julian of Norwich averred that she "saw no hell but sin"; and St. Catherine of Genoa said that the eternal fires were no other than the light of God, seen by those who rejected it.

In pointing out parallels of this kind, I do not mean to suggest that Charles Williams got his ideas out of Dante.

That is a very crude and popular way of putting it. It is also
a manner of speech far too common among the Damaris
Tighes of scholarship, who tend to see everything in terms
of sources and influences. That poets derive from other
poets in the same tradition is true, and they have never
been ashamed to acknowledge their debt to one another;
neither was such borrowing ever thought dishonorable
until we decided to make a fetish out of the word *originality*.
But sources and influences and borrowings are not the
whole story; the coinherence found among the practitioners
of the grand art is not of this simple kind. We may say that,
for example, the theology of romantic love would not have
existed in Williams, or not in that particular mode, if Dante
had never written; but we may also say that it did not exist
after that mode in Dante until Williams found it there. In
the tradition—which means the handing over—of the symbols of art, time's arrow flies both ways. That which was
always potentially in the earlier poet may be actualized in
the later poet, and, once it has been actualized it becomes
and remains actual in the poet of its origin. In a letter that
the late J. D. Sinclair was kind enough to show me, Williams wrote (apropos of the allegory of the Beatrician Pageant in *Purgatory*, xxix–xxx), "My chief point, though I
should be cautious how I made it to the world in general, is
that poets think of something that they then discover to
have relevance all-around. It is perhaps a little unfortunate
that they so rarely bother to explain all the relevance. This
has caused lesser poets than Dante to be called obscure."

Since Williams was cautious of disclosing this fact about
poets, it is perhaps a little treacherous of me to do so behind, as it were, his back; but I will hope that he does not
regard you as "the world in general." What he says is exceedingly true, as I myself can bear witness. A poet creates
a character, a situation, a phrase for a particular purpose
and, after having done so, realizes that he has created a universal symbol, applicable in a far wider sense than that
which he immediately intended. Thenceforth he uses it,

with or without bothering to explain all its relevance, in the wider context to which he has found it applicable. But it sometimes happens that it is not the poet himself, but another, who discovers the wider relevance. If so, he is justified in so interpreting it in the place where he finds it; for the relevance was always potentially there, and once seen and recognized it is actually there forever. This does not, of course, mean that we can read into poets anything that we jolly well like; any significance that contradicts the whole tenor of their work is obviously suspect. But it means that in a very real sense poets do sometimes write more greatly than they know; and it also means that every poet's work enriches not only those to whom he transmits the tradition, but also all those from whom he himself derived it.

It is here that we find ourselves returning, by a slightly different road, to that sense of poetic timelessness that enabled Williams to break down Dante's isolation and treat him quite freely and naturally as a poet among other poets. I do not think that this had ever been done for Dante in quite the same way before. His debts to earlier poets have, indeed, been thoroughly investigated—verbal borrowings from Vergil and Ovid, Statius, Boethius, and the Scriptures, parallels from Guido Guincelli, Guido Cavalcanti, and other lyricists of the *dolce stil nuovo* allusions to the *Song of Roland* and the Romance writers of the Arthurian cycle, affinities with the troubadors of Provence, and all the rest of it. His philosophy and theology have been tracked to their sources in Aristotle, Aquinas, St. Bernard, the Victorines, in the Gnostic pseudo-Scriptures of the second century, and in the Jewish Cabbala. All this is the daily bread of research scholarship; and very exciting it can be, especially when it is carried out with sympathetic understanding of the workings of the poetic mind, as was done by John Livingston Lowes for Coleridge in that astonishing book *The Road to Xanadu*.

Equally, of course, the influence of Dante upon later poets has been duly noted—the quotations, the borrowings, the overt repudiations, denunciations, and eulogies. There have also been some sporadic attempts to compare—rather externally and superficially—Dante's hell with Milton's, of his Satan with Goethe's Mephistopheles. But it is only Williams who, in discussing Dante's poetic theme and treatment, will readily, and, as it were, casually, bring in Shakespeare, Milton, Wordsworth, Coleridge, Bernard Shaw, Coventry Patmore, George Fox, Sir Thomas Browne, Spenser, Keats, Kierkegaard, Raymond Lully, and Christopher Marlowe, to exchange ideas with him as though they were all democratic citizens of one and the same poetic Athens. I have taken these names from *The Figure of Beatrice*, in which they all appear; in conversation, Williams was equally ready to illuminate any passage in Dante from Browning, Tennyson, or Gerard Manley Hopkins, and for aught I know, he would have been prepared to illustrate him from Kafka, James Joyce, or Dylan Thomas, or them from Dante, had the occasion arisen. We are accustomed to deal thus with our own poets—Shakespeare is not too great for such treatment, nor Chaucer too remote; but believe me, it is rare to find any critic of Dante using this pleasant familiarity with him. "It might not be unwise," says Charles Williams, speaking of the perils of the Beatrician way, "to point to a few extracts from Mr. Shaw's *Arms and the Man* . . . in every edition of the *Commedia*." Others have solemnly warned us of these perils, but who except Williams would ever have proposed such a prophylactic?

The death of Beatrice is the figure of a spiritual disillusionment: "This state," he adds, "has been put to us most clearly in two places in English verse; the first is in Shakespeare's *Troilus and Cressida*; the second in Wordsworth's *Prelude*." Or again: "The forest itself has different names in different tongues—Westermain, Arden, Birnam, Broceliande." Meredith, too, drops in to the poetic party, adds a word to the discussion, and drops out again. Across the centuries, the poets hold communication.

In the same way, and quite apart from formal criticism, we find Dante discoursing with his fellows in the body of

Williams's tales and poems. Here, for example, is a short passage from *The Calling of Taliessin*. Merlin and his sister Brisen, the figures of time and space, are beginning the magical operation that is to call in the spiritual powers to the founding of the kingdom of Logres in Britain.

The cone's shadow of earth fell into space,
and into (other than space) the third heaven.
In the third heaven are the living unriven truths,
climax tranquil in Venus, Merlin, and Brisen
heard, as in faint bee-like humming
round the cone's point, the feeling intellect hasten
to fasten on the earth's image; in the third heaven
the stones of the waste glimmered like summer stars.
Between wood and waste the yoked children of Nimue
opened the rite; they invoked the third heaven,
heard in the far humming of the spiritual intellect,
to the building of Logres and the coming of the Land of the Trinity
which is called Sarras in maps of the soul.

For the full elucidation of this beautiful and complex image I must refer you to C. S. Lewis in *Arthurian Torso*. Briefly, as he says, "we are in fact watching the impregnation of Nimue by her pattern"—that is, of the earthly ectype by its heavenly principle. We know the heavenly principles—the Platonic ideas; we have met them in *The Place of the Lion,* there called down wrongly for selfish ends and in their own naked power; here invoked to a right end and in the right way, that is, through the earthly ectype. The earth's shadow—"as we all know," says Lewis, though perhaps he flatters us—is a cone of darkness, extending through outer space and touching with its apex the third heaven, the sphere of Venus. We have met that shadowy cone in the *Paradiso,* though it there fulfils a different symbolic function. The third heaven in the *Paradiso* is that heaven of love and poetry and therefore a very suitable source for this poetic image of the impregnation of matter by form—"matter yearns toward form as a woman yearns toward a man," according to the saying of the Schoolmen.

Lewis adds that "Williams is here (perhaps unconsciously) reproducing the doctrine of the Renaissance Platonists that Venus—celestial love and beauty—was the pattern or model after which God created the material universe." But "what resides in the third heaven . . . is called by [Williams] 'the feeling intellect' or *mens sensitiva*. The expression 'feeling intellect' is borrowed from Wordsworth's *Prelude* (xiv. 226), and the whole passage in which it occurs is a comment on the later poet's meaning." (I am still quoting from Lewis.) Plato, Dante, the Renaissance Platonists, and Wordsworth have thus all contributed to the passage, while Merlin, Taliessin himself, and the phrase "the summer stars" belong to the ancient poems of the Arthurian cycle. And we might add two further points. First, about the "feeling intellect," which a few lines later is called the "spiritual intellect," Lewis notes that "the important difference between the two poets is that where Wordsworth is thinking of a subjective state in human minds, Williams is thinking of an objective celestial fact."

And here we can scarcely help remembering—as Williams can scarcely have helped remembering—how Dante speaks of the tenth heaven, the empyrean or heaven of God's presence, from which all the other heavens derive their being, as "pure intellectual light fulfilled with love"—*"Ince intellettual piena d'amore."* This intellectual love or loving intellect is the ultimate objective celestial fact—a greater thing than Wordsworth's "feeling intellect" and incomparably greater than the *mens sensitiva*. Secondly, we shall recall the combination of intellect that love in the opening line of Dante's great ode addressed to the celestial intelligences: "You that *by understanding* move the third heaven—*Voi che intendendo il terzo ciel movete"*; and perhaps also that of the still more famous sonnet *"Donne ch'avete* intelletto *d'amore*—Ladies that have *intelligence* in love." The words *source* and *borrowing* are inadequate for this close fusion of poetic images, gathered over twenty-one centuries from

Greece and Italy, Wales, and England. It is nothing in itself unusual; it is the way in which the poet's mind habitually deals with images, and the process is partly conscious and partly subconscious.

The point that I am trying to make is that Williams's critical approach to Dante is of precisely the same kind as his poetic approach—and the same, no doubt, holds true of all the books listed in his biography as "literary criticism." It is not a scholarly approach at all, and it is not the kind of thing that has any real place in a history of literature. It is a poet's approach: creative, vital, existential, seminal, timeless—and therefore, in a sense, without perspective. For this reason it is always, quite understandably, a little suspect by purely academic standards, and received with some reserve by those whose view is powerfully influenced by that awareness of historic perspective to which we have grown accustomed. And where Dante is concerned, it is (very naturally) vigorously repudiated by those who are only too anxious to have Dante's experience thrust firmly back into those remote Middle Ages to which they feel it should belong.

Williams's approach to Dante was able to be thus peculiarly intimate because he shared with him certain kinds of experience—a poetic experience, an experience of romantic love, and (so far as one can tell with either man) a mystical experience of the affirmative way—in addition to sharing with him a common religious faith. That combination of shared experience is rare among Dante's interpreters—in fact, I will venture to call it unique. He also shared with him something else, namely, a temperament capable of the experience of heaven and hell. It is well to say a few words about this because it is a matter very [open] to misconception. The capacity for joy and the capacity for something like despair tend to be found together; sometimes, as in Williams or Blake, joy appears to predominate and to communicate itself the more readily to the outside world; in others, as in Hopkins or T. S. Eliot, we receive on the whole a stronger impression of the suffering than of the joy. In a few men, as Traherne on the one hand, and James Thomson of *The City of the Dreadful Night*, either the hellish or the heavenly element seems to be almost entirely absent.

In Dante's writing, the balance inclines to the side of joy (all the rubbish about the grimness and cruelty and "the poet of hell" is a piece of Gothic fancy inherited from the eighteenth century); though in his private life one gathers that he was rather reserved and severe except among his intimate friends. Or perhaps he was merely absent-minded, like a good many other people given to very close mental concentration. In general it remains true that a very strong awareness of horror attends upon any very strong awareness of joy. Note that I say *joy* and not *happiness*—they are by no means the same thing. Indeed it would scarcely be untrue to say that people of a happy temperament are seldom capable of joy—they are insufficiently sensitive. The word *joy* is a favorite word with Williams, as the word *gioia* with Dante; beneath the coruscations of that joy, the blackness and squalor of the pit open and run down to the center.

This tension between joy and the opposite of joy is, once again, something that is viewed with a certain distrust by an age committed to the pursuit of happiness. It can be readily pigeonholed as lack of adjustment or, in severe cases, as a psychosis. In very severe cases it may indeed be a psychosis. But we must not disguise from ourselves that happiness is a gift of the heathen gods, whereas joy is a Christian duty. It was, I think, L. P. Jacks who pointed out that the word *happiness* does not occur in the Gospels; the word *joy*, on the other hand, occurs frequently—and so do the name and image of hell. The command is to rejoice, not to display a placid contentment or a stoic fortitude. "Call no man happy until he is dead," said the Greek philosopher; and happiness, whether applied to a man's fortunes or his disposition, is the assessment of something extended in time along his whole career. But joy (except for those saints who live continually in the presence of God) is of its nature brief and almost instantaneous; it is an apprehension of the eternal moment. And as such, it is the great invading adversary that can break open the gates of hell. In *Descent into Hell* there are two moments when Wentworth might have saved his soul by accepting what one might call a Dantean vision. The first is a Beatrician moment, the vision of joy.

There was presented to him at once and clearly an opportunity for joy—casual, accidental joy, but joy. If he could not manage joy, at least he might have managed the intention of joy, or (if that were also too much) an effort toward the intention of joy. The infinity of grace could have been contented and invoked by a mere mental refusal of anything but such an effort. . . . He could enjoy; at least he could refuse not to enjoy. He could refuse and reject damnation.

With a perfectly clear, if instantaneous, knowledge of what he did, he rejected joy instead. He instantaneously preferred anger, and at once it came; he invoked envy, and it obliged him.

The second moment is when Wentworth is almost arrested at a much later and lower stage of his descent into the hell of self-absorption by the simple appeal to his professional integrity. This is the vision of Vergil.

All this may be read, and was perhaps intended by Williams himself, as an imaginative gloss upon two incidents in the *Commedia*. The first is Beatrice's mission to Vergil described in the second canto of the *Inferno*, where she says, "Dante has sunk so far in sin that he can no longer hear my voice—do you go and recall him." Later on she says in Dante's own presence:

> "With inspirations, prayer-wrung for his sake,
>   Vainly in dreams and other ways as well,
>   I called him home; so little did he reck"—

and therefore, she says, she was obliged to send Vergil. These correspond to the two offers of possible salvation, by the way of spiritual joy, and by the way of natural duty. The other incident is the dream of the siren, in which

Dante's fascinated gaze upon "that ancient witch," who is Lilith and the succubus, is broken by the discreet lady, calling upon Vergil to unmask the siren and show her for the hell-born obscenity that she is.

And along with the two passages of the *Commedia*, and the two passages from *Descent into Hell,* we may set the critical comment on the siren in *The Figure of Beatrice*—Beatrice known in her opposite identity of hell: "If sloth overtakes Love, Beatrice is lost in the Siren, the romantic Image in the pseudoromantic mirage." He goes on:

She [the siren] has been called the image of sensual pleasure, but this (it would seem) need not be the whole significance. She is as much—let us say—ideal gratification, all the sighs that lament the imperfection of a man's actual mistress, the verses that sweetly moan over her failure to live up to his dreams (or the other way round), the self-condolences, the "disillusions"—all these are the siren's song. She takes flesh and color and music within the night reveries of laziness; she is then—what? what we want; and that is? we do not rightly know, but certainly a siren and a song.

The siren is, therefore, the image of the false joy, and it is significant that in *Descent into Hell* the succubus appears to Wentworth immediately after his deliberate rejection of the true joy.

We may be inclined to ask: "But is that really what Dante meant? One sees what Williams meant, and one can see how he contrived to extract it from Dante's words. But is not this merely a reading into the text subtleties that a medieval poet could never have thought of?" The only answer we can well make is something that Williams himself saw and pointed out: the appearance of the siren and the opening words of her song are a deliberate echo, and almost a parody, of the subsequent appearance and words of Beatrice. In the dream, Dante gazes upon the siren until she becomes beautiful and "puts on the hues of love," and then she sings: "*Io son, io son, dolce sirena*—I am, I am, the sweet siren." Beatrice, appearing, veiled, to Dante in the sacred forest, addresses him: *"Guardaci ben—ben sem, ben sem Beatrice*—Look on us well, we are, we are Beatrice."* Once again we have Dante's trick of the corresponding and contrasting images. We must be prepared, I think, to believe that supreme artists do not produce these elaborate symmetries by accident.

Thus we return to the point from which we set out—the peculiar quality of Williams's interpretation of Dante and the reason why it offends some people as much as it delights others. To say that it offends by being Christian is a great part of the truth, but it is not the whole truth.

You will perhaps have noticed that criticism today tends to divide itself into two schools, which (as usually happens in such cases) diverge as they develop. One, of which we have already spoken, may be called the historical school; and its attitude may be roughly but not altogether unfairly summed up by saying that it considers a poet's meaning to have been important in his own day, but to be of no importance to us except as a part of the historical perspective. This is the more academic and scholarly kind of criticism; and its great virtue is that it does oblige us to consider what the poet's language actually meant to himself and his contemporaries.

There is, however, another school, which may be called the school of interpretative criticism. This pays little attention to what the poet himself, or his contemporary readers, may have thought he meant; it is almost exclusively concerned with the psychological symbolisms and overtones that we can contrive to extract from it. The great virtue of this school is that it does demand some kind of contemporary relevance and so keeps the work of the past present to us as a living force; its weakness is that its interpretations become purely arbitrary—they cease, as C. S. Lewis has said, to be right or wrong and become more or less brilliant executive performances: variations, so to speak, upon a theme suggested by the poet's words. This kind of interpretation is by no means new; it is in fact almost exactly the way in which the allegorists used to treat biblical texts. What Isaiah or Daniel intended to say about contemporary Israel was discarded or ignored in favor of the mystical or moral significations that might be put upon it for the purposes of Christian devotion.

Now, both these methods of criticism are perfectly legitimate, and indeed indispensable, so far as they go. But you will have noticed that they have one thing in common: Both alike, although for quite opposite reasons, dispense us from any obligation to take the poet's meaning seriously. If his language is sufficiently ambiguous to mean almost anything, we can give it our own meaning, and this does not matter. If his language, like Dante's, makes his meaning as unambiguous as it is unwelcome, we can shut him up firmly in the prison of the past, and because it is of the past his meaning does not matter.

Now, to my mind—and I am not alone—any critical method that altogether nullifies the poet's belief and intention is bad for criticism and bad for poetry. A writer in the *Sunday Times*, in reviewing Stephen Spender's *The Making of a Poem,* has observed: "Despite the blandishments of Dr. I. A. Richards, poets can neither regard the beliefs of dead poets as pseudostatements, nor themselves exist on psychologically valuable delusions." Poets themselves desire and need a different kind of criticism, which shall allow them not only, in Middleton Murry's words, "to mean what they say," but to go on meaning it.

Charles Williams's criticism is of this kind. He is a poet in criticism—a poet's critic. Of this kind of critic Dante has hitherto had too few; and that is why *The Figure of Beatrice* and the other books seem to me to usher in a new era of Dante criticism. But since this kind of criticism undermines the assumptions of both the fashionable schools of criticism, we can scarcely be surprised if it is received in some quarters with hostility and contempt. And all the more so because the meaning that it thus drags out to confront us from the cage of the past and the decent mufflings of psychologically valuable delusion is a Christian meaning. For

Christianity also rests upon the assumption that the Word uttered in the past meant something then and means the same thing now. There is an unseemliness about the Easter appearances of something that has no business to be alive. We cannot really be surprised if some people find it more comfortable to sit down to a quiet, objective, laboratory examination of the grave clothes.

STEPHEN SPENDER: *THE MAKING OF A POEM*

If you have not as yet read this book of Spender's, I most strongly urge you to do so. The first two essays in particular throw a most revealing light upon the situation of the poet in the contemporary world, and are curiously tinged with resentment against the advanced type of critic, hailing (this is Spender's identification, not mine) from "Cambridge, Eng. and Mass."

I can only quote now a few short passages that bear more or less directly upon our subject. His thesis is summed up in this reaction to I. A. Richards's statement that modern poetry must learn to exist "in a complete severance from all beliefs":

When the poet abandons the belief which connects visible with invisible worlds, he is left with nothing but a problem of adjustment through poetry to the situation of man in the surroundings of alien nature. He is in a cage with bars that are mirrors reflecting only himself, and there is no possibility of entering through the imagination into the factual realities outside.

In other words, Spender sees the poet shut up with the siren—the projection of his own desires. And here we may remember Vergil's dry little scholastic statement, in the Discourse on Love in *Purgatorio* xviii, that love is excited "by the apprehension of some real fact"—it is directed, that is, to something actually existing outside the self—to a real other. In the absence of the real other, there is only the projected image, the mirror-bars of the cage.

Spender notes "the attempts of the poets, in the cage, to

find—even within the cage—an *unconditioned center."* He adds:

After the collapse of the attempts to put poetry back into the symbolism of creeds or politics, and even make it an alternative religion or way of life, we now find poets accepting the idea that the imagination has no autonomy, is completely conditioned by circumstances. Writing and criticism have become closed systems, and it is considered bad taste to relate the work that is written back to the view of life from which the writer's attitude derives. Yet unless the questions and answers on which the present attitude is based are reopened, poetry will not find a way out of its cage.

He goes on to speak of poets such as Blake, Wordsworth, and Yeats, "who expressed in their poetry mystical experiences which they believed to be true and to which they bore witness":

Now to accept or interpret all such statements as being only "psychologically true" is to understand them in a sense the opposite of that in which they were intended. The effect of this kind of acceptance of the past on terms which those who lived then would regard as their rejection, may be justified by science, but to the poetic mind, which has its own kind of literalness, it is an extremely dubious proceeding. There is always the danger of turning the present into a kind of prison of our own, science and ideologies and analyses where every idea that enters from outside is doctored and treated with our modern machine that renders it—in its own, historic terms—meaningless. . . .

Thus the situation envisaged by I. A. Richards is one in which the poet finds himself shut out from God and the past, and inside the cage of contemporary attitudes.

In another paragraph, Spender is in almost exact agreement with C. S. Lewis in his Cambridge inaugural: "The really important distinction today is not between different creeds but believing and not believing."

This testimony seems to be extremely important, and especially because nobody can dismiss it as Christian propaganda.

The Writing and Reading of Allegory

ALLEGORY, of late years, has been suffering from what is popularly known as a bad press. Almost any reference to it in contemporary critical writing tends to be both slighting and superficial and to use such expressions as "artificiality," "chilly abstractions," "frigid allegorical conceits," "tedious didacticism," "conventional and bloodless personifications." Still more significantly, the term itself is often used as a mere pejorative; thus, a reviewer may say: "The book never degenerates into allegory, but is, on the contrary, a rich and evocative work of the imagination." Or finally, the word may be applied, quite at random, to something that is not allegory at all, but which happens to contain some religious or moral teaching that the critic dislikes or fails to understand. When C. S. Lewis published his novel *Perelandra* (since reissued under the title *Voyage to Venus*), which is a fantasy of the kind we now call "space fiction," recounting quite straightforwardly the beginnings of rational life on that planet, and how a new fall of man was prevented by the intervention of a voyager from our own earth, to prevent misunderstanding he wrote in his preface, "All the human characters in this book are purely fictitious, and none of them is allegorical." Notwithstanding, one reviewer, after describing the actual journey through space, abruptly concluded his review: "Then the allegory begins." Having, that is, deliberately filed away the book in the wrong pigeonhole, he took it for granted that about a work of that kind there was nothing useful to be said.

Now, when a whole department of literature is thus unanimously and, as it were, automatically condemned for the mere crime of being itself, and excluded from serious critical attention, it is pretty safe to say that we have simply forgotten how to judge it. It is extremely improbable, to say the least of it, that a genre that, in the past, produced such acknowledged masterpieces as *The Divine Comedy*, *The Faerie Queene*, and *The Pilgrim's Progress*, is altogether worthless. Neither it is probable that a genre that enjoyed so many hundreds of years of popularity corresponds to no fundamental need in human nature. It is much more likely that we have fallen out of touch with it, so that we no longer remember how this particular literary game should be played—what its intention is or what its rules are—and thus are in no position to tell whether it is well or badly done, or what it is all about. We are in the same situation as an American, who, not knowing the first thing about cricket, is planked down in the pavilion at Lord's to watch a test match. The only impression he is likely to carry away is that this is a slow and formal game, and not in the least like baseball. He will have only a very vague notion of what everybody is so earnestly trying to do, and the finer points of the play will escape him altogether.

So with allegory. Most of us are, to be sure, a little more advanced than the reviewer of Dr. Lewis's novel; we know that an allegory is a story that says one thing and means another; whereas, on that occasion, Dr. Lewis meant exactly what he said, neither more nor less. But we may well wonder why a writer should choose what seems to us this very roundabout way of expressing himself. And further, the whole question is obscured for us by a great deal of argument about myth and symbol, imagery and fantasy, figures and archetypes, and so on, which gets mixed up with the subject and makes it difficult to see the wood for the trees.

Perhaps the simplest way is to start by saying that allegory is a distinct literary form, whose aim and method are to dramatize a psychological experience so as to make it more vivid and more comprehensible. Parable and fable are two other literary forms that do much the same thing. Each of them tells a literal story that is complete in itself, but which also presents a likeness to some spiritual or psychological experience so that it can be used to signify and interpret that experience; and the story is told, not for its own sake, but for the sake of what it signifies. At the bottom of all such stories there lies this perception of a likeness between two experiences, the one familiar and the other unfamiliar, so that the one can be used to shed light on the other. "Whereunto shall we liken the Kingdom of God, or with what comparison shall we compare it? . . . And another parable spake he unto them: The Kingdom of Heaven is like unto leaven, which a woman took, and hid in three measures of meal, till the whole was leavened." Usually the story is a good deal more elaborate than this, as for example the parable of the sower. A number of events occur, each one of which can be interpreted with reference to the real (i.e., the figurative) meaning; but throughout, the two stories remain distinct and parallel—corresponding at all points but never intruding on one another.

In the fable, which is usually a story ostensibly about animals but actually about human beings, the figurative meaning is as a rule compressed into a moral at the end:

The mice held a meeting to decide how they could best protect themselves against the cat. A young mouse proposed that a bell should be tied to the cat, so that they might hear her coming.

"That is all very well," said an old mouse, "but who is to bell the cat?"

Moral: It is easy to propose impossible remedies.

Both these forms of figurative narrative are, of course, very ancient—more ancient than *allegory,* whose distinctive feature is that the personages of the literal story are personified abstractions. Here is a little tale that sits, as it were, on the fence, halfway between fable and allegory.

Fire, Water, and Reputation went on a journey together. Before starting, they thought it would be well to arrange how they should find one another in case they should get separated. Fire said: "Wherever you see smoke, there you will find me." Water said: "Wherever the grass is greenest, there you will find me." But Reputation said: "Beware how you lose me, for a lost reputation is not easily recovered."

It is evident that the third speaker in this dialogue is of a different kind from the others. Fire and water are concrete things, however much personified, but reputation is not a *thing* at all; it is a personified abstraction.

Since this is the sort of personification with which allegory characteristically deals, it is fairly evident that it is not likely to appear except in an advanced civilization, one in which people are already learning to think in terms of abstract concepts.

It is in the reign of Augustus, at the latter end of the period which we call "B.C.," that we begin to notice something rather peculiar happening to those Olympian deities whom the Romans had taken over from the Greeks. Instead of being fully characterized, self-sufficient, superhuman personages, enjoying a communal life, with emotions and interests and adventures and somewhat unedifying love affairs of their own, they are beginning to turn into abstractions. Mars, for example, in the old days, though he was the patron of war, was never simply and solely war; he had leisure and interest to spare for other things. He had a love affair with Venus; and when Vulcan, her husband, caught them at it and cast a net over the erring pair and dragged them into the presence of the other gods, there was much merriment on high Olympus. If he interfered in a human war, he did so by coming in to support one side or the other for personal reasons—to avenge an injury or to assist some hero in whom he was interested. But in the *Thebaid* of Statius, who wrote in the beginning of the Christian era, we find Mars fulfilling quite another function. Jupiter wants a war started to punish the city of Thebes; accordingly he sends for Mars and tells him to go and stir one up. Mars does so, and, having carried out this order, departs to stir up wars elsewhere. In all this, Jupiter is still behaving like a mythological deity; he has personal reasons for being offended with Thebes. But Mars has no interest in Thebes one way or the other; he simply exists in order to stir up strife at the command of fate. He has ceased to be the god of war; he has become the personification of warfare. Later in the poem, semidivinized attributes enter in their own persons to play the kind of part that would formerly have been played by some god or other. Allegory has come into being.

Our natural reaction is to say that this is a great pity. The mythological Mars is clearly much more picturesque and poetical than an abstraction called warfare. But human souls cannot live by picturesqueness and poetry. Under the empire, the old gods were already dying; they had been dying for many years. It was no longer possible to interpret human destinies and human behavior in terms of the Olympians. The Romans were, in fact, developing a new kind of moral consciousness.

The Greeks, incurably intellectual, had in their philosophy always tended to take it for granted that to be good it was sufficient to know the good. Like certain more recent thinkers, they rather took the line that all evil dispositions could be cured by education. But in this period of crisis and confusion, the Romans, always incurably moral, were discovering within themselves that inner dislocation between knowing and doing right that we call the divided will and sometimes the sense of sin. They knew, with the painful conviction of experience, what it meant to say, "I see and approve the better, but follow the worse." In this dilemma, neither the ancient, cult religions of Rome nor the newer gods of Greece would give them any help. They turned to the Eastern mysteries, with their offer of release and redemption from the self and integration in the one. Christianity, arriving literally, one might say, at the psychological moment, with this divided will at the very center of its doctrine of human nature, spoke to their condition. But Christianity did not induce that condition in them; it was there already.

It is thus not surprising that man, becoming acutely aware of a conflict within himself, should look for a literary mode of expressing these new feelings. He feels his life to be not so much a battle against forces without as a battle between forces within him; and he begins to personify those forces and dramatize the conflict. Allegory becomes his poetic medium, and the allegories of this period most frequently take the form of a *psychomachia,* a soul battle, fought between the vices and the virtues. The tradition of the psychomachia proved exceedingly tough and vital; indeed it has so passed into our current speech that we can scarcely get away from it today. When we use expressions such as "he was torn between greed and fear" or "his curiosity overcame his sense of decency," we are making a psychomachia—an allegorical combat between personified qualities. We may tell ourselves, in our more philosophical moments, that abstractions such as fear and curiosity have no independent existence—there is only one actual person who fears or is inquisitive; but it is very difficult not to speak, or even to think, as though our personality were a battleground for emotions distinct from and stronger than ourselves.

There are, of course, certain technical difficulties about writing a psychomachia on a big scale. The personified qualities, having no personal existence outside those qualities that they personify, are likely to be somewhat limited in their activities and conversation. This is a disability of all allegory, which occasions and to some extent justifies the charges of frigidity and artificiality; we shall see later how the great masters of allegory get over it. Moreover, while warfare is an occupation well suited to such vices as wrath, jealousy, and cruelty, and to such virtues as courage, fortitude, loyalty, and the like, there are other qualities— especially such mild and Christian virtues as patience, meekness, humility, pity and so on—that do not take kindly to the profession of arms. Some of the combats in Prudentius, for instance, turn out rather grotesquely. Other suitable subjects had to be found for allegory—for example, the epithalamion or marriage between selected virtues, each accompanied by a suitable train of followers. And so forth. We should undoubtedly find these early experiments very tedious to read and should sigh for the elasticity and many-sided humanity of the old gods. But to these pioneer writers, allegory was no dull convention—it was a new and exciting medium by which to explore undiscovered regions of the soul, and to make their first adventure into analytical psychology.

They found also another use for it. Allegory became an instrument for interpreting, not only the present but also the past. By its help, pious pagans could find a satisfying meaning for those mythological tales that had begun to shock thoughtful men by their immorality and inconsequence; and pious Christians could perform a like office for the mythical and historical portions of the Old Testament. Thus seen, the old stories glowed with a new light. Indeed, the allegorical interpretation of Scripture enjoyed a surprisingly long life; modern theology has found a better way of dealing with religious myths, but there can be few people of my age, who were brought up to hear sermons, who have not been made familiar with spiritual exercises of this kind. To be sure, many of the interpretations were tasteless and unconvincing, but it does not do to judge any literary form by its sufferings at the hands of devout persons intent on edification. And if one insists on allegorizing a story that was not originally written with that end in view, there are bound to be moments when the interpretation becomes forced and unnatural. Nevertheless, this business of, as it were, allegorizing backwards must have been of great assistance to those who were writing original allegory for its own sake; it enlarged the field of experiment and suggested a wider variety of literal story to carry the allegorical signification.

From what we have been saying, we should be led to expect that allegory, as a literary fashion, would tend always to accompany any profound change in men's psychological outlook. And this does indeed turn out to be the case. The golden age of allegory in Europe sets in with that remarkable psychological upheaval that was produced in the twelfth century by the discovery of romantic love.

We are so much accustomed nowadays to take it for granted that romantic love between the sexes is one of the most important and sacred things in life, that it is hard to believe that, before the twelfth century, such an idea never entered anybody's head—and, if it had, it would have been considered not only immoral but also ridiculous. That human beings did in fact fall in love, with very disturbing effects, was of course a fact that nobody in any age could possibly overlook; but it had never been customary to admire them for it. On the contrary, passion, as distinct from a decent conjugal affection, had always been held to be a bad thing, both in men and in women—but especially in men, since it overthrew their sovereign reason, made them behave like lunatics, and (still worse) caused them to submit to the caprices of the inferior sex. On this point, pagan and Christian were agreed. The passionate adoration of woman was a weakness, and worse. Ovid had written a satire on the subject called *The Art of Love*, in which he sacrificed the foolish lover who made himself a woman's slave, and sarcastically advised him as to the best methods of making a public fool of himself:

> Go early ere the appointed hour to meet
> The fair, and long await her in the street.
> Through shouldering crowds on all her errands run;
> Though graver business wait the while undone.
> If she commands your presence on her way
> Home from the ball to lackey her, obey!
> Or if from rural scenes she bids you, "Come,"
> Drive if you can, if not, then walk, to Rome.*

And so on.

At the same time, Christian preachers never wearied of warning young men against the wiles of women and the snares of love. To be sure, they disagreed somewhat as to whether the pleasures of sex were evil in themselves. Sex, as such, could scarcely be evil, since God had ordained it; but it should perhaps be accepted merely as a necessary means for keeping up the population, and not enjoyed—for that was to know no better than the beasts. Some theologians took the more cheerful view that the pleasures of love were all right so long as they were confined to the senses and did not get the upper hand of one's reason. But all were agreed that the sort of passion that overthrows a man soul and body, making him indifferent to all other earthly (and indeed heavenly) considerations, was altogether evil and shameful. And every layman, gentle or simple, while doubtless holding matrimony profitable and wenching excusable, would heartily have agreed with the fathers of the Church that the very idea of a man prostrate with devotion before the feet of a young woman was silly, degrading, and a reversal of the proper order of things.

And then, almost unimaginably, starting among the troubadours of Provence, and singing its way across Europe in all the romance languages, came the new cult of courtly

---

* Ars Amatoria ii. 223 (*trans.* C. S. Lewis)

love. We cannot now stop to inquire what brought it into being; it is enough that it came, that it spread like wildfire, and established itself, changing the whole aspect of men's lives, and effecting one of the very few genuine social revolutions in history. It sprang from, and registered, and in so doing helped to produce, profound psychological changes, which demanded political expression. Writers were concerned to examine and dissect this entirely novel interior experience; and allegory, which had already proved itself useful in the spiritual laboratory, was again pressed into the service. By a curious irony, Ovid's *Art of Love*, written as a satire, was accepted as a serious textbook for the correct conduct of a love affair, and with this in their hands, the courtly poets settled down to work out a complete art and science of the passion of love. Whole poems were devoted to debates in the court of love, in which the niceties of amorous conduct were thrashed out with as much earnest hairsplitting as prevails in a court of law; and a correct ritual of devotion to one's lady was devised, with so perilous a likeness to the devotions prescribed by the Church as to occasion scandal and accusations of blasphemy.

Not that the poets confined themselves to mere didacticism; they by no means neglected the duty of telling an exciting story. The literary material on which they laid hands for this purpose was that rich traditional deposit of wonder and adventure that we call the matter of Britain, or, more popularly, Arthurian romance. Tales like that of Tristan and Iseult, or of Owain, which dealt with such matters as love potions, or the carrying off and rescue of distressed ladies, obviously provided just the kind of basic material that was needed. The tales were ruthlessly modernized, expanded, and added to when required, and made a vehicle for the new and fashionable ideas. Most of the time, the poet was content to tell a straightforward story; but when a character has to choose between two possible courses of action, we find a tendency to drop into allegory. Thus, in Chrestien de Troyes's *Romance of Lancelot*, the hero, who

has lost his horse, is told that if he wants news of his lady,
Queen Guinevere, he must submit to being carried in a
common cart. Lancelot hesitates a moment before mounting
upon this unknightly and undignified conveyance, and his
hesitation takes the form of a debate between Love and
Reason:

> Reason, who does not judge like Love,
> Bids him not mount, and warns him off
> By chiding and admonishing
> That he should ne'er do anything
> Whence he might get shame or disgrace.
> The mouth and not the heart's the place
> Where Reason dwells, that dares him chide.
> But Love sits closeted inside
> His heart, and doth command and say
> He ought to mount the cart straightway.
> Love wills it so; so must it be;
> For of the shame nought reckoth he
> When such is Love's command and will.*

It is interesting that the *Tristan* of Thomas the Anglo-Nor-
man, in which the poet attempts long passages of direct
psychological analysis, with scarcely any resort to allegory,
seems never to have achieved any very great popularity in
its own day. To us, Thomas's approach appears more modern and straightforward than Chrestien's; but his contemporaries probably found it obscure and lacking in drama, in
the absence of those personifications that we stigmatize as
tedious and unreal. Thomas, in fact, was ahead of his time,
for, from the twelfth to the fourteenth century, allegory is
preparing to take its place as the dominant form in literature.

So, from romances of adventure, with allegorical passages, we come to poems that are conceived as allegories
from start to finish. Some are allegories of courtly love,
some are religious allegories, others again are huge and

confused compendia dealing with everything that an educated person ought to know. Fortunately, one of the best and most influential examples of pure allegorical form presents itself very handily for our study, since it was translated for us by Chaucer. This is the first part of the *Romance of the Rose*, written by Guillaume de Lorris about the middle of the thirteenth century. Its allegorical significance is as simple as possible: it is the story of a young man falling in love with a girl. In the literal story, the girl never appears at all; she is made known to us only by the allegorical personages who typify various aspects of her character. The only actual human being who appears in the poem is the Lover himself. Like so many medieval allegories, the story is cast into the form of a dream, told to us by the dreamer. The Lover dreams, then, that he is just getting up on a fine May morning.

> In time of love and jollity,
> That all things ginneth waxen gay.

He washes his hands and dresses himself, lacing up his sleeves with a silver bodkin, and goes out to amuse himself in a meadow "soft, sweet, and green," through which runs a clear river. Presently he comes to a garden by the waterside, full of beautiful trees in which the birds make melody, and surrounded by high walls. This garden represents the courtly life, and on the outside of the walls are painted figures of those qualities that unfit one to live that life—vices such as Hate, and Felonye, and "Villainy" (which means Churlishness), Covetousness and Avarice (for a courtier must be free with his money), and Envy, and Prudery—and also Sorrow, Old Age, and Poverty, for these are not welcome in the playground of noble youth. The Lover is, of course, eager to get into this delightful place and, finding at last a wicket gate, he knocks repeatedly. At length the door is opened by an elegant lady called Idlenesse. She is beautifully dressed and looks like a person unaccustomed to work, for, says the poet, when she has done combing her hair and arranging herself to perfection, she "calls it a day."* Idlenesse informs the Lover that the garden belongs to the Lord of Mirth, and at his earnest prayer lets him in. The place is so enchanting, and so melodious with birds, that it seems to him like an earthly paradise; and here he finds a goodly company engaged in dancing—Courtesy, who welcomes him as he approaches, and Mirth with his lady Gladness; Beauty and Riches with their lovers; Largesse, and Franchise, and Youth; and among them is the God of Love himself with his squire, Sweet-Looking, who carries his bow and arrows. There is no time to read the descriptions of all these attractive people, nor yet of the many trees and fresh flowers adorning the garden that the Dreamer now sets out to explore. He comes eventually to a fountain, at the bottom of which are two crystal stones. And the crystal is a magic crystal, for, gazing into it, one can see reflected the whole garden and everything that is in it. And there he sees a rosebed full of roses, which so much attracts him that he immediately sets off in search of it. When he comes there, he says:

> The savor of the roses swote
> Me smote right to the hertë roote,
> As I had all embalmed be.

One particular rose—a half-opened crimson bud—overwhelms him with desire to pluck it; but the rosebed is set about with a thick and thorny hedge, and he does not know how to come near the rose.

Now, all this while, unseen by him, the God of Love has been following him, bow in hand. And when he sees the Lover's desire thus fixed upon the rose:

> He took an arrow full sharply whet,
> And in his bowe when it was set,
> He straight up to his ear draugh
> The strongë bowe that was so tough,

---

*Thenne had she don al hir journe.

> And shot at me so wonder smart
> That through mine eye and into mine heart
> The tackle smote, and deep it went.

The arrow is called Beauty; and the god follows it up with four others: Simplicity, Courtesy, Company, and finally Fair-Semblance,

> The which in no wise will consent
> That any lover him repent
> To serve his love with heart and all,
> For any peril that may befal.

Thus stricken, the Dreamer surrenders to Love, who binds him to his service and admonishes him, in a speech of considerable length, on the whole duty of a lover.

So far, the allegory is very easy to follow. A young man goes to court and enjoys the gay and luxurious life there. He is rash enough to gaze into a lady's eyes (this is the episode of the crystal stones in the fountain), and sees there the promise of further delights (the rosebed). In particular, he feels that it would be delightful to win the lady's love (the rose). While he is lightheartedly pleasing himself with these thoughts, he falls deeply and genuinely in Love.

Now we come to something a good deal more subtle. As the heartsmitten Lover is gazing wistfully through the hedge, there comes up to him a cheerful, young man called Bialocoil (Fair-Welcome), who says that, provided he behaves himself like a gentleman, he will be charmed to let him through the hedge to see the rose closer, and do him any services in his power. This obliging youth is the first of the Lady's personal qualities; and here we begin to see the advantage of the allegorical device, for, though we can sense immediately what Bialocoil represents, we can hardly put it into words without a lot of clumsy periphrasis. He is, one may say, the Lady's instinct to be pleasant to people, she thinks it agreeable of the Dreamer to be so obviously attracted and she receives his attentions amiably—to put it in

one word, she shows him "Fair-Welcome," Bialacoil. The
allegory, which looks like the longest way around, is really,
you see, the shortest way home in these matters.

So Bialacoil lets the Lover through the hedge. He cannot,
he explains, do as much for him as he would like to do, for
fear of the three guardians whom Chastity has set to keep
watch on the rosebed. The first of these is Shame, the
daughter of Reason and Trespass; and once again, this parentage seems to me to convey very accurately our curiously
ambiguous attitude to sexual modesty. The others Male-
bouche (Wicked-Tongue), the fear of slander; and Danger,
of whom more in a moment. Bialacoil ventures, however, to
present the Lover with—not the rose, but a leaf that has
grown near it; the Lady, that is, grants some favor or token
of kindness or compassion. This emboldens the Lover to
ask if he may pluck the rose. But at this, poor Bialacoil is
terrified, and out of the grass where he has been lurking
there starts up Danger—a hideous black-faced churl who
frightens Bialacoil away and thrusts the Lover back through
the hedge. The young man, in fact, has gone too far; the girl
is seriously shocked and affronted and rebuffs him with
that kind of primitive roughness and brutality that can easily be aroused in any woman by a sudden, direct approach
which presumes upon her kindness.

This is, of course, only the beginning of the story, which
soon becomes more complicated. Reason tries in vain to
dissuade the Lover from his attempt; Venus (physical passion) intervenes on his behalf to undermine the Lady's resistance; Suspicion (Jalousie) is aroused; a wall is built
about the rosebed, and Bialacoil is banished to a dungeon.
Guillaume de Lorris never finished his poem; it was completed later at unwieldy length by Jehan de Meung—a poet
of much greater power, but much less skill in handling allegory. But the fragment we have shows how delicate and accurate an instrument allegory could be in the right hands. It
is also remarkable for the extreme purity of its form; there is

no confusion between the figure and the thing figured—no intrusion of flesh-and-blood persons upon the personified abstractions who play all the roles in its tiny drama.

And here we are reminded of two cautions that Dante gave about the proper way to read and write allegory. Defending this allegorical handling of Love in his early book, the *Vita Nuova*, he says that a reader "might be in a difficulty as to what I say concerning Love, as if he were a thing in himself, and not only an intelligent being but a corporeal being. Which thing, according to truth, is false; for Love exists not as a being in itself but is a *quality of a being* (an accident in a substance)." And he goes on to say that those who write allegory "should not speak this without having some interpretation in their minds of what they say; for deep shame it were to him who should rhyme under cover of a figure or of rhetorical coloring and afterward could not, if required, strip such vesture from his words, in such a way that they should have a real meaning" (*Vita Nuova* xxv). We must not, that is, be led away by our own eloquence into attributing to abstractions the kind of reality that belongs to actual persons. And we must also take care that the literal and the figurative meanings can be so separated as to form two independent stories, corresponding at all points, but each coherent and complete in itself.

Dante himself is, of course, the greatest of all allegorists; but his is a special case. In *The Divine Comedy* he invented a method so individual that no one has ever really succeeded in using it on the grand scale again. All his characters do, indeed, represent qualities in a person; but he has used, instead of personified abstractions, actual historical or mythical personages who are fitted to serve as natural symbols of those qualities. Thus the various kinds of pride are represented, not by a lady called Superbia or by a giant called Orgoglio, but by such people as Capaneus, Farinata, Umberto, Aldobrandesco, Oderisi the Painter, and Provenzan Salvani. Thus at one stroke Dante abolishes the limitations that fetter the conversation and behavior of abstractions and regains something of the freedom that belonged to the mythological treatment of the gods. Yet, although so penetrated with symbolism, and set in a great symbolic framework, *The Comedy* can be interpreted allegorically at no fewer than three levels, without any encroachment of the figure upon the thing figured, or vice versa. But nobody has ever been able to bend Dante's bow, and it is easier to study the pure classic outline of allegory in the works of the lesser masters. We may notice, however, that for his literal story Dante has chosen a scheme that was to become very popular and very rewarding—that of a journey or pilgrimage.

It is the fourteenth century that allegory becomes a dominant form in literature. Almost anything that a writer wanted to say, on any subject whatever, was crammed, as though into a hold-all, into an allegorical romance of some kind. Similarly, in the nineteenth century, a writer's heterogeneous views on life in general emerged, almost automatically, from his or her mind in the shape of a sentimental novel; that is, whatever the book was really about, it purported to be the sentimental history of Jack and Jill. Whenever any literary form achieves dominance, the result is the production of a huge mass of works, some bad, some good, and many mediocre; and the classical outline of the form becomes distorted—bulging like the hold-all, under the pressure of bulky contents that strain it out of shape.

By the time we get to Spencer's *Faerie Queene,* allegory has got about as much as it can carry and is already falling out of fashion. This Spencer knew, as he showed by making deliberate use of an archaic style of language. For his literal story he uses a background of the old Arthurian romance—not as the twelfth century knew it, but in the fantasticated development it had undergone in the hands of Boiardo and Ariosto, in which adventure is piled upon adventure, story interlocked with story, in a way that allows of immense richness of description and variety of detail. Spenser's method is genuinely allegorical and often contains allegory within allegory—as where the House of Alma presents us with a self-contained allegorical picture of the human body, packed within the allegory of temperance that forms the subject of the second book. He has also interwoven with the moral allegory the strands of a political allegory; and the very word *interwoven* is a way of saying that the pure form of allegory is becoming blurred.

One cannot strip the poetic lendings from the political sense of *The Faerie Queene* and present it as a complete and coherent entity. It makes its appearance only in patches; the levels of interpretation are becoming confused. Nor is it always possible to distinguish clearly between person and personification, between the figure and the thing figured. Is Sir Guyon, for instance, a temperate man or the virtue of temperance in a man? His palmer seems certainly to be rather a quality than a person, but when Guyon suddenly produces an iron lock, a stake, and a hundred iron chains with which to bind Occasion and Furor, we cannot help wondering how these objects came to be in the possession of a knight and a palmer wandering on foot through open country. The allegory is intruding into the literal story with disquieting results.

Not that such things need trouble our enjoyment very much so long was we keep in mind while we read that the allegorical meaning is the real and important meaning. But if we try to forget the allegory and read only for the story, or for what people call the poetry, we shall be faintly disturbed by a kind of incongruity that we never feel in reading either the *Comedy* or the *Romance of the Rose,* on the one hand, or the irresponsible absurdities of the *Orlando Furioso,* on the other. In Spenser, the flower of allegory has opened to the full, and the petals are beginning to fall apart, though its scent and its beauty are incomparable. After this, sustained allegory disappears as a narrative genre; though in many moralities the pure allegorical form contrives to hold the stage to a surprisingly late date. *Everyman,* at the end of the

fifteenth century, is as unmixed as *The Romance of the Rose*
three hundred and fifty years earlier, and its personified
qualities are as humanly, though perhaps not quite as
subtly, characterized. "What!" says Beauty, aghast to find
herself accompanying Everyman on a journey that ends in a
grave, "Should I smother here?" and when assured that this
is so, she adds hastily:

> I cross out all this: adieu by St. John!
> I take my cap in my lap and am gone.

Whereas Strength plays the part of the common-sense, can-
did friend:

> Yea. I have you for enough conveyed;
> Ye be old enough, I understand,
> Your pilgrimage to take on hand;
> I repent me that I hither came.

But for the most part, as we move on into the sixteenth
and seventeenth centuries, men have grown sufficiently
aware of their conscious mental processes to be able to represent them directly, without allegorical simplifications.
There was, however, one region of the psychological field in
which the simple, if not the learned, came to need help in
making themselves clear to themselves.

The great theological disturbance that had its center at
Geneva transferred the sensitive area of religious experience
from confrontation with a transcendent God without to the
workings of the spirit within the soul. As always, a strong
sense of sin—a vivid awareness of the divided personality—called for some kind of dramatic expression. In England the acute consciousness of this inward crisis induced
by the struggles and persecutions of the late seventeenth
century bore fruit in the works of John Bunyan—especially
in *The Holy War* and *The Pilgrim's Progress.*

It is difficult to say what were Bunyan's models for these
books. To say that he was steeped in the Bible explains
nothing; for the Bible, though rich in myth and parable, is

almost barren of allegory. It is doubtful whether Bunyan ever read an allegorical poem or saw a morality play—yet if these had never been, his own books would have been different. For all the characteristic features are there: the personifications, the pilgrimage or psychomachia, the debates between abstractions, the dream framework. Probably the tradition of allegory, fixed in men's minds through many generations, was handed down in sermons from preacher to preacher. *The Holy War* is as classically pure in form as *The Romance of the Rose; The Pilgrim's Progress* is of the mixed Spenserian type in that there are moments (as with Mr. Greatheart or the Interpreter) when we cannot be perfectly sure whether we are dealing with persons or abstractions, and moments when (as with the martyrdom of Faithful at Vanity Fair) there is a slight confusion between the literal and the allegorical story.

The Holy War has never enjoyed the same prestige or evoked the same affection as *The Pilgrim's Progress;* but this, I think, is due not so much to its austerity of form as to the obvious fact that warfare, particularly siege warfare, cannot possibly provide such a variety of entertaining incidents as a journey. The psychomachia, though the most obvious machinery for an analysis of the divided will, has never in the long run proved satisfying. But the one book displays just as brilliantly as the other Bunyan's supreme gift as an allegorist—his genius for investing abstractions with a homespun, humorous, and convincing humanity. Consider, for instance, the defense of Mr. Incredulity when he is put on trial as a prisoner of war for resisting the forces of the divine King Shaddai. Incredulity is not an original inhabitant of Mansoul, but a member of the occupational forces of Diabolus, settled there when Diabolus first took over the town.

Then said Incredulity: "I know not Shaddai; I love my old prince: I thought it my duty to be true to my trust, and to do what I could to possess the minds of the men of Mansoul to do their utmost to resist strangers and foreigners and with might to fight against them. Nor have I, nor shall I change mine opinion for fear of trouble, though you at present are possessed of place and power."

The defense is disallowed, but it is the defense of a human being, not a frigid and abstract conceit, and we have heard many very like it in recent war trials.

Bunyan is the last of the English allegorists in the great tradition. After him, we get a hundred and fifty years of rationalism and common sense, the integrated mind, and the omnipotence of education. Or if there were men like William Blake, or groups like the Romantics, who were aware of their own inner dissensions, their protests did not voice themselves in formal allegory, but in symbolism, or prophecy, or in direct exposition and argument.

But toward the end of the nineteenth century, the sense of spiritual cleavage and insecurity, produced by disturbing new scientific views of man's place in nature, evoked a fresh attempt at allegory on the large scale—Tennyson's *The Idylls of the King*. This is a most interesting work, which has been treated with absurd frivolity by twentieth-century critics who, ignoring its claim to be allegory, and ignorant or contemptuous of allegorical form as such, have consistently mistaken its virtues for defects and condemned it accordingly.

It is indeed very fumbling and uneven in its allegorical technique. This is partly because by that time the art of writing and reading allegory had been forgotten, and partly because the composition of the *Idylls* extended over forty years, and the first few stories were not undertaken with any definite allegorical intention in mind. It was only as he went along that Tennyson became fully conscious that he was writing, as he says in the *Dedication*, an allegory "of sense at war with soul." On the whole, Tennyson is at his worst when he is merely rewriting Malory, and at his best when he is deliberately allegorizing on his own account. In the opening Idyll, *The Coming of Arthur*, which stands first, but was one of the latest to be written, both allegory and poetry are at their best.

Like Dante (whom he knew well), he has chosen to use not personified abstractions but traditional personages in whom those abstractions may be symbolized; and like the twelfth-century romancers and Spenser, he has chosen the matter of Britain for the subject of his literal story. He has been sneered at for turning Arthur's knights into Victorian ladies and gentlemen—but here Tennyson is right and his critics wrong. An allegorist must write in terms of contemporary problems. Tennyson is doing with the Arthurians what the romancers did when they turned them into medieval devotees of courtly love, and what Spenser did when he turned them into Elizabethans with a sound Protestant morality. No writer can in fact really assume the whole habit of mind of another age—or, if he could, he would merely produce pastiche. However we may dress the production, Shakespeare's Lear is no legendary king of folktale, but a complicated man of the Renaissance.

Neither is it very sensible to talk contemptuously about "the painful snuffle of Tennyson's blameless king."* We may not find King Arthur very lovable—but then, neither did Guinevere; and that is what the allegory is about. For the central image that dominates the poem is the marriage of Arthur and Guinevere. Unless (this is the whole argument) the Soul (Arthur) can retain the allegiance of the Heart (Guinevere), it cannot consolidate its rule over man's Nature (Logres), for the realm will be "betrayed by what is false within." The fault is indeed in Guinevere; yet it is necessary that her treason should not be merely perverse. There is in Arthur, as there is indeed in all idealism, something that the undisciplined heart may easily find repellent. Tennyson's real error here has been to fall at one point into the allegorist's besetting sin of confusing the figurative with the literal story. The sexual relations between Arthur and Guinevere are only the image of the relations between Soul and Heart; but in the Idyll called *Guinevere* he has slipped into treating the problem as though it were really only a question of sexual ethics—of whether a man holding a public position would be justified in openly condoning his wife's adultery.

---

* Graham Hough: *The Last Romantics*.

But it is difficult to see how the Soul can publicly repudiate the Heart for the sake of setting a good example—unless on a dualistic and ascetic view of life, which Tennyson certainly did not accept. I did not say it would be impossible to make out a case for the allegorical interpretation here; but it would require a good deal of ingenuity and would still seem strained and unnatural. The whole tone of the passage rather suggests that Tennyson, confronted with the facts of the literal story as he finds them in Malory, has slid aside from his main allegory into discussing a different problem—that of forgiving the sinner and, at the same time, not only condemning the sin but also making it clear that one does so. It is wrong, I think, to stigmatize Arthur as a sanctimonious prig; he is concerned (as we are today perhaps too little concerned) with maintaining public standards of conduct; and we cannot dismiss a very real dilemma by merely using words such as *smug* and *hypocritical*. But I think it is fair to say that the story, as Tennyson handles it, does not quite fit in with the main allegorical structure of the poem as a whole.

On the other hand, in *The Coming of Arthur*, the long argument about Arthur's parentage—whether he is

> the child of shamefulness,
> Or born the son of Gorlois after death,
> Or Uther's son, and born before his time—

is a fine and imaginative translation, into the terms of the traditional allegorical debate, of the heart searchings aroused by evolutionary theory. What was the soul? Was it of heavenly descent, or evolved out of animal instincts, or the offspring of self-delusion? Has it any right at all to claim sovereignty over the rest of man's nature, or is that claim mere usurpation? And the debate ends in Merlin's account of Arthur's mysterious arrival at Tintagel—the storm, and the ship like a winged dragon, and the naked babe carried to the shore in a whirl of fire and water—

> . . . and presently thereafter followed calm,
> Free sky and stars.

Tennyson is too honest a writer to answer his own question, except by implication. Merlin, who stands for the intellect, will not pronounce:

> Where is he who knows?
> From the great deep to the great deep he goes.

The whole idyll is a magnificent piece of allegorical writing, precise, subtle, and on the very highest plane of technical accomplishment. Equally good, though thinner in allegorical texture, are *Lancelot and Elaine,* and *The Holy Grail,* both dealing with the morbid effects of an unbalanced idealism: on the one hand, retreat into a fantasy of egotistical emotion; on the other, flight into an overspiritualized religion.

I have chosen *The Idylls of the King* to represent this period for two reasons. In the first place, because the issue there is a simple one, and we need not be confused as we are in discussions about, for example, *Peer Gynt,* with talk about myth, imagery, and symbolism. In the second place, because the poem and its present status illustrate so clearly what happens when the whole habit of writing and reading allegory has fallen into decay. Tennyson's own touch is uncertain—he is seldom quite sure what kind of poem he is writing or whether he ought not to apologize for writing allegory at all. And the effect on critical appreciation has been disastrous, since, too ignorant or too contemptuous of allegory to take it seriously, writers have based their judgment on totally irrelevant standards. For we have now reached the period when it is sufficient to give a thing the bad name of allegory and leave it without further ado. Thus, a recent writer quotes Yeats as saying: "I find that though I love symbolism, which is often the only fitting speech for some mystery of disembodied life, I am for the most part bored by allegory, which is made, as Blake says, by 'the daughters of memory,' and coldly, with no wizard frenzy." And he comments: "Symbolism is the only possible expression of some otherwise inexpressible spiritual essence, while allegory is *an arbitrary translation of some principle that is already familiar, of something that has already been expressed in other terms.''* *

Historically, we have seen that this is quite untrue. Allegory, in a journeyman's hands, may (like symbol itself) come to be used to translate the already familiar; but it always begins as an effort to express something for which terms have not yet been invented.

So long as we remember this, we may readily agree that symbolism springs from, and stirs, profounder and more primitive levels of the soul; indeed, as we said to begin with, allegory is not primitive, neither is it possible for primitive minds to produce it.

If there is any truth in the contention, which we have been so far putting forward, that a strong and disturbing awareness of psychological dislocation tends to result in the production of allegory, what are we to say about our own times? For we have seen that allegory is despised and misunderstood as a literary form—and yet there can never have been a period in which our sense of the divided psyche was so acute. Ought we not to be experiencing a vigorous revival of allegory? Why should it obstinately stay dead under the very conditions that ought to give it life?

The answer is, quite simply, that we *are* experiencing a revival of allegory, though not quite in the place where we are accustomed to look for it. The resurrection in fact took place before the critics had got around to burying the body, and was brought about, not by the poets, but by the psychoanalysts, particularly those of the Freudian school. I am not now referring to the odd and sometimes perverse use that they have made of primitive myth, but to the interesting vocabulary that they have found themselves driven to use in expressing their experimental conclusions about the psychology of the unconscious. This vocabulary is not scientific, but poetical, and imposes a poetical and indeed fictional form on the whole presentation of their subject.

* Graham Hough: *The Last Romantics*, p. 228.

[Freud's] conception of the mind (says Professor J. C. Flügel) is essentially dynamic. He regards striving or conation (to use the generally accepted psychological term) as the real function of mind, and the opposition between different parts of the mind can, he thinks, best be expressed as a conflict between inconsistent and opposing mental tendencies or "wishes."*

This is plain enough. Like the pioneer explorers of the conscious, the pioneer explorer of the unconscious can only think and express himself effectively in terms of a psychomachia. This device is taken up and used by his successors, Adler and Jung. A whole rout of personified abstractions take part in the conflict, some new to us, others already familiar under other names: the Libido (who in some aspects corresponds closely to the medieval Cupidon), the Censor (who in Dante sits at the threshold of assent but in Freud at the lower threshold of consciousness), Eros and Agape (again closely corresponding to the earlier Venus and Amor), the Will-to-Life, the Will-to-Death, and the Will-to-Power (who form a kind of family group, like Spenser's Sansfoy, Sansloy, and Sansjoy, though of course bearing no other resemblance to them), and that other allied trinity, the Ego, the Superego, and the Id. The assault of disreputable Wishes upon the House of Consciousness, their encounter with the Censor, who firmly opposes their entrance and repressively imprisons them in the dungeons below the Threshold, their escape in disguise through the ivory gate into the Garden of Dreams, the impish tricks that they play upon those respectable inhabitants, Mind and Behavior, and the long process by which the good magicians Analysis, Transference, and Sublimation unmask them, convert them, and eventually bring them under control of the Conscious and make them swear fealty to Person (the integrated personality) forms an exciting episode worthy to adorn the pages of any allegory. It is, in fact, allegory, with all the illuminating persuasiveness, and some of the dangers, of alle-

---

*Outline of Modern Knowledge, p. 375.

gory. The chief danger of allegory, as Dante was careful to point out, is that we should be led into mistaking its poetic truth for concrete fact. The writer previously quoted says, speaking of the "unconscious morality" by which we tend to conform to received conscious standards of thought and conduct:

This morality is [now] regarded as a definite entity within the mind, and is called the *Superego*. It is, as it were, at the behest of the Superego that the Censor does its work.

His loose employment of the philosphic term *entity* must not mislead us—and if we are trained in the interpretation of allegory it will not mislead us—into supposing that the *superego* or any other personified quality really is an *entity*: i.e., an independently existing being.

Which thing, according to truth, is false; for Love (or any other such personification) is not a being, but a quality in a being (an accident in a substance).

Provided that we remember this, and do not attribute a self-existing objective and demonic reality to each of the complex activities of the single psyche, we can easily accept these modern allegories as helpful pictures of our interior difficulties. If not, the allegories of modern psychology will end by becoming as stereotyped and unreal as those of the older faculty psychology, or as dangerous to the personality as the Manichaean duality between matter and spirit.

It would be strange if the allegorical apparatus of the new psychology did not, after all, find its way into literature. And so in fact it does. A great deal of modern poetry and fiction teases us by seeming to carry some kind of allegorical significance; but we find it very hard to "strip," in Dante's phrase, "the vesture from the words in such a way that they shall have a real meaning." For one thing, the images are not the traditional ones; neither does the writer help us as a rule by giving his characters explanatory names, as the old allegorists did when they personified Bialacoil, Duessa, or Giant Despair; they do not even use openly the allegorical figures of the psychoanalysts. Further, both the writers themselves and their apologists seem to avoid the label *allegory* as though it were an obscene word, preferring expressions such as *myth* or *symbol*, which, when accurately used, mean something different.

As an outstanding example of the modern allegorist, we may take Franz Kafka, who died in 1924. His two longest and most important novels, *The Trial* and *The Castle*, are efforts to find a satisfactory allegorical expression for man's awareness of a relation to some power beyond himself. He feels, obscurely, that this power claims his entire allegiance, and that it claims to sit in absolute judgment upon his thoughts and actions; but he cannot understand its claims or the values by which it judges him. He can never get into direct touch with it; and all the intermediaries who purport to provide channels of communication with it only lead him into labyrinths of nonsense, frustration, disorder, or mere filth. Yet the compulsion to find the way and establish the relationship persists and makes any easy accommodation with the life of everyday things impossible. Throughout, there is a suggestion that it is precisely the man's determination to intellectualize his situation and justify himself that stands in the way of his success. Both books were left incomplete by their author; and no complete solution to this heartbreaking mystery is offered.

A key to Kafka's enigmatical writings has been furnished by Herbert Tauber (*Franz Kafka: An Interpretation of His Works*). It is perhaps not complete; it may here and there be mistaken. (After all, it has taken us some six hundred years to wrestle with the problem of Dante, and we are not out of the woods yet!) The point that concerns us now is that this key treats the books frankly as allegories. Tauber says: "Kafka avails himself of the old laws of poetic license, using landscapes to symbolize states of mind, houses and rooms as symbols of personality, men and animals to symbolize aspects of their own ego, and even representing Fate as a function of character." He then goes on: "All these characteristics, particularly extolled by the surrealists as a new discovery, and used by them as a polemic deliberately opposed to the 'old' world of reality, are to be found in Kafka's work." He might have added that, though these characteristics are not to be found in the "realistic" novel, they are so far from being a new discovery as to be found in all allegorists from the first century onwards. Any work of fiction that personifies states of mind and aspects of the ego is in fact an allegory, whether or not it also avails itself of myth and symbol.

There are, I think, three chief errors to avoid when reading allegory. The first is a finicky insistence of finding a significance for every word in the text, even in passages that are obviously only put in to give vividness and verisimilitude to the literal story. If Dante says that he took no more than three paces to come up with somebody, it is quite unnecessary to attach allegorical importance to the number three and an allegorical significance to each separate step; nor is it sensible to try and find a paticular meaning for every tree that grows in Guillaume de Lorris's garden. Flat-footed literalism of this kind, much indulged in by many medieval and some modern commentators, has been largely to blame for the disgust and irritation that the very word *allegory* excites in people's minds. Common sense and a sensitiveness to poetic expression will usually tell us whether we are dealing with figurative speech or mere decor; and it is a sound rule that any significance that seems forced or arbitrary is probably not in accordance with the writer's intention.

The second error is that of confusing the allegorical with the literal meaning. This may sometimes, we have seen, be the fault of the writer; but it is also an error into which the reader may slip on his own account. A little practice in reading the great masters of allegorical form will soon enable one to avoid being drawn away by red herrings, and also to detect where the writer has accidentally crossed his own trail.

The third error is much more fundamental and is an infallible recipe for weariness of the flesh and vexation of spirit. I mean the very widespread notion that the best way to enjoy allegory is to read for the sake of the poetry, or the literal story, and not bother about what it signifies. That is the direct opposite of truth. If we read, for instance, Dante's *Inferno* merely as a desciption of literal torments in a physical hell, we are likely to find ourselves baffled and repelled before we are halfway through, and in no mood to appreciate its rare moments of pure lyricism. But if we see it as, primarily, an exploration into the infinite possibilities of evil that lurk in the depths of the psyche, we shall discover its unexpected relevance to the human situation and its uncomfortably piercing insight. This is true, not only of poems as austere as Dante's, but also of those that, like *The Romance of the Rose*, or *The Faerie Queene*, are gaily adorned with "quaint and pleasant devices"; it is only when we see what the whole thing is really about that we can take intelligent pleasure in the thousandfold beauties that accompany and enhance the significant figures of the story. For we are so made that we soon grow weary of ornament for sake of ornament, and even of beauty that makes no appeal to the heart or the understanding.

Oedipus Simplex:
Freedom and Fate in Folklore and Fiction

So POWERFUL is the impression made upon our minds by
the devotional literature of the Freudian cult that if you
were to ask the first person you met what the story of Oedipus was about, he or she would quite probably reply that
it was a story about incest. And indeed it is natural enough
that in this legend of the man who, quite unwittingly and
altogether unwillingly, killed his father and married his
own mother, Freud and his followers should have seen an
allegory of the alleged unconscious impulse in the human
male to do that very thing. But this is an allegorical interpretation of the story; it is not the story itself. The psychoanalysts have allegorized the myths in exactly the same
way that Christian preachers and mystics have allegorized
the Old Testament, seeing in Leah and Rachel types of the
active and the contemplative life, in Noah's Ark a type of
baptism, in The Songs of Songs a signification of the love of

Christ for the Church. This allegorizing tendency is something thought to be peculiarly medieval, but it is in fact found whenever a new trend in psychology, lacking a ready-made technical vocabulary, is forced to express itself indirectly in poetic images. The allegorizing of the Old Testament begins with the early fathers; Julian the Apostate, struggling with the problem of a new, conscious morality, allegorized the Olympians; the Renaissance allegorized Vergil; Freud and Jung, wrestling with the problems of an unconscious immorality, have allegorized the folktales. The practice is ancient and highly respectable, and it is based on an assumption fundamentally sound, namely, that all art and mythmaking disclose the universal pattern of things and may therefore be taken as symbolic presentations of truths greater than themselves.

But this kind of interpretation belongs to the sphere of devotion and edification and not of historical criticism. The modern Bible critic will not permit us to suppose that the story of Jacob's two wives was originally written about a couple of abstractions, or that the writer of The Song of Songs was proleptically thinking about Christ when he composed his love poem. The allegorical interpretation of Scripture has fallen out of fashion, and so it is easy for us to distinguish between the story and the symbolism imposed upon it; but where the allegorical method is still in force the distinction is less readily made. It is quite easy to slip into the belief that the Oedipus story really is about the Oedipus complex.

But it is not. No incestuous passions are displayed in action; it is not about incest as the tale of Phaedra or Myrrha is about incest. No parricidal passions are displayed in action; it is not about parricide as the story of Orestes is about matricide. It is about something that lies upon the very surface of the story and may, for that reason appear at first sight to be simpler. That is why I have called it the Oedipus simplex. But it is really far from simple. Philosophically, it goes beneath the roots of the great riddle of fate and free will to the most unfathomable of all mysteries—the inscrutable nature of time. And to the writer it presents, as we shall see, a literary problem of a very peculiar and exacting kind.

Oedipus belongs, in fact, to a very widespread group of folktales whose theme may be compendiously summed up as man's vain attempt to cheat the oracle. It is very noticeable that from the majority of these tales the incest motif is completely absent, and that when the parricide motif occurs it does not always involve the killing of an actual father. One is tempted to say that these atrocities have been put into the Oedipus legend "just to make it horrider"—as though the storyteller had deliberately set himself to discover the most revolting consequences that could possibly be extracted from his theme. I do not seriously suggest that he did anything so self-conscious, and it is a curious fact that the earlier version of the story lacks both the appalling sense of guilt and also the catastrophic ending that to us seem inseparable from it. Oedipus kills his father and marries his mother, and yet survives to rule in peace over Thebes. But to a tragic poet bent on arousing pity and terror in his audience, the legend (however it first started) is a gift. No more horrid situation could well be devised by the wit of man; and, exploited as Sophocles exploits it, with a brilliant detective-story technique that unfolds one ghastly *anagnorisis* after another until the tension is well-nigh unbearable, it leaves us with an oppressive sense of doom and agony, frustration, and above all of bodily and spiritual pollution. But the *Oedipus* is unique of its kind; nearly all the other members of its groups are cheerful stories with happy endings.

The outline of the plot is invariable. A child is born, of whom it is prophesied that he (or she) will bring about some disaster. The prophecy is duly fulfilled despite every effort to avert it, the disaster being often precipitated by the very precautions taken against it.

The details vary considerably. The child is usually

(though not invariably) a boy, and the predestined disaster
is frequently (though not always) the killing of a king, who
may be the child's father, grandfather, or no relation at all.
The attempts made to avert the doom may be by imprison-
ing or exposing the child (seldom by killing it outright,
which would involve the pollution of infanticide, though
this variant does sometimes occur as in the very primitive-
type tale of Kronos and Zeus). The fulfilment of the prophecy is brought about frequently by accident, or in ignorance, though sometimes the subject of it is fully aware of
what he or she is doing.

In *Oedipus*, the Delphic Oracle foretells that to Laius King
of Thebes will be born a son who will slay his father. According to Sophocles, this is the whole content of the original prophecy—the further prediction, that the boy will
marry his mother, is made only at the second consultation
of the oracle, when the separation of the child from his
parents has made it possible for this catastrophe to come
about without his knowledge. In the Perseus legend, it is
prophesied to King Acrisius that his daughter Danae will
bear a son who will kill his grandfather. Acrisius imprisons
Danae in a brazen tower, and here she bears a son to
Zeus, who visits her as a shower of gold. Acrisius sets
mother and child adrift on the sea in an open chest, and
they are rescued by Dictys the fisherman.

This very common exposure-and-rescue motif is found
also in the story of Oedipus, who is exposed upon the
mountains, rescued by a shepherd, and taken to Polybus,
King of Corinth, who brings him up as his own son. The
legend told by Herodotus about Cyrus the Persian has close
affinities with the Perseus legend. King Astyages dreams
that his daughter Mandane will have a son who will usurp
his throne. He tries to avert this by marrying her to a com-
moner, but after the birth of her son he has a second warning dream. He tells his steward Harpagus to destroy the
child; Harpagus hands it over to the herdsman Mitradates

with orders to expose it; but Mitradates takes it home and brings it up as his own.

In the German folktale of *The Three Golden Hairs,* a poor woman gives birth to a son, of whom it is prophesied that he will be very fortunate and marry the king's daughter. The king, hearing of this, offers to take care of the boy. He puts him in a box and sets him adrift on the river; he floats down to the mill dam and is rescued by the miller and brought up by him. Later, the king comes to know who the boy is and again attempts to get rid of him by sending him to the queen with a letter ordering the bearer to be put to death at once. The youth is taken by robbers, who find the letter, and substitute another commanding that the bearer shall be married immediately to the king's daughter.

An Indian variant, containing the marriage motif and the substituted-letter motif, is *The King Who Would Be Stronger than Fate;* and the substituted letter turns up again in a Serbian story, *The Three Wonderful Beggars,* where the place of the king is taken by a rich merchant, who tried to get rid of the Child of Fortune by throwing him over a cliff in a snowstorm. In the English folktale of *The Fish and the Ring,* the child is a peasant girl, fated to marry the son of the local baron, and the denouement is once more brought about by means of a substituted letter.

In all these tales, the expected disaster is connected with some kind of usurpation, whether of wealth or power, though it by no means always involves the death of the person who has tried to cheat the oracle. There is nothing surprising about this. Autocrats have always lived in terror of being assassinated or deposed. It is one of the risks of their profession, and we need not invoke parricidal impulses to explain it. Even today, if a rich person dies in suspicious circumstances, the first question the police ask is: "Who comes in for the money?" On the other hand, in the Indian story of *Chandra's Vengeance,* which contains the "exposure by setting adrift in a box," the child is a rajah's daughter, and the prophecy is that her hair will one day set her native country ablaze—some solar myth of fire myth being presumably involved. In none of these stories is there any suggestion of incest.

Let us go back for a moment to Perseus. He after many adventures, returns to his native land and there competes in the games. A gust of wind seizes his quoit, which strikes the aged King Acrisius and kills him. The prophecy is fulfilled by pure accident—or, more precisely, by direct interposition of the gods; the resulting pollution is purely formal and is purged by the usual ceremonies, since no evil intention was behind the slaying. Neither did Perseus, like Oedipus, help to bring his doom upon himself either by taking steps to avert it, or by indulging in violent temper, or by unwittingly invoking a curse upon the slayer.

This at once raises the question of the underlying morality of all these tales. The will of the gods must be done, that is certain; but how far is the manner of its accomplishment related to the attitude of the persons concerned? Did the Greeks feel it to be presumption to try and cheat the oracle? Supposing that Laius and Jocasta, the Oedipus himself, had resigned themselves to the divine will, would the prophecy have been fulfilled harmlessly? Would the slaying have been accidental as in the case of Perseus? Might Oedipus, succeeding peaceably to his father, and devoting himself to the well-being of Thebes have been said to have "wedded himself to his mother city," so that in the word the prophecy might be both broken and fulfilled?

Some such riddling fulfillment of dark prophecies is by no means unknown in classical folklore. In the third book of the *Aeneid*, the Harpy announces that before the voyagers reach the end of their adventures they will be reduced to "eating their trenchers." They come to Latium; they partake of a picnic meal of meat and fruit served on cakes of barley bread and end by thriftily eating the bread as well. The boy Iulus cries jestingly, "Why, we have eaten trenchers!" and the fulfillment of the prophecy is accepted as a good omen.

Still more significant is the tale of Deucalion, the classical counterpart of Noah, as we find it in Ovid's *Metamorphosis*. Deucalion and his wife Pyrrha are the sole survivors of a flood that has drowned the whole world. They consult the oracle of Themis and are told to depart and, as they go, to "throw behind them the bones of their great mother." Pyrrha is horrified at the idea of so offending the spirit of an ancestress and at first refuses to obey. At length Deucalion says: "Either my wit is at fault, or else (for oracles are holy and never counsel guilt) our great mother is the earth, and I think that the bones that the goddess speaks of are the stones in the earth's body." This pious attitude is rewarded; the stones that they throw behind them are turned into men and women, and the earth is repeopled. We notice here both the suggestion of an outrage offered to a parent, and also the insistence that the oracle must be obeyed and "cannot counsel guilt."

Twenty centuries of Christian tradition have so conditioned us to look upon the source of power as identical with the source of ethics that it is extremely difficult for us to enter into the mind of the Greeks in this matter. For them, sin and pollution, which for us are ethical terms, so often appear to have meant something merely extraneous and mechanical. One was polluted by even accidentally committing incest or parricide, just as one would be physically polluted by accidentally falling into a cesspool. But in this story we recognize an explicit connection between the will of the gods and that which is right. In the form in which I have quoted it, the legend has passed through a Roman mind; and Roman religious feeling was always, I think, more consciously moral than that of the Greeks.

But not so emphatically so as that of another ancient race. It was the Jews who, from very early times, were most conscious of the will of God—not of "the gods" but of really-truly God in the sense we attach to the word. A divine prophecy was fulfilled, not merely because it had to be, but because it ought to be. In their folk literature, the great cheat-the-oracle story is the story of Joseph, and it is as un-like the Oedipus story as Jehovah is unlike Apollo. Yet in outline it agrees with all the tales of its class. Joseph has two prophetic dreams that seem to indicate that his father and his eleven brothers will one day do homage to him (the usurpation motif). The brothers attempt to get rid of him. At first they suggest killing him, but Reuben dissuades them, and they drop him into a dry well (the exposure motif). Finally they sell him to some passing merchants (a variant of the rescue theme). He is taken to Egypt and be-comes Pharaoh's overseer. This leads to the story of the famine and of how the ten elder brothers first and finally the youngest brother and the father himself have to come and beg for corn and bow before him as Pharaoh's repre-sentative. There are no killing and no incest; Joseph knows what he is doing and amuses himself by playing tricks on his brothers.

What is constant in this as in the other tales is the fact that the very means taken to confound the prophecy lead directly to its fulfillment. It is the gayest and most charming of all the cheat-the-oracle stories. I am bound to admit that many of the Old Testament worthies seem to me rather an unpleasant lot of people; but if anybody maintains that Jew-ish legend is entirely compact of gloomy ferocity and that classical legend is unadulterated sweetness and light, let him compare the story of Oedipus with its corresponding story of Joseph, and he will see that the cheerful piety is not all on one side.

There is never any doubt in the Jewish mind that true prophecy is, in the most pregnant sense of the words, "of God"—whether it conveys a divine command or exhibits that pattern in the nature of things that reveal the shape of the future. Christendom is the heir to this tradition; it could scarcely be otherwise, founding itself as it does on Scrip-tures that resound from end to end with the phrase, "That it might be fulfilled which was spoken by the prophet." In those Scriptures, the historical events of the Gospel are consistently presented as an acceptance of prophecy and a total obedience to the will of God, whatever apparent disasters that submission might entail.

This Judaeo-Christian concept has probably to some extent influenced and modified the European folklore of cheating the oracle, and has quite certainly influenced and modified the conscious handling of the theme in literature. It is to the literature that I now propose to turn. But I ought, perhaps, first of all to say a word about the whole idea of prophecy as such.

It has, I think, always been generally held that true prophecy, insofar as it involves the prediction of future events, is uttered unconsciously—that is, without any clear or detailed knowledge of the manner of its fulfillment. Sometimes, as in the case of the Delphic sibyl, the prophet is held to speak in a trance—she is possessed by the god and acts only as a mouthpiece or medium for the divine voice. Sometimes the prophet, though conscious, is aware that the words he utters are not his own: "The word of the Lord came to me." The poet—for every poet was once considered a *vates*—felt himself to be inspired by the Muse. (It is only in comparatively recent years that the poet has declined into mere self-expression; in his palmy days he expressed something a great deal more important than himself.)

And nearly always—and this is the characteristic of true prophecy—his words were fulfilled in a manner that he could not and did not foresee. What he said in one sense came true in a totally different sense, and the thing he foretold was not in the least the thing he thought he was writing about. He was not like a man running a pin down a list of names to pick a Derby winner. He was more like a man picking "Jet Pilot" to win, who has all his windows blown out next day by a supersonic bang. He was right about the name, but greatly underestimated its significance. When a university professor solemnly writes that Vergil's fourth eclogue was—wrongly—accepted in the Middle Ages as a prophecy of Christ, the word *wrongly* has no meaning. If a prophecy is fulfilled, it is fulfilled; iit does not matter in the least that Vergil supposed himself to be writing about a possible son of Octavian or Mark Antony—he is a prophet, not a tipster. No doubt the Harpy in the *Aeneid* supposed herself to be uttering not merely a prophecy but a curse; her words were fulfilled as she neither foresaw nor desired.

At the bottom of all this lies that assumption to which I have already referred—that the poet or prophet has *insight*. He is a seer, who discerns the underlying pattern of things. It is in this sense that the unknown inventor of the Oedipus legend may be said, if you like, to have been a prophet of the Oedipus complex. That is one of the fulfilments of his pattern, though it is not what he discerned at the time.

The last folktale I will deal with is the Icelandic story of *Ingebjörg*. In this, the Queen, under the influence of an evil magician, becames jealous of her own daughter and casts a spell upon her that she shall burn down the place, kill her father, and marry a terrible giant. The machinery of the story is at this point a trifle confused. I have not seen a primitive version of it, and it looks as though there might originally have been some sort of incest motive, though with complete inversion of the Oedipus complex both as to sex and generation—i.e., mother jealous of a daughter, instead of son jealous of father. In any case, the girl is good and virtuous, and, in order that she avert this doom she runs away from home. However, she meets her fairy godmother, who instructs her that the evil is to be overcome with good: "The king's palace I cannot save," she says, "but neither your father nor your mother shall be hurt . . . neither need you fear the giant." When the king and his courtiers are out hunting, the fairy and the princess send the servants away, carry all the treasure into safety, and set fire to the palace, thus fulfilling and breaking the spell. Subsequently the girl meets the giant, who turns out to be a handsome, young prince who has been bespelled by the magician. She breaks the spell and duly marries him as prophesied. The interesting point here is the breaking of the original spell by deliberately setting out to implement it.

Let us now abandon Oedipus and folklore and see what happens to the cheat-the-oracle theme when it is handled by a conscious artist addressing a sophisticated audience. The literature of the subject is too vast to permit anything like a full examination. Fortunately, there is one very well-known work that provides in itself a handy compendium of almost all the possible ways of dealing with prophecies, favorable or unfavorable. The plot of *Macbeth*, as distinct from the study of criminal psychology that it carries, is that and nothing else.

The witches in *Macbeth*, although directly dominated by the powers of evil, are represented as true prophets. In some manner the divine voice speaks through them. The atmosphere of the play can scarcely be called overtly Christian; but the writer and his audience were Christian people and would doubtless have been prepared to accept the theological proposition that even the evil powers are ultimately the instruments of an overruling Providence bringing all things into subjection to itself. It is tacitly taken for granted, that is, that the scheme of things is monarchist and not dualist. The playwright does not obtrude this question on us. All that matters is that we should accept the witches as telling the truth for evil ends—just as the serpent in Genesis tells the truth for evil ends.

At the first meeting with Macbeth and Banquo on the blasted heath, the witches make three prophecies—two about Macbeth and one about Banquo. Having shown that they know Macbeth by hailing him as "Thane of Glamis," they go on: "All hail, Macbeth! hail to thee, Thane of Cawdor! . . . "All hail,Macbeth, that shalt be King hereafter!" And of Banquo they prophesy: "Thou shalt get kings, though thou be none." Of these three predictions, two are welcome to Macbeth; the third comes to seem to him most unwelcome; on his manner of dealing with them the whole action of the play hinges.

About the first, "Hail to thee, Thane of Cawdor!", he does nothing. He has not time to do anything, for it has already been fulfilled in the preceding scene; and the announcement that Cawdor has turned traitor and been deprived of his title and estates in Macbeth's favor follows immediately upon the prophecy. This might and should have shown Macbeth that the witches knew what they were talking about, and that to get everything he wanted he had only to sit still and let things happen. As we know, he does nothing of the sort. The oracle fits in too well with his own secret thoughts, and he is ready to be persuaded that it supplies a sanction for murder. So he proceeds to implement the prophecy; not, like the virtuous Icelandic princess, in order to break it in the fulfillment and so purge out the evil, but simply to force the hand of destiny by his own efforts, and that in the most evil manner possible. Up to that point there is nothing to suggest that Macbeth might not, somehow, have succeeded peaceably to Duncan; it is by the will of Macbeth and his wife that the evil that is potential in the witches is assented to and called, by that assent, into actual existence and operation.

Duncan is murdered, and Macbeth seizes the throne. But now there is Banquo. Just before the murder, he had said to Macbeth,

> I dreamed last night of the three weird sisters.
> To you they have showed some truth.

The accent is on "you"; the implication is "and to me?" Macbeth suggests that he and Banquo should some time talk the matter over, adding

> If you shall cleave to my intent, when 'tis,
> It shall make honor for you.

Banquo replies,

>   So I lose none
> In seeking to augment it, but still keep
> My bosom franchised and allegiance clear,
> I shall be counseled.

It seems he is not to be tempted into implementing prophecy by murder and treason—though perhaps it was rash of him to say so. After Duncan's murder, he unburdens his mind in a soliloquy, and his tone is a little changed:

> Thou hast it now—King, Cawdor, Glamis, all,
> As the weird women promised; and I fear
> Thou playd'st most foully for 't. Yet it was said
> It should not stand in thy posterity,
> But that myself should be the root and father
> Of many kings. If there come truth from them—
> As upon thee, Macbeth, their speeches shine—
> Why, by the verities on thee made good,
> May they not be my oracles as well
> And set me up in hope?

Now that the obstacle is no longer a legitimate king but a usurping and suspected murderer, is Banquo thinking, after all, of taking a hand in his own fate? We are not quite sure, but Macbeth has no doubts at all. We are now back in the classic myth of the threatened king and the child of destiny. As usual, the king plots to destroy the predestined heir, adding the murder of Banquo for good measure. As usual, though Banquo is murdered, the child of destiny escapes. Oddly enough, Fleance, the traditional linchpin of the plot, appears only once and says nothing; the crown passes to Malcolm. Nor are we ever told how Flenace becomes ancestor to a line of kings. But that he will in fact do so we are assured both by the fact of his escape and also in the second prophecy scene when the witches call up the spirits from the cauldron. This time there are four prophecies: the first: "Beware Macduff"; the second: "None of woman born shall harm Macbeth"; the third: "Macbeth shall never vanquished be until / Great Birnam Wood to high Dunsinane Hill / Shall come against him"; the fourth is the shadow show of Banquo's royal issue.

Macbeth is now prepared to accept whatever the witches tell him. The fourth prophecy merely fills him with a kind of helpless horror; he is unable at the moment to do anything useful about the first, for he hears that Macduff has fled to England, and he can only execute a savage butchery of his wife and children. But he receives the second and third prophecies with a credulous confidence. In the end they are fulfilled, but riddlingly, after the manner of the Harpy's curse; and their fulfillment brings about the fulfillment of the first prediction.

Thus we have four methods of dealing with prophecies: (1) To do nothing about them, with the result that they are fulfilled harmlessly in the ordinary course of things (the Cawdor prophecy and Banquo's issue); (2) to implement them by crime (Duncan's murder) with disastrous consequences; (3) to try to escape them at all costs (Banquo's murder and the attempted murder of Fleance), altogether in vain; (4) to trust them (the riddling prophecies) and be betrayed by them.

We must now pass over much entertaining and profitable matter to come quickly to modern times, in which a number of efforts have been made to examine the phenomena of precognition along scientific and statistical lines.

In 1927, J. W. Dunne published a book called *An Experiment with Time*, in which he put forward a theory about time and precognition, founded on the examination of a number of apparently veridical dreams. This book, which was succeeded by another called *The Serial Universe*, stimulated the imagination of more than one writer of fiction. J. B. Priestley used it as the basis of two plays—*I Have Been Here Before*, which postulates a cyclical or spiral time, returning upon and repeating itself at vast intervals, and *Time and the Conways*, which postulates a kind of spatial or simultaneous time. Neither of these directly concerns us, since they do not handle the question of foreknowledge. But the same book suggested to John Buchan the plot of *A Gap in the Curtain*, which does, and which, like *Macbeth*, presents us with a kind of survey of the various methods of cheating, or otherwise manipulating, the oracle.

In the Dunne story, five men concentrate on visualizing a page of *The Times* newspaper for that day twelve-month.

The first, who is a financier, sees headlines about a merger of two big industrial companies. He realizes that this means that a certain mineral will become very valuable, and sets about buying the controlling interest in a moribund mining venture. Many of the shareholders live in wild and inaccessible places, and his quest involves him in great risk and trouble. At the moment of his triumphant success, a new chemical discovery makes the shares worthless, and though the merger duly takes place, he cannot profit by it. He is a good gambler and takes the disappointment cheerfully, losing only a few thousands, which he can well afford.

The second man, a member of Parliament, sees the name of a new prime minister. He too tries to profit by the information and plans his political adherences accordingly. He is an egotistical, prudent, and calculating man; but a sudden, unexpected coalition upsets the whole political picture. He finds he has backed the right man, but the wrong policy. No party now wants him, and his parliamentary career is ruined forever. "If he hadn't been so clever," says a colleague, "he would have been at No. 10 today . . . he was shrewd enough to spot the winner, but not the race it would win."

The third story is pure comedy. A young man of the world sees an announcement that he has joined an exploring expedition to Yucatan. He firmly resolved to do nothing of the sort—especially as his publicschool education has left him with the notion that Yucatan is in the east, and he takes a poor view of the Orient. Unfortunately he gets entangled with an overpowering young woman and, in order to escape marrying her, agrees to go at a moment's notice on a voyage with a friend who is an explorer. "But not east," he says; "I absolutely refuse to go east." The friend assures him that they are going in the opposite direction. The next morning he finds himself on a ship sailing for Yucatan.

The fourth and fifth men see their own obituary notices. One of them becomes obsessed by this and, eventually, dies of sheer fright. The fifth makes a gallant struggle against fate, but is fighting a losing battle when he falls in love with a girl and confides in her. The girl falls seriously ill about a month before the fatal date, and in his love and anxiety for her, the young man altogether loses his fear of death. "He saw all things in a new perspective. Death was only a stumble in the race, a brief half in an immortal pilgrimage. He and Pamela had won something which could never be taken away." The girl recovers and they are married. On their wedding morning the obituary notice appears in *The Times* and turns out to apply to another man of the same name.

Here again, the writer has run the whole gamut of possible reactions, emerging this time with the conclusions that to implement, resist, or submit to fate are all equally vain, and that the only safeguard against futurity is to fix one's heard upon that which is not subject to time.

Now it will be seen that our whole attitude to divination, whether in life or in literature, is paradoxical. We desire to know the future, in order to control it—for if we cannot control it *at all*, to know it would be at best a tedium and at worst a horror. But if we can control it so completely as to evade it, then it is not the future. We desire the prophecy to come true, otherwise the story is pointless; but unless the manner of its coming true is affected by human behavior, there is no story to tell. A universe in which everything is determined from moment to moment reduces to nonsense not only every action but also every emotion; on the other hand a universality of randomness affronts our sense of order. And a universe in which every man's will was entirely free from restriction would be formless—a mere chaotic flux of incompatibles. What in fact we desire is that the will should be both bound and free; the future at the same time fixed and indeterminate, foreseeable, and unexpected. This may be irrational, but it is artistically right, and in fact all good stories about true prophecy are so constructed as to content this paradoxical appetite for inevitability combined with surprise. That is why such tales exercise so powerful a fascination, and why we are all, willy-nilly, enthralled by the palmist, the crystal gazer, the astrologer, the gypsy with the tarot pack, and the seventh son of a seventh son who has the gift of sight.

"Of course," we say, "it is all nonsense, but—." And the moment we come to the word *but,* a curious note of satisfaction creeps into our voice. True prophecy may be pure illusion; yet a tale about a prophecy that turned out to be merely false would afford us no entertainment at all, but only a sense of anticlimax. (In real life, of course, these futilities frequently occur.) Now, in order to enjoy and write oracle stories, we must find some consistent philosophy to which we can relate them, if we are to keep our intellectual self-respect and avoid being called backward, unscientific, superstitious, escapist, adolescent, and similar ugly epithets. What we need to justify our artistic enjoyment is a theory of time and fate that will combine necessity with freedom—necessity as to the end and freedom as to the means. Such a theory we will now proceed to construct.

I do not myself think we need to postulate, with Mr. Dunne, a series of observers, nor yet an infinite series of dimensions of time. All such bad infinities have something unsatisfactory and faintly nonsensical about them; moreover, they offend against Ockham's razor, by needlessly multiplying entities. Neither do we really need the cumbrous concepts of cyclic or spiral time, both of which have the grave disadvantage of moving far too slowly to be handled. All we actually require is two observers: the infinite Observer, to whom Mr. Dunne himself has to come in the end, and the experiencing self. These are enough, provided that each is triune, that is, subsisting in three hypostases, each a mode of the whole self, and in virtue of which the self is, acts, and knows its act and being. Neither do we need more than two kinds of time: real time and created time. This duality of time has the advantage of being empirically known to us. Every novelist and every reader of a novel take it so much for granted that they never give it a thought. Real time is the rhythm or dimension in which the author himself has his being; created time is the time that takes place inside the story—known to the characters in it as a linear movement in one direction, but to the author as a simultaneity in which all its moments are present at once. The two times have nothing in common, except that they are both known to the author; there is no sense in which it can be said that the time inside the story I am writing coincides with *my* time in which I am living—they are related in the way in which what we call "time" is related to what we call "eternity."

I write "the next seven years passed happily"; those years have extension for the people in the story, but they have none in mine. They are only a curve in a created pattern that I perceive simultaneously in all its parts. Further, the future of the characters is known to me simultaneously with their past; to them it appears future; but it may be the thing that I began, and which, unknown to them, conditions their past. Every event in their world is governed by two chains of causation: the created causation known to them, which provides that each of their events shall develop logically from events in their past, and the real causation, known only to their author, which may work backwards in their time so that their acts are the consequences of their own effects. This sounds confusing, but in practice every author deals casually and competently with double time and double causation without the least hesitation or confusion in his own mind. The reader also, though he does not share the author's omniscience, is aware of the double time scheme. He says to himself: "Let's see—Henry must be about thirty-seven by now—isn't it getting on for teatime?"

But note that the author, though his is the only ultimately effective will and the only real time or causation concerned, is to some extent bound by the laws he has made for his own creation. He must not reverse or confuse the time sequence within the story; neither must be make his created people behave otherwise than in accordance with the natures he has bestowed upon them. Even in an imagined story the characters have a certain simulacrum of free will that the author must needs respect; and this encourages us to suppose that in the actual created universe a measure of free will may be compatible in the creature with the infinite author's knowledge of the pattern. I say *knowledge*, not *foreknowledge;* to the author, human or divine, there is neither before nor after: each event is known in its own place. It is only in the creature that we can speak of foreknowledge, if any such knowledge is available to him—as, for our purpose, we must assume that it is.

Given thus the created pattern, with its two operative wills, its double time scheme and its double network of causation, we have to find room in it for both necessity (that is to say, the absolute and unconditioned will of the creator) and potentiality (that is to say, the free but conditioned will of the creature). We shall also have to account for those moments of apparent foresight that, though at the time they seem to have the quality of true prophecy, yet remain unfulfilled or are only partially fulfilled or fulfilled in riddling and ambiguous ways.

Let us then picture the totality of things as a web spread out in as many dimensions of time and space as we may find it easy and convenient to imagine. We shall observe in it certain fixed points; these are the nodes of necessity, through which the lines must pass in order to make the pattern. The nodes are determined by the artist, but the lines are self-determined and may take any direction they choose, subject to two limitations: (1) However they bend and turn—even if they start off in the opposite direction— they are bound eventually to go through the fixed points. (2) Every movement they make modifies and is modified by the movements of the neighboring lines. The will of the maker readily submits to all these modifications, since the necessity laid upon the lines to come to the nodes means that all the possible modifications can only in the end produce a conditioned necessity of their own—just as, in a game of croquet, the path of every ball, however wildly it may diverge under the impact of a bad shot, or the disturbing shot of the adversary, is governed by the absolute external necessity imposed on both sides alike of going through the right hoops in the right order.

Thus: Oedipus must kill his father; that is the fixed node through which the lines must pass. But the manner of their passing is tragically determined by the folly of Laius and Jocasta, by the sins of Oedipus himself, by the very virtues of the shepherd and Polybus. The lines that seemed to run away are brought home by the master hand, the chain of primary causation always adapting itself, link by link, to the chain of secondary causation, as the concave curve follows the curve of the convex and is identical with it.

Let us take another example: the tale that, if it is not true history, is at any rate the greatest of all myths. Most races have cherished the prophecy that, in some manner or other, the divine should become human and share human experience. Given that all men are mortal, it becomes necessary that the human experience should include the experience of bodily death. Birth and death are thus, presumably, the essential nodes of the pattern. But time, place, circumstances, and in particular the manner of the death are determined by the course of human history; for though all men must die, comparatively few die violent deaths, and fewer still by judicial murder. This was recognized by certain medieval thinkers, who pleased themselves with the fancy that if Christ had not been crucified, he would have laid down his life by a natural death at the age of eighty, which they considered to be the perfect age.

At the rim of the pattern, then, the lines of potentiality lie wide apart and may take almost any course toward the node. But as they close in, the area of available choice becomes narrower and narrower. The decision of man in general becomes the decision of an empire, of a nation, of a court of law, and eventually the decision of particular persons—all moving to one end, under pressure of the history of decisions in the past. But the element of personal choice remains to the last moment: "the Son of Man goeth indeed as it is written of Him, but woe unto that man by whom the Son of Man is betrayed." Some measure of indeterminism, though limited at length to Pilate's simple choice between yes and no.

On this hypothesis, then, an inescapable prediction, like that of the Oedipus story, will mean that the seer has been vouchsafed a sight of one of the nodes, though all the lines of potentiality are veiled. I would add that, in order to make a good story, it is advisable to keep the lines veiled; otherwise one will not achieve the desired effect of inevitability combined with surprise. What makes the boding dreams or warning visions of fiction both dull and incredible is an excessive accumulation of veridical detail, as, for example, in the allegorical dreams so common in medieval moral tales, or the monstrously elaborate dream in Wilkie Collins's *Armadale*, which is punctiliously fulfilled in episode after episode. Both in real life and in fiction, it is, as we have seen, the mark of convincing prophecy to be fulfilled "all wrong"—that is, along lines of potentiality that neither the prophet nor his contemporaries every foresaw or guessed at. Thus, Vergil's fourth eclogue is a convincing prophecy of Christ just because, not in spite of, the fact that he supposed himself to be writing about somebody quite different.

When, however, a vision that appears to have equality of prophecy remains unfulfilled, or only partially fulfilled, we shall say (on the same hypothesis) that the seer has been looking along one of the lines of potentiality. He has seen the future, not as it will be but as it might be. the lines of potentiality may be modified if we care to take the risk; but if what we have seen turns out to be one of the nodes, then we take liberties with it at our own peril. And it may be said on behalf of the more conscientious kind of fortune-tellers that, if closely pressed, they will not as a rule claim more for what is written in the stars or on the cards than a very high potential.

The trouble is, of course, that before we undertake to meddle with fate, we want to know whether we are looking at the nodes or one of the lines of potentiality. Unfortunately, no one can tell us that, except the author of the pattern. When contact is established with the mind of the author, then the vision is properly called not foresight but revelation, and as such it forms no part of our subject. For the ordinary person, it is wisest to leave the whole thing alone—a disappointing conclusion, in which the church, the law, and most of the writers of cheat-the-oracle stories unreservedly concur. So do most scientists, though not altogether for the same reason. The statistical experiments carried out by Professor Soal and others, being directed only to discovering whether veridical foresight does in fact take place, are as potentially harmless or harmful as other scientific experiments—with nuclear fission or what not. It is always interesting to know what lies within our power; it is when we begin to make use of the knowledge that the balloon is likely to go up.

At this point we come up against another type of prophecy altogether—the type that William Blake recognized, and which is founded, not on foresight, but on insight. It begins by saying: "The universe is so made that if you insist on doing so-and-so the consequences will be such-and-such"; and it frequently goes on to say: "and knowing you as I do, I can confidently predict that you will do it and the inevitable result will follow." The only objection to this kind of prophecy is that it seldom flatters our hopes, and cannot, by its nature, offer us much in the way of dramatic surprise. Yet it, too, may have its false prophets, for insight may be as unreliable as foresight; we are, for example, less sure than we were of the inevitable evolution of human perfection. Moreover, the stories in which it figures are for the most part of a deadly serious and edifying kind, like the *Industrious Apprentice* and *Eric, or Little by Little*. We do not invite Jeremiah to entertain us at parties, or pay astrologers to inform us that by honest thrift we may gradually amass a genteel sufficiency. What we want to hear is something quite different: "The eight of swords is a journey by water"; "Your twenty-first year will be perilous—I see Mars and Venus opposed, and Saturn threatening the House of Life"; "Cross the gypsy's palm with silver";

> I dreamed a dream, a weary dream
>   Ayont the Isle of Skye;
> I saw a dead man win a fight,
>   And I think that man was I.

But when it comes to taking action about them, we fall into perplexity. What is it expedient to do? And what is our moral duty? And here, the prophecy of insight casts a damper on our hopes of dealing with the prophecy of foresight. If I dream that the 9:30 to Liverpool Street is due to be wrecked tomorrow, I can refrain from traveling by it. But is it my duty to rush to the station and dissuade other passengers from traveling? My knowledge of human nature suggests that I shall have but little success. Am I to ring up British Railways and peremptorily summon them to cancel the train? Alas! my knowledge of the way government departments work pronounces that this is a node that there is no untying. With a delicious shudder we may remember Max Beerbohm's A. V. Laider, who reads the hands of all the passengers in a railway compartment and finds that all, except himself, are foredoomed to die in the same imminent catastrophe. He has not the courage to pull the communication cord—and the next thing he knows is waking up in a hospital.

"Tell me," says the acquaintance to whom he narrates this painful episode, "was it marked in your hands that you were not going to pull that cord?" . . . "It was marked very clearly," he answered, "in *their* hands."

Until prediction becomes an exact science—and how dull life will be when it does—it is probably best to take the thrill and let the profit go. We do not know enough; and the gods have a sardonic sense of humor that it is rather rash to provoke.

The Faust Legend
and the Idea of the Devil

IT IS NOTORIOUS that one of the great difficulties about writing a book or play about the Devil is to prevent that character from stealing the show. Any actor will tell you that the role of the Devil in any handling of the subject is sure-fire. And it is likely to be sure-fire—not only in the sense that the Devil is a picturesque figure of color and action; that is true of any vigorous villain. But it is also true in the sense that the Devil is only too likely to capture the sympathy of the house.

This is a serious matter, either for the artist, or the audience, or both. Or perhaps it would be better to say that it is always a serious matter for the audience; for the artist, it may be serious in one of three ways. Either he knows what he is doing and intends it (in which case there is something wrong with him spiritually as a man), or else he is, as Blake said of Milton, "of the Devil's party without knowing it" (in which case the spiritual evil is deeper and more incurable), or there is simply a failure of communication in his art.

It is not, of course, surprising that the devil should appear attractive, or that he should be made to appear so in a work of the imagination. It is precisely the Devil's business to appear attractive; that is the whole meaning of temptation to sin. And unless the artist conveys something of this attraction, his Devil will be a mere turnip-ghost, exciting either boredom or derisive laughter, and in no way conveying or communicating the power of evil. But it is important artistically as well as theologically to ascertain whether the artist is able to view his own creation critically, or whether he has fallen, consciously or unconsciously, under the power of his own spellbinding.

There is, indeed, a grave theological difficulty about the Devil, which we had better look at first and clear out of the way (so far as that is possible) before going on to the artistic side of the subject. It is the old difficulty about omnipotence and free will. If God is almighty and created everything, how do we account for the existence of the evil power, or of any sort of evil in creation? One answer—that of the Manichaeans—is to deny that God is omnipotent and to allow the coexistent presence of two powers: good and evil, light and darkness. Even in this scheme of things, it is generally supposed that the good will eventually conquer the evil. But the supposition behind it is that the evil and darkness are as primary as the good and the light. A variation of this is that the darkness is primary; that it existed in chaos or the abyss before the light got to work upon it, and that the light—what we mean by God—is continually engaged in building up creation toward the good against the backward drag that seeks to reduce all things to the primeval chaos. This position is unorthodox and, strictly speaking, heretical. It lies behind a good deal of Berdyaev's philosophy; and it seems to have a good deal also to do with the fashionable doctrine of emergent evolution, by which God is

supposed to be evolving himself out of chaos in an enormous time process.

The orthodox Christian conception is more subtle and
less optimistic; it is also much less involved in the time process. For it, the light and the light only is primary; creation
and time and darkness are secondary and begin together.
When you come to consider the matter, it is strictly meaningless to say that darkness could precede light in a time
process. Where there is no light, there is no meaning for the
word *darkness,* for darkness is merely a name for that which
is without light. Light, by merely existing, creates darkness,
or at any rate the possibility of darkness. In this sense, it is
possible to understand that profound saying, "I form the
light, and create darkness; I make peace, and create evil; I
the Lord do all these things" (Isaiah 40:7).

But it is at this point that it becomes possible for the evil
and the darkness and the chaos to boast: "We are that
which was before the light was, and the light is a usurpation upon our rights." It is an illusion; evil and darkness
and chaos are pure negation, and there is no such state as
"before the light" because it is the primary light that creates
the whole time process. It is an illusion; and that is the primary illusion inside which the devil lives and in which he
deceives himself and others. That primary illusion is stated
with perfect clarity by Goethe's Mephistopheles:

> Ich bin ein Teil des Teils, der Anfangs alles war,
> Ein Teil der Finsternis, die sich das Licht gebar,
> Das stolze Licht, das nun der Mutter Nacht
> Den alten Rang, den Raum, ihr streitig macht.

That is the Devil's claim, the exact statement of the pride by
which he fell from heaven. It sounds extremely fine; and
when it is set forth in attractive language, it is sometimes
difficult to remember that the Devil is a liar and the father
of lies. In *Paradise Lost,* we find Satan making the same
claim; he "feels himself impaired" because of the authority
of the Son of God. He believes, or affects to believe, that he

himself is anterior to the Son, and ought not, therefore, to be subject to him. In the subsequent argument with Abdiel, he shows himself a poor logician, but we may, if we like, suppose that by this time he really believes in his own claim, or has argued himself into the illusion of belief—for the corruption of the will saps the intellect, and the Devil is ultimately a fool as well as a villain. He is, let us believe by all means, the victim of his own illusion. But Milton is not; Milton knows, and says, that the Son is anterior to Satan, and is, in fact, the very power by whom Satan was created.

In the orthodox Christian position, therefore, the light is primary, the darkness secondary and derivative; and this is important for the whole theology of evil. In *The Devil to Pay*, I tried to make this point; and I remember being soundly rapped over the knuckles by a newspaper critic, who said in effect that after a great deal of unintelligible pother, I had worked up to the statement that God was light, which did not seem to be very novel or profound. Novel, it certainly is not; it is scarcely the business of Christian writers to introduce novelties into the fundamental Christian doctrines. But profundity is another matter; Christian theology is profound, and since I did not invent it, I may have the right to say so. These are the lines spoken by Mephistopheles, in the presence of the Judge before whom a lie cannot live:

> FAUSTUS: Who made thee?
> MEPHISTOPHELES: God; as the light makes the
> shadow.

That is the acknowledgment of derivation. Later follows:

> FAUSTUS: What art thou, Mephistopheles?
> MEPHISTOPHELES: I am the price that all things
> pay for being.
> The shadow on the word, thrown by the world
> Standing in its own light, which light God is.

And whether or not those lines are good verse, they do bring us up against the fundamental problem. Evil is "the price that all things (i.e., all created things—God is not a "thing") pay for being"—that is, for existing in created and material form. There is, for them, along with the reality of God, the possibility of not-God. For things inorganic, this is only known as change, and not as evil; for creatures organic but not self-conscious, there are both change and pain—and here there is a very great mystery, which we are scarcely in a position to solve because we know nothing of what pain may be like to the unself-conscious organism. But to the self-conscious creature, the not-God is known as change, as pain, and also as intellectual error and moral evil; and it is at this point that it actually becomes evil in the profoundest sense of the word because it can be embraced and made active by the will. The possibility of evil exists from the moment that a creature is made that can love and do good because it chooses and not because it is unable to do anything else. The actuality of evil exists from the moment that that choice is exercised in the wrong direction. Sin (moral evil) is the deliberate choice of the not-God. And pride, as the Church as consistently pointed out, is the root of it; i.e. the refusal to accept the creaturely status; the making of the difference between self and God into an antagonism against God. Satan, as Milton rightly shows, "thinks himself impaired," and in that moment he chooses that evil shall be his good.

That is what the orthodox Catholic doctrine is. I do not want to argue it here because that would lead us away from our subject; but I want to make clear what it is. Evil is the soul's choice of the not-God. The corollary is that damnation, or hell, is the permanent choice of the not-God. God does not (in the monstrous old-fashioned phrase) "send" anybody to hell; hell is that state of the soul in which its choice becomes obdurate and fixed; the punishment (so to call it) of that soul is to remain eternally in that state that it has chosen.

In the Christian *mythos*, the original head and front of this offending is not placed among mankind. It happened first among another order of created beings. The devils are fallen angels. Satan and his followers chose the not-God, and when they had it, they found that it was hell. In that obduracy they suffer; and into that suffering they endeavor to drag the rest of creation—of which man in particular concerns us. Their whole will is to hatred and negation and destruction, and, if they could accomplish that will wholly, they would be none the happier, since happiness is not in them—they have destroyed their own capacity for happiness. The lust for destruction in no way increases the happiness of those who indulge in it—if anything, the more successful they are in it, the more miserable they are—but they persist in it because they have destroyed their own will for anything else. This is, of course, a witless state of mind; but then the intellect is one of the first things that the evil will destroys. That it is not an impossible state of mind is quite apparent—for we can see it existing in human beings today—and sometimes can find it only too clearly in our virtuous selves: for example, in jealousy, that searches avidly for fresh occasions of the distrust that torments it; or in our savage resentment against those we have injured, which prompts us to renew the injury and so increase the miserable resentment.

I apologize for this long theological preliminary, which seemed necessary in order that we might examine the subject of the devil in literature. Because one of the most important things we have to do is to distinguish the Devil as (in the sight of God) he is, and the thing that may be called the "diabolic setup." The underlying actuality is miserable, hideous, and squalid; the setup is the facade that the devil shows to the world—and a very noble facade it often is, and the nobler, the more dangerous. The devil is a spiritual lunatic, but, like many lunatics, he is extremely palusible and cunning. His brain is, so to speak, in perfectly good working order except for that soft and corrupted spot in the center, where dwells the eternal illusion. His method of working is to present us with the magnificent setup, hoping we shall not use either our brains or our spiritual faculties to penetrate the illusion. He is playing for sympathy; therefore he is much better served by exploiting our virtues than by appealing to our lower passions; consequently, it is when the devil looks most noble and reasonable that he is most dangerous. And here the poets have sometimes become his unconscious or even his conscious allies. And in order to be fair to the poets, it is very necessary that we should find out whether the illusion is in them or in us.

I should like to take two or three examples of the Satanic setup from the work of the poets who have dealt with the subject—including those who have dealt with the Faustus legend and the theme of the devil's bargain.

In the original Faustus legend, there is no setup, except of the most obvious kind. It is a plain story of the man who barters his hope in the next world for success or power in this, knowing quite well what he is doing. Such setup as there is in this and in the medieval mystery plays may be found in the traditional clowning and horseplay of which the Devil is always the center. The theology is correct enough—the devil is a fool and is outwitted in the end—but I suspect that he was, for the audience, a "favorite character" for the sake of the comic relief. On the whole, this was probably wholesome; at any rate, at the time. Laughter is a blessed thing, and the Devil's pride does not easily endure it. "The Devil, the proud spirit, cannot endure to be mocked" (Sir T. More). It was only much later that the Devil was to make his profit out of these medieval floutings. But in Marlowe's *Dr. Faustus* we begin to come to something different.

Marlowe is said to have been, or claimed to be, an atheist; but his handling of the legend is orthodox enough. Faustus makes his bargain with open eyes and is duly damned. And it is interesting to see what the bargain is. A nineteenth-century editor* of *Faust* has remarked, "The Devil

---

*Calvin Thomas.

of any age or people is the enemy of what that age or people regards as supremely good." That is only partly true. In *Dr. Faustus*, the Devil's offer is precisely of something that Marlowe's age regarded, or was coming to regard, as supremely good—knowledge and especially the power acquired by knowledge. Sensual pleasures are, indeed, included—Faustus demands "girls and gold," but, above all, adventure, romance, and power in their most splendid forms; and knowledge as a means to these things.

> emperors and kings
> Are but obeyed in their several provinces,
> Nor can they raise the wind or send the clouds;
> But his dominion that exceeds in this
> Stretcheth as far as doth the mind of man,
> A sound magician is a mighty God.

That is Faustus coming to the study of magic; and then

> Had I as many souls as there be stars,
> I'd give them all for Mephistopheles.
> By him I'll be a great emperor of the world,
> And make a bridge through the moving air,
> To pass the ocean with a band of men:
> I'll join the hills that bind the Afric shore,
> And make that country continent to Spain,
> And both contributory to my crown,
> The emperor shall not live but by my leave.

And when the bargain is struck, Faustus—soon wearying of the merely academic learning of astronomy (which he dismisses as trifles) is next found touring the world. What the Devil is actually offering him is the immediate future—the splendors of the Renaissance, the triumph of power politics, the opening of the economic era—the new humanism—the exaltation of the mind of man. The devil is on the side of all the grand new things—of expansion and progress, and all the gods of the age to come. But on which side is Marlowe?

Formally, on God's side. The gifts are the Devil's gifts, and Faustus goes to hell. Faustus proclaims that, "This word *damnation* terrifies not him. For he confounds hell in Elysium. His ghost be with the old philosophers." But in the end he is both damned and terrified. Marlowe's own sympathies may be with Faustus, but in fact he condemns his own sympathies. So far, so orthodox. But a new note comes in the presentation of Mephistopheles:

FAUSTUS:
> Where are you damned?

MEPHISTOPHELES:
> In hell.

FAUSTUS:
> How comes it then that thou art out of hell?

MEPHISTOPHELES:
> Why this is hell, nor am I out of it:
> Think'st though that I who saw the face of God,
> And tasted the eternal joys of heaven,
> Am not tormented with ten thousand hells
> In being deprived of everlasting bliss?

To which, so grand is the language, the audience is moved to rejoin heartily, "Oh, poor creature!" Faustus, it is true, sneers at Mephistopheles and adjures him

> "Learn then of Faustus manly fortitude
> And scorn those joys thou never shalt possess."

That advice will be taken by Milton's Satan. But in the meanwhile, we observe the structure of the Satanic facade already going up. It is true that Mephistopheles is comparatively frank about the origin of his sufferings:

FAUSTUS:
> Was not that Lucifer an angel once?

MEPHISTOPHELES:
> Yes, Faustus, and most dearly loved of God.

FAUSTUS:
> How comes it then that he is prince of devils?

MEPHISTOPHELES:
> O by aspiring pride and insolence
> For which God threw him from the face of Heaven.

But somehow the suggestion is already there that Satan and his followers are rather noble in their suffering. It is only a suggestion, conveyed rather by the sound than by the sense of the lines; but the suggestion is there. It is the beginning of what we may call the Promethean setup—the sympathetic picture of the sad, proud sufferer defying omnipotence.

In Milton's Satan, this setup is magnificently completed. "Nobility" is Satan's line, and he runs it for all it is worth. He is "impaired," his pride is hurt, he has been deprived of his rights, his sufferings are acute, but he bears them superbly, he presents himself as the champion of all noble rebels, he is the indomitable spirit

"Who durst defy th' Omnipotent to arms"—

and the whole thing is so grand, and sad, and stoical as to deceive the very elect. What Satan does not mention (though Milton does) is that Satan did not in fact suffer any wrongs and undergoes no torments except those he has deliberately chosen. He plays for sympathy, and he gets it. As a friend of mine observed on this subject: "One can't help admiring anybody who fights so courageously a battle he knows to be hopeless, against somebody else who is omnipotent." Indeed, one is so lost in admiration that one is led to overlook the fact that the battle was undertaken without any necessity and in a totally unworthy cause.

It has for some time been the fashion to pretend that Milton was the dupe of his own eloquence, and really was "of Satan's party without knowing it." I hope that Charles Williams and C. S. Lewis have sufficiently disposed of that pretense. Milton was no dupe. It is true that he could summon up sufficient imaginative sympathy with Satan to present his case with a diabolic plausibility—but imaginative sympathy is not moral approval. Milton knew very well that the setup of the "grand infernal peers" was only a setup—the reality was the hideous obscenity

"Squat like a toad, close at the ear of Eve"—the hissing

serpent crawling on its belly, the monstrous paramour of sin and father of death. Milton did not deceive himself.

I think, however, there is some excuse for those who imagine that he did—and it is simply a literary excuse. I think that the magnificent and ordered grandeur of Milton's style was perhaps not quite a satisfactory instrument for communicating squalor and beastliness. It communicates beauty in spite of its author. Flexible as it is within its own compass, it cannot sink quite so far as to the real deep of hell. But I do not want to enter upon the great Milton row, with which the older universities are still ringing. I will only note that within the last couple of centuries this particular Satanic setup has been accepted at its face value by a great number of critics who should know much better.

The noble sufferer setup achieved its most forcible expression when it became the Byronic setup and stormed and attitudinized through the *Sturm und Drang* period of heroic Satans and Satanic heroes. By this time the poets themselves had become thoroughly duped. Their poetry was hardly the better for it, and the setup (in that form) has now become a laughing-stock, though it is still naively accepted, in another form, by a number of simple-minded people who suppose that there is something noble in being agin' the government of the universe, and that heresy is in itself a proof of superior understanding.

With Goethe, we come to a different form of the setup, and that which has the merit of raising a very central theological difficulty. It is integral to Christianity to affirm that Christ (and in him, all Christians) can so redeem evil as to make of it a greater good. *O felix culpa!* The sin of Adam is the occasion of the Incarnation; redeemed man is something more poignantly blessed than innocent man could ever have been. That is the glory of the God who was made man, and that is Catholic doctrine. But at the same time, evil is no less evil because it can be in the literal sense made good. "The Son of Man goeth . . . but woe unto that man by whom the Son of Man is betrayed." Evil may be made the occasion of good, but in itself it remains evil and damnable.

That is the doctrine. But from this it is but a single false step to making the assertion that evil is a good thing because it is the occasion of good. And from that assertion the new facade is built up. In this setup, the Devil becomes, as it were, a part of the divine process, playing the same part in the cosmic constitution as the advocates of the party system assign to the opposition. His job is to stir up the people on the governmental side of the house and keep them from going to sleep on the job.* This view of the matter is put by Goethe plainly enough into the mouth of God,

> Des Menschen Tätigkeit kann allzuleicht erschlaffen,
> Er liebt sich bald die unbedingte Ruh;
> Drum geb' ich gern ihm den Gesellen zu,
> Der reizt und wirkt und muss als Teufel schaffen.

We must therefore suppose that to the extent Goethe himself was "of the Devil's party"—and not without knowing it.

The new kind of Devil is certainly a most happy relief from the Byronic Devil, and a very great deal healthier. We have got rid of the notion that obstinate opposition to the order of life is something to be proud of. The spirit of negation is exposed in its barrenness, its futility, and also in its vulgarity—for Goethe's Mephistopheles, for all his cynical charm, is at bottom a low-minded person. The bubble of the Satanic nobility is well and truly pricked. And on this occasion it is true to say that the Devil is taken to represent the enemy of what the period accepts as its best good. The era of progress and perfectibility is coming in; and the Devil is seen either as the grit that clogs and stops the wheels, or—and here we must vary the metaphor—as the roughage that irritates and stimulates the system to perform its work of metabolism. It is the optimistic view of an op-

---

*Cf. the Book of Job, in which "Satan" appears to exercise precisely this function. Here, however, he is not represented as a spirit of evil in the sense in which we use the words when we speak of "the devil."—D.L.S.

timistic age, stirring with all the vigor of a new life and confident in its own power to assimilate the toughest morsels and turn them into vital sustenance.

Something, however, has been lost, and dangerously lost. We may perhaps see what it is if we compare the Devil's bargain in *Faust* with that in *Dr. Faustus*. Faustus makes a choice; Faust makes only a wager. Faustus may say that he does not believe in the immortality of the soul; but in reality he knows what he has done and that it is a thing irrevocable. Faust makes a bet, confident that he will win it, and is very little tormented with the fear of hell—for he has not chosen hell; he has merely defied it. The author sees to it that the Devil is cheated of his bargain—correctly enough in one sense, seeing that the will of Faust does not consent to evil. But what is getting lost is the sense of the dignity and finality of choice, and of the reality and evilness of evil. Faust gains heaven by striving—and in the end by striving to do some good in the world; but for all his remorse about Margarete, there is little real conviction of the ravage of evil or of the cost of its redemption. The price of accepting the progressive setup is that in the end it persuades us not to take evil very seriously.

I must be fair to Goethe. In the famous speech that I have already quoted, there is a reservation:

> Von allen Geistern, die verneinen,
> Ist mir der Schalk am wenigsten zur Last—

It is suggested that there may be other and worse spirits of evil than the irritant Mephistopheles. But the suggestion is not, I think, elaborated; and it is certainly fair to say that Mephistopheles never for one moment is represented to us as a spirit in torment, and that the appearance of hellmouth in the final scene is, almost admittedly, pure decor. Mephistopheles does, in fact, admit it:

> Ihr tut sehr wohl, die Sünder zu erschrecken;
> Sie halten's doch fur Lug und Tug und Traum.

Hell has become a picture to frighten sinners with; it is not felt as a real possibility.

Whatever our theological views about the possibility of final damnation may be, it is, I think, true to say that the age of progress and perfectibility from which we are now emerging did bear certain marks of this particular Satanic setup. It did hold to a belief that somehow good would emerge of itself from the world process so long as we kept on going on; it did play down the actuality of sin and the intolerable nature of evil; it did deprecate the idea that any act or choice could be final or irrevocable; and the result of these things was, in fact, a slackening of the rigid sense of personal responsibility in the face of eternal fact.

If I now say a word or two about my own *Devil to Pay*, it is not because I think that I am suitable company for poets such as Marlowe and Milton and Goethe, but because it was an endeavor to bring the fable of the Devil's bargain to the interpretation of the interwar period. In my play, Faustus's transactions with the Devil go through two phases. In the first, the idea that evil is a means to good reaches its almost inevitable conclusion; i.e., it is *consciously* accepted and exploited. Faustus, sickened by the human suffering about him, tries to take the shortcut to a remedy, and to cast out bodily evil by invoking the aid of spiritual evil. Many builders of earthly utopias and new orders seem prepared to do the like. When this endeavor to make Satan cast out Satan fails, he reacts into the next phase, which is to repudiate the actuality of evil, and, with it, the whole personal responsibility for the redemption of evil. The illusion of Helen is the illusion that it is possible to go back before the Fall and regain the simple animal innocence that Walt Whitman admired, or pretended to admire—the innocence that does not know evil:

> Serpent of Eden, take thy curse again,
> Undo the sin of Adam, turn the years
> Back to their primal innocence.

But the years cannot be turned back. We cannot, as Mr. Charles Williams has said, return to primal innocence by simply removing our aprons of fig leaves. When the human will consented to sin, and so-called evil into actual existence, it learned to know the existing good as evil; and the corollary was that, in the absence of the knowledge of evil, it could no longer know either good or evil. Faustus bargains for animal innocence—that is his choice, and he gets it. His soul becomes the soul of an animal, knowing neither good nor evil, and irresponsible. In this irresponsible mood, he is the instrument of all mischief—as the whole of innocent and inorganic nature is the instrument of the evil will. The evil will uses him for the making of war, as it uses all nature's innocent and irresponsible forces. In the moment of death he calls upon Christ and upon Lisa, and in that last lucid moment is saved—but so as by fire, having to undergo in purgatory that redemptive suffering that he repudiated.

It is not for me to say whether I have been the dupe of my own setup—I hope not; but of course, if I have, I do not know it. My Mephistopheles starts as a plausible humanitarian, breathing contempt upon the inefficiency of God; that is his setup. In the sequel, he is vulgar and cruel—and he is fooled, because the bargain into which he entered destroyed the identity of the soul he wanted for his own; he falls himself into the inefficiency to which he claimed superiority. He is made to work God's will, but in spite of himself. So far as it goes, the theology is, I think, sound—though in a play so short it would be impossible for even a great writer to plumb the deeper issues.

As to whether the idea of the play was suited to the time in which it appeared, I will say only this: first, that a great number of people expressed the opinion that it would have been better had Faustus chosen to remain in his animal state to all eternity, rather than redeem his human soul by purgation; secondly, that the play ran for only a few weeks

in London—largely because of the imminence of the war
that we had been largely instrumental in bringing about
through a refusal of responsibility and through a determined refusal to believe in the possibility of a deliberate
will to evil.

From this very brief and hasty sketch, there is one poet
whom I have very conspicuously left out. You are probably
wondering why—at least, you ought to be—and wriggling
in your seats with anxiety to shout at me (but that courtesy
restrains you) that from this portrait-gallery of the Devil the
most important example of all is missing.

I had not forgotten. The greatest poet, the most exact
theologian, the most adult intellect of all ought, chronolog-
ically, to have been taken first; but I have left him to the
last, because if, now, we are going to begin once more to
take evil seriously, he is the one with whom we shall have
to reckon. He was never taken in by the Satanic setup; nor
did his verse—that amazing and flexible instrument that
could move at will and almost in a breath from the raptures
of paradise, "all air and fire," through the homeliest earth-
iness, to the extreme of infernal dirt and squalor and beastliness—nor did his verse ever offer his readers the smallest
excuse for finding the devil anything else but diabolical.
Down the great sterile circles of perverse and petrified
choice, hell goes narrowing to its frozen center, deep after
deep; at the top are the irresponsibles, who refused choice;
below them, the people who incontinently lapsed into evil
through failure to control their choice, blown on the winds
or sodden in the marshwater of their passions; then the deliberate hardening of the will to the choice of the wrong
made in full knowledge—the will to violence, the will to
deceit—circle below circle of fire and filth and disease,
down to the ultimate treachery in which all feeling, all intellect, every conception, are frozen. And, fixed in the ice at
the bottom, the ultimate corruption, resentful and despair-
ing, passive and rebellious, petrifying and petrified, fixed

for ever in a misery without dignity, the grotesque and ghastly reality behind the facade. In a sense he still appears not less than archangel ruined; but the ruin is here complete; the beauty does not shine through the corruption: it is the corruption of beauty itself:

> S'ei fu si bel com' egli e ora brutto
> e contra il suo Fattore alzo le ciglia,
> ben dee da lui procedere ogni lutto.

"If once he was beautiful as now he is hideous, and lifted up his brows against his Maker, well may he be the origin of all sorrow." He chose to ape the glory of the Trinity, and he has his choice; the monstrous three-headed parody lies fixed there in his inimitable self-will, champing the traitors in its jaws; the six wings of his immortal seraphhood beat savagely, powerless to lift him out of the ice of his obduracy, and increasing that ice by the wind of their beating.

> Quindi Cocito tutto s'aggelava;
> con sei occhi piangeva, e per tre menti
> gocciava il pianto e sanguinosa bava.

"Hereby all Cocytus was frozen; with six eyes he wept, and down his three chins gushed tears and bloody foam."

That is the thing at the bottom: the idiot and slobbering horror. At the entrance to his realm stand the two dreadful sentences:

"Here dwell the wretched people who have lost the good of the intellect."

and the fearful paradox of the corrupted will:

"All their fear is changed into desire."

That is the picture seen by the poet who took evil seriously. And we cannot evade Dante by saying that we do not believe in that particular kind of judgment after death. For he himself said that his poem was indeed, literally, an account of what happens in the world beyond the grave, but allegorically an account of what happens within the soul. His hell is the picture of an eternal possibility within the heart of man; and he adds that the gate to that hell always stands wide open.